COMMERCIALIZATION OF INNOVATIVE TECHNOLOGIES

With regard to errors in general, either falling under the denomination of mental, typographical, or accidental, we are conscious of being able to point out a greater number than any critic whatever.

Encyclopaedia Britannica, 1771 edition

COMMERCIALIZATION OF INNOVATIVE TECHNOLOGIES

Bringing Good Ideas to the Marketplace

C. JOSEPH TOUHILL
Touhill Technology Management Corporation

GREGORY J. TOUHILL
United States Air Force

THOMAS A. O'RIORDAN
The Raytheon Company

A JOHN WILEY & SONS, INC., PUBLICATION

For general information on our other products and services or for technical support, please contact
our Customer Care Department within the United States at (800) 762-2974, outside the United
States at (317) 572-3993 or fax (317) 572-4002.

Wiley also publishes its books in a variety of electronic formats. Some content that appears in print
may not be available in electronic formats. For more information about Wiley products, visit our
web site at www.wiley.com.

Library of Congress Cataloging-in-Publication Data:

Touhill, C. J., 1938–
   Commercialization of innovative technologies : bringing good ideas to the
marketplace / C. Joseph Touhill, Gregory J. Touhill, Thomas A. O'Riordan.
      p. cm.
   ISBN 978-0-470-23007-7 (cloth)
   1. Technological innovations. I. Touhill, Gregory J. II. O'Riordan, Thomas A. III. Title.
   T173.8.T68 2008
   658.5'77—dc22
                                                                    2007030013

Printed in the United States of America

10 9 8 7 6 5 4 3 2 1

To our wives and children

CONTENTS

FOREWORD

I have known Joe Touhill since we were college classmates in the class of 1960 at Rensselaer Polytechnic Institute. The characteristics that impressed me most about Joe were his eagerness to take on a challenge, his common sense, and his ability to size up an issue and then lay out a logical plan for resolution. Most important, then and now, is his ability to follow through to a conclusion. Joe and coauthors, Greg Touhill and Tom O'Riordan, have produced a book that is focused on one of the most exciting and rewarding challenges of our time: ***commercialization of innovative technologies***. Economists pretty much agree that innovation on a commercially attractive basis is one of the key economic drivers of our capitalist system. This means having an atmosphere that promotes innovation, with appropriate rewards and incentives flourishing freely. Our system is based on the premise that incentives really do work!

Entrepreneurship is a popular and growing topic in the business world today. There is a buzz about it. The topic is red hot and is a rapidly emerging course of study on most technology and business school campuses. You cannot pick up a business magazine without finding an article on innovation. Furthermore, it is one of the key metrics that analysts look at in rating an organization. How efficient organizations—research, business, government, military and educational—are in utilizing resources to develop innovation is a crucial question. The authors have educational backgrounds in engineering and the sciences with subsequent business training and experience. They have had genuine exposure and responsibility in the world of development on a results-oriented and profitable basis.

The book hammers on the concept of the ***innovation team*** and its importance to a consistent and repetitive commercialization process. It identifies the players, their characteristics, how to deal with their idiosyncrasies and what to expect as the commercialization process moves ahead. The book brings all the touchy topics into play: compensation and incentives as well as recognition, rewards, and celebration. The maestro (entrepreneur) inevitably is leading an orchestra of highly strung talented individuals. Embarking on a development process without a realistic understanding of these points is foolishness and costly.

The Wall Street Journal suggests that the overwhelming number of innovative ideas since the end of World War II have been commercialized by U.S. citizens. The book suggests that this is changing. Intuitively, we know that creativity is not the sole province of the USA. Because of improvements in global communications, we are seeing global teams put together for the development of ideas. Much of this team building is to take advantage of lower costs in different parts of the world. The innovation team of the future will be looking for the best ideas no matter where they come from. Global teams that we are beginning to see develop is a perfect lead into the topic that this book features uniquely—the innovation team—and understanding how important this concept is.

The book will not turn a poor idea into a profitable one. But it will ensure that attentive readers get a good commonsense strategy in place for identifying, funding, and developing truly good ideas. Of equal if not greater importance, the book will lead you to set up a screening system so that you can quickly identify ideas that do not fit into your strategy and goal profile. If you come away from reading the book with only one idea—the concept that early elimination of time-wasters is crucial to success on a consistent basis—reading it will have been worthwhile. Time really is precious, and things are moving at an ever-accelerating pace. The book takes you through all the steps in sufficient and understandable detail for ease of implementation. It will help you to avoid wasting time and bring discipline to the creative process. Although this may seem like a contradiction in terms, what is business really, if not the application of discipline? The tension between creativity and discipline is discussed candidly. Healthy solutions can only come about with awareness and knowledge. Good things do not happen by accident.

The book does not shy away from difficult questions such as "Can entrepreneurship be taught"? Addressing difficult questions is a hallmark of this book. Anyone who has been through the commercialization process will recognize immediately that the authors have been there. There is considerable benefit to be derived from their experience. The book is proactive about looking at things that did not go well. How else do we learn if not from our mistakes?

The book is recommended for both students and practitioners (investors, inventors, entrepreneurs, and managers). It will serve as a text for students and as a comprehensive resource for practitioners: those trying to bring innovative ideas to market on a commercially sound basis. The table of contents will serve nicely to direct you to those parts of the process in which you have the most interest.

ROBERT B. SHEH

Managing Partner
Alta Group, LLC
Redondo Beach, CA

ACKNOWLEDGMENTS

Many people and career experiences helped us in writing this book, and it would be a very long acknowledgment indeed if we attempted to identify them all. Thus, at the risk of missing those who truly were influential in guiding our effort, we will thank only a few for their direct intervention and contributions to this endeavor.

Dr. Herbert M. Clark, professor emeritus of physical and nuclear chemistry at Rensselaer Polytechnic Institute, encouraged us in writing this book, challenged us to make it thoughtful and insightful, dispensed considerable wisdom in the process, and as the author of several books, provided us with sound advice on the mechanics of publication.

Dr. Gary F. Bennett, professor emeritus of biochemical engineering at the University of Toledo, wisely guided us to appropriate people at the American Institute of Chemical Engineers (AIChE) who helped us to get the book published.

Dr. Richard D. Siegel, environmental consultant, also a friend and colleague from AIChE, gave us important insights that were valuable in getting ready for publication.

Dr. Kenneth L. Mulholland, president of Kenneth Mulholland & Associates, Inc., and author of *Identification of Cleaner Production Improvement Opportunities*, provided beneficial information related to his favorable experience in publishing his book through the AIChE–Wiley affiliation.

Stephen M. Touhill, vice president of Clearspring Technologies, Inc., was especially helpful in his review of Chapter 3, and in providing insights into the evolution of emerging high-technology startups.

The U.S. Central Command Air Forces (USCENTAF) team, which was awarded the 2006 U.S. Air Force Science and Engineering Achievement

Award for the work cited in Chapter 17, is recognized for its outstanding efforts under very trying conditions. We would like to single out the following officers for their special contributions: Colonel Marty Edmonds, Squadron Leader Patrick Del Guidice, and Major Robert Sylvester.

Disclaimers

The views in this book expressed by coauthor Gregory J. Touhill are his alone and are neither endorsed by nor necessarily reflect those of the U.S. Department of Defense or the U.S. Air Force. Similarly, the views of coauthor Thomas A. O'Riordan are his alone and are neither endorsed by nor necessarily reflect those of the Raytheon Company.

1

ESTABLISHING PERSPECTIVE

> During the last 100 years, we have created more wealth, reduced poverty
> more, and increased life expectancy more than in the previous 100,000
> years. That happened because of entrepreneurs, thinkers, creators, and inno-
> vators. They are the heroes of our world.
>
> Johan Norberg[1]

How many people do you know who when asked "What would you like
to be doing five years from now?" answer by saying that they would like
to have their own business. In our experience, the percentage is very high.
Perhaps this is because the desire to be free, independent, and in control of
one's destiny is innate. However, realization of such a vision is not nearly
as frequent as the desire. Key stumbling blocks are that people don't have
the knowledge, resources, energy, or discipline to convert their dream into
reality. This book is intended to help provide thoughts on how to bring
good ideas to the marketplace. It focuses on and emphasizes technology.
Technological innovations can be simple or complex, hardware or software, manufactured products or technology-based services, even systems

---

[1]Johan Norberg, "Entrepreneurs are the heroes of the world," *Cato's Letter*, Winter 2007,
Vol. 5, No. 1.

that combine existing technology in a unique and imaginative way, but the pathway to successful commercialization is similar for all good ideas.

In addition to the huge audience of budding entrepreneurs who dream of starting their own businesses (including many who are actively involved in doing so now), there are many others who will find this book useful. Virtually all leading universities now have centers of entrepreneurship and teach courses on the subject to eager management and engineering students.[2] Today's investors are seeking ways to enhance their investment returns because the return earned from current stock, bond, and mutual fund investments is lower than it has been historically, and it appears that investing in real estate has taken on considerable risk. Hence, venture capitalists and consortia of investors[3] continue to look at the potential that innovative technology can have in realizing their target aspirations for significant returns on invested capital.

Another group of significant size that can benefit from this book are those who submit proposals to various federal agencies that award Small Business Innovative Research (SBIR) and Small Business Technology Transfer (STTR) contracts. SBIR is a program that encourages small businesses to explore their technological potential and provides an incentive to profit from its commercialization. STTR is a program that reserves a specific percentage of federal research and development funding for award to small businesses and associated nonprofit research institution partners. Because the risk and expense of conducting research and development can be beyond the means of many small businesses, STTR combines the strengths of small businesses and nonprofit research laboratories by introducing entrepreneurial skills to high-tech research efforts. Its intent is to transfer technologies and products from the laboratory to the commercial marketplace.

The U.S. Small Business Administration, Office of Technology's Web site (http://www.sba.gov/SBIR/) provides detailed information on how to become aware of proposal opportunities from agencies that award SBIR and STTR contracts. The Web site answers frequently asked questions and has a master schedule of release dates for solicitation announcements. Additionally, the Web site includes helpful links to agency/department SBIR and STTR program solicitations. Any small business interested in

---

[2]See Section 1.4 for a discussion of programs and curricula at leading universities that teach entrepreneurship and commercialization.

[3]These consortia, especially those that focus on smaller companies, commonly are referred to as *angel investors*. Interestingly, in 2004, angel investors financed nearly 45,000 startup companies to the tune of $24 billion. The majority of the startups were high-tech companies. These 225,000 active angel investors outspent venture capitalists, who funded $22 billion in high-growth startups. Angel investors are described in some detail in Chapter 4.

TABLE 1.1   Federal Agencies with SBIR/STTR Programs

Agency	SBIR	STTR
Department of Agriculture	×	
Department of Commerce	×	
Department of Defense	×	×
Department of Education	×	
Department of Energy	×	×
Department of Health and Human Services	×	×
Department of Transportation	×	
Environmental Protection Agency	×	
NASA	×	×
National Science Foundation	×	×

submitting proposals to federal agencies that fund SBIR/STTR programs is strongly encouraged to use this valuable resource for determining what agencies may be interested in their technological innovation, matching that interest with formal solicitations, and learning how to submit proposals.

There are 10 federal agencies that award such contracts (Table 1.1). Contract amounts are significant. For example, during fiscal year 2004, $2,015,000,000 was awarded for SBIR programs and $208,700,000 for STTR programs. One of the requirements of both SBIR and STTR is that proposers must demonstrate that their planned effort, if successful, will be commercialized. Thus, we envision that this book can serve as an inventor/innovator manual, a university textbook, an SBIR/STTR reference, or as a technology investment handbook. Additionally, business executives and management students will find it helpful in explaining the life cycle of product innovation and the dynamics of bringing good ideas into practice.

Unfortunately for all of these people, the old truism, "build a better mousetrap and they will beat a path to your door," doesn't always work. In fact, our experience shows that unless you know how to commercialize good technological ideas, people won't take your mousetrap even if you gave it away for nothing. The four key ingredients that make commercialization of good ideas successful are:

- Teamwork
- Planning
- Discipline
- Perseverance

We emphasize the first three ingredients explicitly throughout the book; the perseverance part is implicit, and truthfully, is learned best through experience. Of the key ingredients, we think that teamwork is the most crucial.

This is because we believe that the best chance for commercial success is through the formation of an *innovation team*. Surely there are occasional extraordinary people who alone can bring the germ of an idea to full commercialization, but these geniuses are few. In Section 1.2 we explain our rationale regarding teamwork in more detail and show how teamwork was an essential element in the birth of that great American phenomenon—Silicon Valley. Throughout the book we emphasize that an innovation team cannot succeed without a plan, and we spend time describing how strategy is formulated and how a plan is built. Finally, we stress that it requires discipline to follow a plan and wisdom to know when to amend it.

1.1   ORGANIZATION OF THE BOOK

We believe that enhancement of the human condition depends on thoughtful creation and implementation of innovative technologies. In these times of rapid technological expansion and global communications, most people recognize and understand the basic importance of intellectual property. Moreover, they understand the need for the entrepreneurial spirit to launch new enterprises. The winners will be those who know how to exploit good ideas and put them into practice. Our book defines a strategy for doing so and outlines an approach to commercializing innovative technologies successfully.

In the first three chapters we deal with *strategic* issues, answering such questions as:

- What is the audience for this book?
- Why is it so important to form an innovation team?
- Who are members of the innovation team, and what are some of their traits and characteristics?
- What does a strong and flexible commercialization plan look like?
- What are our objectives in developing a strategy for success, and how do we assess, develop, and manage promising technologies?
- How do we develop an endgame?
- What are key elements in executing the strategic plan?

In Chapters 4 through 16 we address *tactical* issues, such as how we find, fund, assess, develop, design, and demonstrate innovative technology. Whereas the first three chapters reflect boardroom decision making, the tactical chapters deal more with on-scene issues and problem solving. In Chapters 17 and 18 we focus on both strategic and tactical decision making related to how a successful technology can be improved and what happens after our goal of successful commercialization has been achieved.

Some people claim that any worthwhile enterprise rests on a three-legged stool comprised of strategy, tactics, and operations. For our purposes in this book we have chosen not to address detailed operational matters explicitly. We leave this important area to others. Others have recognized the growing strong interest in entrepreneurship and commercialization of innovative technology, and some very good books on the subject have been published recently. Our book is different because we emphasize (1) the importance of the innovation team, (2) the wisdom of building a portfolio that spreads risk, and (3) the strong input required from technologists in the commercialization process.[4]

1.2   THE IMPORTANCE OF VIEWPOINT

It is extremely rare that a single person can conceive of an idea and then, alone, carry it through to successful implementation and commercialization. As technology increases in complexity and governmental rules and regulations become more pervasive and onerous, it is difficult to see how one person could bring a good idea to the marketplace without a lot of help. One of our main themes in this book is that successful commercialization is best achieved through teamwork. We believe that building an innovation team is crucial to the process of commercializing good ideas. Our conception of the innovation team that is best equipped to commercialize technology is one comprised of several personalities or roles, each with a different image of the idea or concept that we intend to implement[5]:

- Inventor/innovator
- Investor
- Technologist
- Entrepreneur

[4]Although the two junior authors have been or are associated with the U.S. Air Force, our primary audience is not defense contractors, but rather, people who are highly entrepreneurial and eager to make new ideas grow and go. The book subtitle, "Bringing Good Ideas to the Marketplace," reveals that we are focused on nascent ideas rather than mature technology that characterizes much of the defense community. Not that defense contractors won't find the book useful: To the contrary, many contractors would benefit from reading it, to find and promote new ideas. We see the typical reader as being young in spirit, eager, and bursting with energy and zeal. We hope to provide them with a road map and the benefit of a lot of experience.

[5]Accountants, lawyers, and bankers, among others, are important supporters of the innovation team, but are not regarded as core team members within the context of this book.

It takes all four of these personalities to identify and evaluate good ideas and concepts and then bring them to the marketplace profitably. The best pathway toward successful commercialization requires that the innovation team be flexible and interact well, focusing on the common goal of profitable commercialization. Sometimes people will switch roles as an idea is evaluated, matures, and is developed. Thus, each role, whether undertaken individually or in combination, is vital to successful commercialization.

The Birth of Silicon Valley:
The Traitorous Eight

During 1996, Public Broadcasting aired a television show called, *Caesar's Writers*. It was riotously funny, but more impressive was the story of how a group of very talented writers made it possible for an outstanding comedy ensemble headed by Sid Caesar to capture the relatively new medium of television by storm. *Your Show of Shows*, produced in the early 1950s, remains for many people the gold standard of television comedy. Where Milton Berle's slapstick captured the nation's funny bone, Sid Caesar and his cast taught us the meaning of wit. The truly amazing part of the 1996 reunion of Sid Caesar and his writers was the identity of the writers[6]: Mel Brooks; Larry Gelbart; Gary Belkin; Sheldon Keller; Carl Reiner; Aaron Rubin; the Simon brothers, Danny and Neil; Mel Tolkin; and a very young freelance contributor of jokes—Woody Allen. The show itself was terrific, but to recognize the incredible talent of the comedy writers and what they accomplished collectively over the years was astounding. Just suppose that there is a parallel story in high technology. Well, there is!

In December 1947, two scientists, John Bardeen and Walter Brattain, at Bell Telephone Laboratories in Murray Hill, New Jersey, observed that when electrical signals were applied to contacts on germanium crystals, the output power was greater than the input. Their boss was the magisterial William Shockley. Shockley sought to find an explanation for the phenomenon, and with great insight over a short period, he not only explained the effect on semiconductor materials, but also, and more important, developed a crystal that became known as a junction transistor. By 1951, Shockley and his crew had reduced the transistor to practice. In 1956, Bardeen, Brattain, and Shockley shared a Nobel Prize in Physics for their discovery.

---

[6]The great Lucille Kallen was not in the program, although she was an essential part of the writing team.

FIGURE 1.1   The Traitorous Eight at Fairchild Semiconductor in 1959. From left: Gordon Moore, Sheldon Roberts, Eugene Kleiner, Robert Noyce, Victor Grinich, Julius Blank, Jean Hoerni, and Jay Last. (Courtesy of Wayne Miller/Magnum Photos.)

Shockley believed that Bell Labs wasn't moving quickly enough to capitalize on his work, so in February 1956, with financing from Arnold Beckman of Beckman Instruments, Inc., he founded Shockley Semiconductor Laboratory in the San Francisco Peninsula, near Palo Alto. He hired a group of talented young scientists to develop the new technology. During the course of their work, they noted that silicon had many advantages over germanium. Shockley, not a man to act kindly toward criticism even if it was only his perception, reluctantly permitted the young scientists to explore this apparently better route. However, his management style became increasingly difficult for his researchers.

In the words of Gordon Moore, one of these young researchers and eventual cofounder of Intel[7]:

[7]Gordon Moore, "William Shockley," *The TIME 100, Scientists and Thinkers*, Mar. 29, 1999.

Working for Shockley proved to be a particular challenge. He extended his competitive nature even to his working relationships with the young physicists he supervised. Beyond that, he developed traits that we came to view as paranoid. He suspected that members of his staff were purposely trying to undermine the project and prohibited them from access to some of the work. He viewed several trivial events as malicious and assigned blame. He felt it necessary to check new results with his previous colleagues at Bell Labs, and he generally made it difficult for us to work together.

Unfortunately, things went from bad to worse. So in May 1957, eight employees—Julius Blank, Victor Grinich, Jean Hoerni, Eugene Kleiner, Jay Last, Gordon Moore, Robert Noyce, and Sheldon Roberts—went to Arnold Beckman and said that they could no longer work under Shockley's oppressive management. They suggested that they needed a new manager, but said they would not have a problem if Shockley remained as a consultant. Initially, Beckman agreed, but two months later he changed his mind.

That was it. In September 1957, the eight men resigned. Together they were able to scrape up only $3500 between them. They needed help, so Eugene Kleiner wrote a letter to his father's stockbroker in New York. Somehow the letter wound up in the hands of a legendary venture capitalist, Arthur Rock. Rock went to California, liked what he saw, and persuaded Sherman Fairchild, the inventor of the aerial camera, to make the eight young researchers a subsidiary of his company. With a contract for $1.3 million, they became Fairchild Semiconductor and built transistors their way. Shockley was outraged and referred to these men as the Traitorous Eight. He never recovered from losing these talented scientists, and in 1963 he left the electronics industry and went to Stanford University.

What the Traitorous Eight would do next would change history. Committed to development of the silicon-based semiconductor, the eight men set up shop in an area renowned for its apricot groves. They quickly made their semiconductor technology the de facto standard for electric switching devices and produced components that would dominate a wide variety of industries, from consumer electronics to the nascent space program. Within two years, the new Fairchild Semiconductor subsidiary was creating more revenue than that of its parent company.

The eight made Fairchild Semiconductor a huge success, but like Sid Caesar's writers, what the Traitorous Eight became is the best part of the story. They essentially invented Silicon Valley. Victor Grinich became a professor at the University of California at Berkeley and Stanford University; the other seven went on to found notable spin-off companies.[8] Robert

---

[8]The spin-offs and their founders often are called "Fairchildren."

Noyce and Gordon Moore became cofounders of Intel. Eugene Kleiner cofounded the world-renown venture capital firm Kleiner, Perkins, Caufield and Byers. Sheldon Roberts, Jean Hoerni, and Jay Last founded a company that later became Teledyne, and Julius Blank cofounded Xicor.

Their impact on high technology was immense. In the words of Jay Last: "The first 50 years of transistors were very similar to the first 50 years of the Gutenberg press. They happened 500 years apart, and they trace almost the exact same path. Both became mature industries within the same amount of time. The [integrated circuit] changed the world the way the Gutenberg did—but even more so—by giving us this enormous ability to communicate."

The common thread in this story is the value of *teamwork*. It takes a brave person to challenge a Nobel prize winner at his own game, but like the Three Musketeers, the Traitorous Eight truly were "One for all and all for one." Convinced of the value of their technology and their vision of what it could produce, the Traitorous Eight bravely gambled their professional reputations and futures together. Once they had made the break from Shockley, together they began the development of one of the greatest technical transformations in the history of humankind.

Especially notable for the Traitorous Eight is who these young technologists morphed into. Some became seasoned technologists, some venture capitalists, some entrepreneurs (and very good managers to boot), and some even bounced between roles. Clearly, they understood teamwork and exemplify what an innovation team should strive for. These men created an environment that permits high technology to flourish today, and they will remain models to emulate for a long time. The Traitorous Eight were a bold and committed innovation team that changed history.

To build a successful team, the mind-set of each person or role must be understood. Hence, we begin here with descriptions of the traits of the various players in their distinctive roles. For each role we include a brief profile of a person or persons who represents (at least to us) the essential characteristics that we associate with various facets of the innovation team. Note that several of the persons cited assumed multiple roles throughout their careers.

1.2.1 The Inventor/Innovator

Inventors/innovators are a different breed. They see things in ways that most people don't. That's why they are so good at what they do. Even though their ideas or concepts may be technologically based, they don't necessarily have to be scientists. They are usually more interested in practice than in theory. Not that they don't understand the theory—but it's the application that consumes them. A classical example of the consummate inventor is Thomas Edison. Clearly, he was extremely pragmatic in the way he approached his experimentation, but to believe that this brilliant man didn't understand and have command of the scientific principles that were the foundation of his successes would be a grave mistake. Let's look at some of the words that come to mind quickly when we're describing inventors/innovators.

Creative   The characteristic that most people associate with inventors/innovators is creativity. Ideas and concepts that they come up with seem remarkable to us. "Holy cow! How come I didn't think of that?" The reason is that they see things differently within the context of their experience and education. Moreover, and perhaps most important, they can visualize the application and usefulness of what they conceive.

For purposes of this book, we distinguish inventors/innovators from tinkerers, although sometimes it's hard to tell the difference. For example, Floyd Paxton of Selah, Washington became fabulously wealthy by inventing and patenting the plastic clip that is used on bread bags. Although his biography refers to him as an inventor, clearly nothing else he did commercially rivals the success he had with the bread clip. Perhaps he would not qualify for the tinkerer sobriquet either. Nevertheless, our focus here is on the technically oriented person who works in a disciplined way to conceive and develop products and procedures for the technology marketplace. According to one dictionary, a tinkerer is a person who "manipulates unskillfully or experimentally." In our experience, tinkerers today, except in rare cases, simply can't keep up because of the rapid pace of technology expansion. Although Edison hardly was a tinkerer, today his trial-and-error methodologies would be too expensive and time-consuming without consideration and thorough understanding of scientific fundamentals and the shortcuts that they enable.

Inventors/innovators often have lots of good ideas that deal with potential applications in highly varied fields. A good example is Dr. Edward Teller, famed physicist and so-called Father of the H-Bomb, who collaborated with chemists Brunauer and Emmett to develop the famous BET equation, which is the most commonly used method of measuring the surface area of multilayered adsorbent materials. A great strength of Teller was that he had the ability to simplify complex problems, a common characteristic of inventors/innovators. That is a key reason why they are good at generating useful concepts.

The broad interests of inventors/innovators can hamper their creativity. They are diverted easily because of their quick minds and diverse ideas. This often interferes with their focus. Lack of focus is sometimes paradoxical in view of their stubborn single-mindedness most of the time. They also have been accused of being poorly disciplined, due to their occasional inattentiveness. This accounts for the mostly unfair description of "mad scientist."

Passionate   Innovation team members must be acutely aware of the inventor/innovator characteristic of being passionate about their ideas and concepts. It colors their behavior dramatically. When they come up with what they see as a great idea, they believe absolutely that it is the greatest boon to humankind. It's like one of their gifted children. Try to remember that lots of sweat and tears went into the conception of the idea. In fact, many ideas represent generations of failure before the concept is honed into what the inventor believes will prove to be a huge success. So when other innovation team members grill the inventor, we urge that they do so with gentleness and respect just as if they were inquiring into the prospects of the inventor's favorite child.

We are reminded of one inventor we knew who became blinded by his zealotlike commitment to an invention that he had developed over a period of nearly 20 years. He would accept no criticism, even if it was positive. His passion became blindness. Eventually, on the brink of losing everything that he owned, he capitulated and grudgingly permitted an investment group to take ownership of the idea. Fortunately for him, they were decent people who not only paid him a fair price for his asset, but also retained him for many years as a well-paid consultant. Unfortunately, many ultrapassionate inventors are not so lucky and drive investors away. Eventually, their ideas flounder and disappear.

Protective   When inventors/innovators have to seek funding for their ideas, they make it hard to deal with them. All of them believe that if they were independently wealthy, they would fund the entire venture on their own. But they usually run out of their own money[9] and understand that to achieve full commercialization potential they need resources well beyond what they can provide themselves. But here's the problem: They are highly reluctant to share the basis for the inner workings of their idea. In addition, they tend to be suspicious and believe that if they aren't

---

[9]This doesn't necessarily mean that they exhaust all of their financial resources, but it does mean that they have reached the limit that they have established for what they are willing to risk. The risk/reward concept is a key in negotiating with them in sharing ownership and equity.

careful, somebody is going to steal their idea. As a result, they don't want to reveal anything. They want investors to trust them and simply write checks. Clearly, that's not the way things happen.

To inventor/innovators, any darned fool can see what a great idea they have. But those who are going to spend money and time developing the idea and concept have to know how it works and why it works, sometimes in excruciating detail. And what's obvious to the inventor probably isn't all that apparent to the other innovation team members. So inventors/innovators have several courses of action: They can simply surrender their reluctance and trust the other team members; they can use detailed confidentiality agreements and apply for patents; they can structure development agreements that include confidentiality provisions and rights of control of technological intellectual property; they can enter into elaborate consulting contracts; they can move on and try somebody else; or they can try a combination of the above.

In early stages of development, patents aren't the complete answer. Some people believe that patent applications are sufficient protection for nascent ideas. A patent application helps, but what really protects young ideas is the proprietary knowledge of the inventor. Moreover, if the idea is a blockbuster, patents are a road map for those who would reverse-engineer and/or copy and modify the concept.

At the outset, innovation team members often don't know each other that well, so the trust necessary to make the team function efficiently hasn't developed yet. All the legal agreements in the world can't engender that trust. So if all parties believe in the idea and they want to move ahead but are stymied by the inventor's recalcitrance in revealing details, there is another alternative that we have used successfully. It is the concept of a technological trustee, and it works like this. Both parties—for example, inventor and investor—agree that a third party will be the repository for details of the idea or concept. The inventor will reveal all the details of how and why the idea works to the third party, the technological trustee, who is judged to be an expert in the area of application. The trustee, through a thorough probing, will form an overall opinion of the idea and will share this opinion with the investor. Thus, the inventor trusts the trustee to retain the idea and all the details in secret, and the investor trusts the technological opinion of the trustee sufficiently to lend money for development of the idea. For one client we were part of such an arrangement for 13 years. During that period, the concept was developed and implemented. When all parties believed that their interests were protected, they terminated the agreement and released us from our trustee responsibilities. The fact is: All of the innovation team members finally trusted each other.

Because protection of the concept and details of the innovation are so important to the inventor, they should have a strategy worked out in advance of any contact with investor groups. By doing so, everybody will save a lot of time and friendlier negotiations will be promoted.

Persevering   With regard to their favorite ideas, inventors/innovators are like elephants and bulldogs: They never forget, nor do they ever give up. These characteristics have both a positive and a negative side. Endurance causes them to persevere in the face of derision, experimental failures, and monetary problems. They will wait potentially forever for true appreciation of their ideas. Conversely, it makes them stick too long with "turkeys". With them, bad ideas hang around much longer than they would with other innovation team members.

Somehow, inventors have to learn to step back and analyze as objectively as possible where they stand in their quest for commercialization. Moreover, they should try to understand the motivations of other team members. Doing so will help speed the commercialization process measurably. Dedication, perseverance, and endurance are admirable, and they make inventors/innovators tough and thick-skinned. They may also make it difficult to get along and deal with them.

Stubborn   Stubbornness in inventors is a characteristic closely aligned with both passion and perseverance. We already have talked about an inventor's unwillingness to divulge trade secrets, and there are related traits. After reaching an agreement with others to set up an innovation team, it is not uncommon for inventors to be less than eager to make changes in their original concept, even if such a change represents a clear improvement. They are often not very receptive to the ideas of others, especially those who they believe don't have the technical background to understand how and why their concept works. In fact, some very talented inventors who we have encountered think everybody else is stupid. Fortunately, most (but not all) keep that thought to themselves.

It is interesting that despite their foibles, most of the inventors we have worked with are very good negotiators. They may not be particularly good businesspeople, but they are very effective in negotiations because they are willing to walk away if they aren't comfortable with the terms of the discussions. Most inventors have labored long and hard to get to the table, and the last thing they will tolerate is relinquishing more control than they believe is fair. They are the final arbiters of what's fair, so the best way to approach them in any matter that requires negotiation is to appeal to them rationally and intellectually.

Those Who Failed in Their Success:
Philo T. Farnsworth and Allen B. DuMont

Are you ready to appear on *Jeopardy* and identify the inventor of television? The ubiquitous staple of every home today was the product of the fertile minds of Philo Taylor Farnsworth, who invented television technology, and Allen B. DuMont, who invented the capability to mass-produce cathode ray tubes and created the DuMont Television Network to broadcast programs around the country. Both of these men epitomize the attributes we showcase as the hallmarks of inventors.

Farnsworth and DuMont were exceptionally creative from their early childhoods. Farnsworth, born in a log cabin in rural Utah, developed the technical concept of television as a 14-year-old. While plowing fields, he came upon the idea that like the plowed lines of his field, he could create images on etched glass with a focused electron beam. He sketched his design for his high school teacher, and after a year at Brigham Young

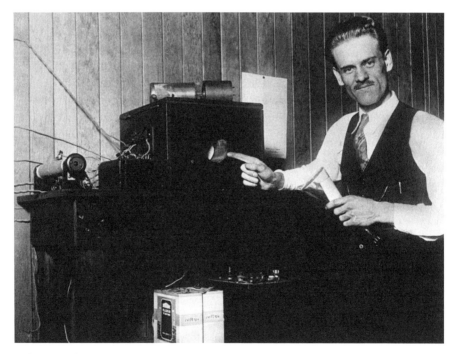

FIGURE 1.2   Philo T. Farnsworth points to his television. (Copyright © Bettmann/ Corbis.)

FIGURE 1.3   Allen B. Dumont. (Courtesy of Institute Archives and Special Collections, Rensselaer Polytechnic Institute, Troy, New York.)

University he created a laboratory in which he soon created the first all-electronic television image. Similarly, DuMont, who was afflicted by polio as a youth, demonstrated his genius early in life by mastering electronics. During his recuperation from polio, he built—and repeatedly rebuilt—radios, incorporating significant improvements in each version. By the time he was 14, he had become the youngest American to obtain a first-class commercial radio operator's license.

Passionate about their work, both men were dogged in their determination to pursue their inventions. Settling in San Francisco after his one year of college, Farnsworth aggressively sought investors and when he was 21 years old set up a laboratory where he created a working television camera (the "Image Dissector") and transmitted the first television image. DuMont rapidly built a reputation as a genius following graduation from Rensselaer Polytechnic Institute. Hired by Westinghouse fresh from college, he quickly transformed their tube production capability from 500 tubes per day to over 50,000 tubes per day. DeForest

Radio enticed him to leave Westinghouse, but soon he felt stifled and left to create his own company, DuMont Laboratories, which became the world's leading manufacturer of high-quality cathode ray tubes. He had just turned 30.

Farnsworth and DuMont were very protective of their inventions, and one might speculate that this was a principal reason that each created his own laboratory to develop and manage their products while retaining complete creative and production control. People typically think of inventors as having struggled for years to perfect their creations; they exemplify endurance. In this regard, Farnsworth and DuMont are not exceptions. For Farnsworth, from concept to creation, the development of a working television system took seven years. DuMont, who toiled in the basement of his New Jersey home to create a long-lasting and reliable cathode ray tube, poured his heart and soul into a company that he would run for nearly 30 years.

Their endurance was matched by their stubbornness. For many years, Farnsworth was engaged in a prolonged and particularly nasty legal struggle with the Radio Corporation of America (RCA) and its president, David Sarnoff. Vladimir Zworykin, who was affiliated with RCA, had received a patent for a device he called an "iconoscope." Ironically, the iconoscope was remarkably like Farnsworth's Image Dissector. In promoting his expanding radio empire and planned television network, Sarnoff scoffed at the thought of acknowledging Farnsworth's invention, let alone compensating him. "RCA doesn't pay royalties," he is alleged to have said, "we collect them." Although the U.S. Patent Office ultimately sided with Farnsworth, it took years of litigation before he received a dime from RCA, and he died penniless and in obscurity.

DuMont also demonstrated brilliance punctuated by stubbornness. DuMont parlayed his success in creating and selling the world's best cathode ray tubes into creation of the DuMont Television Network, the first television network in the world. Facing fierce competition from rivals NBC, CBS, and ABC, DuMont was plagued by lack of a strong affiliate structure. Despite having a few now-famous shows, such as *The Cavalcade of Stars* (featuring Jackie Gleason), Bishop Fulton Sheen's *Life Is Worth Living*, and *Captain Video* (the principal author's favorite), DuMont could not capitalize on his early success and develop the fledging network and make it profitable. Soon he was sinking significant amounts of money from other parts of his company into the television network to keep it afloat. Colleagues and board members alike insisted that in the wake of mounting losses, he terminate or sell the network. DuMont would have none of it and in 1956 was compelled by his corporate board to sell the failing network to Metromedia. Ironically, Metromedia was later acquired by Fox Broadcasting, and many Americans now routinely turn on their local Fox affiliate to watch their favorite baseball or football games. Perhaps DuMont, who died in 1965 with his companies in the hands of others, would be satisfied in knowing that he was right—just ahead of his time.[10]

Human history is rife with stories of inventors such as Farnsworth and DuMont. The common threads are the attributes we find common to all inventors: creativity, passion, jealous protectiveness of their ideas, the perseverance to see their ideas through, and stubbornness in the face of naysayers. Yet, as was true for the inventors we profiled, these attributes are sometimes blessings but may become curses when not managed properly.

1.2.2   The Investor

Investors are persons or groups who furnish money to bring a good idea or concept to a conclusion, either good or bad. Usually, investors enter the picture after the inventor/innovator runs out of funds or time. Remember, inventors/innovators would usually choose to do it all themselves if they had unlimited resources. Investors are allowed in when inventors see the opportunity evaporating; when their patience and enthusiasm are flagging and they are looking to get on with the next bonanza; when they are starting to see weaknesses in their idea; or when they really begin to understand that they need financial and technical help. The contrast between inventors and investors is fascinating. Inventors are creative and emotional, whereas investors are cold and calculating.[11] Yet each of these two parts of the innovation team is absolutely essential to the other.

The first rule in technology investing is to avoid using family and friends as sources of money. Even if such persons are wealthy enough to accept failure, and even if they are eager to help even when we don't ask, it is best not use them if at all possible. Some of the biggest feuds have occurred not when there was failure but when the commercialization went very well and it came time to make critical decisions and to divide up the profits. In addition, and perhaps more important, relatives and friends probably love us a lot more than they love our ideas, inventions, and innovations. Chances are they don't really understand what we are

---

[10]We talk about the importance of timing throughout the book.
[11]Clearly, this is a wild generalization and reflects tendencies rather than absolute categorization.

attempting. Yet somehow they believe that their monetary involvement will give them special privileges in the management of the company, something at which they are probably woefully inept.

Rather than relatives and friends, we urge the use of professional investors who build suites of technology. They understand the science, the process, and the risk better, and they can be far more helpful in making the commercialization work because they are experienced in business and will be much more objective than parents, siblings, and childhood buddies. The enormous success of Silicon Valley investment groups provides abundant proof that working with professional investors enhances substantially opportunities for commercial success. Just as with inventors/innovators, investors have their own set of characteristics that distinguish them as members of the innovation team.

Good Sense of People   Arthur Rock, who coined the term *venture capitalist* (see "The Man Who Turned Apricot Orchards into Silicon Valley" below), says that the key attribute of an investor is the ability to identify successful people and invest in them. "What I'm interested in is investing in people. And I look for people who, you know, everything you could think of. They're honest. They have fire in their belly. They're intellectually honest, meaning that they see things as they are, not the way they want them to be and, and have priorities and know where they're going and know how they're going to get there."[12] Because successful innovation teams begin with visionary people, the investor is always on the lookout for those with the "right stuff."

Well-Connected   Another important attribute of the successful investor is being well-connected with those who present opportunities for success. Many of us look at the recent successes of companies such as Microsoft and Apple and wonder what our lives would be like if we had the opportunity to invest in them early in their development (imagine the return on investment!). Our research has shown that the investor who remains engaged in and connected to the marketplace soon finds that many inventors with good ideas come to them in search of investment. The acme of skill of a discerning investor is to determine which idea is a blockbuster and which is a dud.

Focused on Monetary Return   Many inventors/innovators envision investors as being like the main character in George Eliot's novel *Silas Marner*,

---

[12]http://silicongenesis.stanford.edu/transcripts/rock.htm The quote is in fractured English because it was extracted from an interview, but we believe that the reader can easily see the intent of Rock's response.

who spent a great deal of his time counting gold coins. What they forget is that Silas Marner turned out to be the hero of the novel.[13] Despite the fact that investors don't always have a clear understanding of the technological concept, they do understand money. They understand money as a measure of performance. This perspective is not necessarily bad. In fact, this focus helps to improve fuzzy ideas and prompts creative and beneficial variations and improvements. Members of the innovation team, especially inventors, should listen closely to the probing questions of investors and address their doubts and fears. The reason is simple: To win the game you need a rational and objective scorecard.

Just as it is crucial for investors to focus on return on investment and profitability, they must also keep a tight rein on the spending of money during the entire commercialization and development process. The most important question they can ask when requested to write a check is: "Why?" This helps the entire innovation team to remain grounded in the reason for which they chose to participate to begin with. It also helps everybody to remain committed to the original goals. Be advised, however, that we have found that the most successful investors are not focused completely on monetary return. They are very mindful of monetary return, but their primary focus is to keep the innovation team concentrating on the thing that keeps the team solvent—the most crucial resource of all: human capital.

Impatient   Investors have a reputation for being very impatient with the rest of the innovation team because of the time it takes to evaluate, assess, plan, develop, build, test, sell, fix, and monitor the new idea. There are a couple of reasons for this. First, they usually don't fully understand the technical aspects of the idea, so they don't appreciate the complexities involved in moving toward commercialization. Second, they don't realize the amount of sweat, tears, and emotional, financial, and intellectual sacrifice that went into the early conception and development. Third, from their perspective, time is money, and the longer it takes to reach the goal, the lower the return on their investment. The net result is that they want results as soon as "impracticable." It is essential that this impatience be addressed.

It is important that all members of the innovation team agree at an early stage on a reasonable timetable for accomplishing the various phases of the commercialization cycle. To arrive at such a formal timetable, judgment,

---

[13]Soames Forsyte, the central character in John Galsworthy's *Forsyte Saga* novels, is another investor who ultimately is redeemed despite his consuming focus on "property."

tact, and flexibility[14] are needed when bargaining. One reason is because inventors/innovators especially, and technologists invariably, are overly optimistic in making up schedules and budgets. It is their nature. In fact, the team probably doesn't want to deal with inventors and technologists who are very conservative on these two issues because it's an indicator that either they don't believe in the concept or don't know what they are doing. Once agreed upon, the formal timetable focuses on the tasks at hand and establishes accountability.

In their eagerness to get a quick return on investment, investors sometimes unrealistically push too hard for results.[15] If that becomes a source of acrimony, the team should quickly identify the disconnect and disband the association before the concept becomes bound up in protracted legal battles. Many excellent ideas have been killed due to squabbles that slowed progress to a crawl and lost their time-sensitive window of opportunity.

Capitalistic   Many inventors/innovators are driven, in part, by altruism. They are eager to impart to the world what we referred to earlier as "the greatest boon to humankind." They extend this hyperbole to their characterization of capitalistic investors by suggesting that investors could not care less. The innovation team must help inventors/innovators realize that the goals of their altruism can only be achieved by making the commercialization process work. Hence, they have to come to a reasonable compromise in understanding that free-market capitalism does not exploit people but is really one of the best mechanisms for improving the condition of humankind.

Dispassionate   Investors are most often regarded as being dispassionate about the idea or concept to be developed and really interested only in the money.[16] This isn't necessarily a bad thing. The best characteristics of investor dispassion are objectivity and realism. The innovation team should not subordinate this trait in investors. In fact, they would do well to showcase it.

Dispassion must not be confused with detachment. Detachment can lead to a lack of interest, which in turn can result in a lack of focus, deficient

---

[14]Flexibility is especially important in all phases of the commercialization process and is discussed at length in Section 1.3.

[15]Remember the old story that venture capitalists believe that if a woman can have a baby in nine months, nine women can have a baby in one month.

[16]Once again, the characterization of investors as being money-grubbing troglodytes grossly oversimplifies the situation and usually isn't true. On the other hand, investors are slow to disabuse other team members of this opinion so as to retain close reign over spending.

discipline, and sloppiness. These are deadly sins not just for investors but for the entire innovation team. Conversely, investors must guard against becoming too attached to an idea. Too often, investors become immersed in the thrill of technical developments and lose the objectivity that is necessary to keep the process on track.

Not Interested in Technical Details   Investors often are accused of not being interested in technical details. Lack of interest must be contrasted with failure to understand the technology of a concept. The role of investors should be to understand the big picture of the potential impact of successful development and commercialization. It's not necessary that they be able to derive equations or reproduce experiments, but they should strive to have a good appreciation of what the inventors and technologists are attempting to do and the implications of successful accomplishment. In actual fact, some of the best investors were at one time inventors or technologists. As they became more successful, they envisioned themselves moving up the food chain to the role of investors.

In the course of becoming knowledgeable, investors must guard against micromanagement. Remember that all the roles of the innovation team demand people with strong personalities and convictions, and such people usually regard micromanagers with distain.

Finding Investors   There are many investors who are eager to find good ideas. For example, it is estimated that there are nearly a quarter of a million active angel investors alone, not counting professional venture capital organizations. The trick is how to find the right one to form an innovation team. One way is to go to the Internet and type "venture capitalists" and "angel investors." The problem is that we will probably collect too much information and have too many choices. To refine the broad Internet approach, we suggest that readers try www.en.wikipedia.org as a sort of primer on the subject, then go to the Internet and be more selective. It is usually good advice to seek angel investors and venture capitalists in the region in which the innovators/inventors live and work.

A better approach is to learn as much as possible about the business field that a potential investor wants to enter. Attendance at technology conferences run by professional societies is one good way to create a network of contacts. If we know who the big guns are in our area of interest and do our homework, the list of potential investors will become manageable in a hurry. In addition, we establish our own network of people who can help to identify prospective investors.

The Man Who Turned Apricot Orchards into Silicon Valley:
Venture Capitalist Arthur Rock

In 1957, a group of eight scientists, disenchanted with the management style of their Nobel prize–winning boss, William Shockley, walked out of Shockley Semiconductor Laboratories in Palo Alto. Armed with the technical expertise to commercialize the semiconductor, the foresight to know that their product could change the world, and the drive to make it happen, they merely needed the money to get a new company started. The Traitorous Eight, as they became known, enlisted the help of a visionary investment banker from New York, Arthur Rock.[17]

After his first visit to northern California, Rock became a believer in the group's vision and set out to sell their idea to potential investors. Thirty-five companies turned him down; investing in something at the idea stage was too foreign to them. Eventually, Rock found Sherman Fairchild, an inventor willing to risk some of his family fortune on the venture. With a simple handshake between the two, northern California was changed forever—Fairchild Semiconductor, the first transistor company to work solely in silicon, was born. Later, several spin-offs would emerge, including, with Rock's backing, Intel, now the world's largest producer of microprocessors. Equally important, the idea of stock options for employees and the use of venture capital financing became a standard part of the nascent high-technology industry.

Arthur Rock serves as an excellent example of the ideal investor: having an incisive sense of people, being well-connected in business markets, possessing a sharp eye for the best return on investment, having the ability to take a dispassionate view of the technology and its potential, and lacking interest in the minute technical details. As one of the founding fathers of venture capital, and the man credited with coining the term, Rock was a major player in the development of Silicon Valley. Working with Thomas J. Davis, Jr., in the firm Davis & Rock, as well as on his own (as Arthur Rock & Co.), Rock backed many of the companies that make Silicon Valley what it is today: Teledyne, Scientific Data Systems, Apple Computer, General Transistor, and Diasonics, to name a few.[18]

Rock once described the role of a venture capitalist as someone who hunts for entrepreneurial dreamers possessed of "the potential to change the world." Rock analyzed the potential of a young company by focusing on the entrepreneur. "People, people, people," said Rock, in describing

[17]http://www.alumni.hbs.edu/bulletin/1997/december/rock.html.
[18]Ibid.

how he chose companies to invest in.[19] Once Rock invested in a company, he remained active in its management. He is a director of Intel and Apple, for example, and vice chairman of Diasonics. He stays in close touch with his managers, most of whom recognize that his advice is worth far more than his money. He maintains a delicate balance between guiding them and letting them find their own way.[20]

Rock's professional manner is detached and clinical. He refuses to let his companies waste money and conveys a harsh sense of urgency. He says little at board meetings, and sometimes will squelch woolly ideas by asking abruptly, "What good will it do?" Says his one-time partner, Thomas Davis, a California venture capitalist: "He only wants the right answer." Behind Rock's understated exterior lurks a remorseless will. Notes California financier Max Palevsky: "Arthur makes it clear you had better win and you had better work your ass off all the time."[21]

"Innovation and new ventures fuel the global economy but the spark comes from investment," Arthur Rock said. "Investment is about trust. It's about knowing that the people investors entrust with their money are running ethical, transparent and effective businesses."[22]

1.2.3   The Technologist

As you will discover during the course of this book, we relate most with the role of the technologist. This bias is understandable because that's where most of our commercialization experience is based. Other team member personalities tend to be flashier and at times more volatile, but be assured that technologists have their moments, too. We see the technologist as a strong force that makes an idea work and makes the prototype into something that's practical and affordable. Without that practicality and cost-consciousness, the product is going nowhere. To be viewed as a cohesive team member who works for on-time performance, cost-efficiency, and a useful product that will sell well, a technologist should actually cultivate the trait of quiet rationality.[23]

Sadly, the role of technologist is frequently omitted from the commercialization process, despite its critical importance. This omission can lead

---

[19]http://www.bookrags.com/biography/arthur-rock/.
[20]http://www.time.com/time/magazine/article/0,9171,949965-2,00.html.
[21]Ibid.
[22]http://www.law.stanford.edu/news/pr/3/.
[23]Or at least should convey an appearance of "quiet rationality."

to incomplete development of the idea, faulty products, or outright failure. The reason given most often for not having a technologist on the innovation team is that it costs too much money. Our retort is to ask "Why would you skimp on the phase of the commercialization process that is most important to success?" The answer of really accomplished innovation teams is: "We don't skimp on any aspect of the process, especially technology!"

Focused on Technology   The primary role of the technologist is to test the inventor's technology to see if it really is a good idea. If it is a good idea, the next step is to get it to work reliably at the lowest cost. Some investors[24] use technologists as hired guns. They engage a technologist to make a quick assessment to tell them whether or not an idea will work, and then they send them away. In our opinion, that's not a good strategy. If we hire technologists simply to answer questions one at a time, we have to pay each of them to educate themselves or to relearn earlier information. By putting them on the innovation team to begin with, they have the benefit of the entire story and can provide much better and coherent information and assessments. In addition, if they are enthralled with the idea, we can probably get them to work for a piece of the action rather than for a high hourly consulting fee. There is also much better assurance of confidentiality. Not that they would violate their legally binding confidence pledge, but if they understood the full picture, they would be less likely to make an inadvertent slip.

Some technologists can have an early vested interest as a coinventor or part-investor. Such involvement is subordinate to the primary role of technology assessor and developer.[25] It is expected that the technologist is the most objective of all the interested parties. The inclusion on a team of a specific technologist should be made with such an expectation, and it should be nurtured throughout the entire development and commercialization process.

Development-Oriented   Our experience is that if the technologist is convinced that an idea is a blockbuster, we can tempt the person into working for nothing, because the very good ones are driven by the thrill of the chase.[26] They love to figure out ways to make things work better and

---

[24]For this book, venture capitalists and angel investors are subgroups of the investor category.

[25]Recall that we said earlier that there can be shifting back and forth and across the various roles and personalities of the innovation team.

[26]Unfortunately, food, college education, housing, and the like, get in the way of that approach.

at lower cost. The team has to be careful that the technologist does not allow enthusiasm to dim his or her objectivity. A technologist can be so caught up in development as to lose sight of the critical role of looking for pitfalls and avoiding them before they occur.

A favorable relationship between the technologist and the inventor/ innovator is crucial for overall success. In our experience, initial encounters are rocky. The inventor views the technologist as an interloper, and the technologist can't understand how a crackpot like the inventor could possibly get anything done without help. But when the team starts to roll, things usually settle down and grudging acceptance turns into mutual respect. Positive moves must be made by the innovation team to help it happen soon after the two people are thrown together. However, care must be taken that the two parties don't go overboard and become too chummy. The last thing in the world that we need is for them to form a cabal that regards the investor and the entrepreneur as the enemy.

Key attributes of the technologist in the development process are imagination, project discipline, and a willingness to meld the ideas of others, not only the purely technical ideas but also those that touch on operating, financial, marketing, and sales issues. Project discipline refers mainly to maintaining the schedules agreed upon in project planning and to living within the budget.

Interested in Improvements and Ease of Operation   The role of the technologist is not simply a technical one.[27] The technologist must be able to visualize the idea or concept in terms of its overall feasibility in the short term and its market potential in the long term. In other words, will it work, and will it sell? Moreover, these diverse judgments must be made in condensed time frames. Academicians (especially in consulting assignments) tend to draw out evaluation processes, leading to increased costs and often missed opportunities. Technologists have no time to fiddle. Very experienced and accomplished technologists are much like talent scouts for upcoming stars in the arts or sports. They can pick winners in a timely way because of their experience and knowledge of the business.

In addition, they approach evaluation with an eye toward improving on the original idea.[28] They try to visualize the potential of incorporating improvements that will make a product work better, cost less, and function

---

[27]In fact, the best technologists have good common sense and experience in a broad array of areas, including finance, accounting, marketing, operations, and maintenance.
[28]Remember how Mozart vastly improved Salieri's little tune of greeting in the film *Amadeus*?

reliably. Other primary goals are to make the product easy to build and easy to fix. As mentioned earlier, this penchant to improve on an original idea frequently brings them into conflict with the inventor/innovator. Technologists must strive to incorporate improvements with diplomacy and in collaboration with the inventor rather than in an antagonistic atmosphere.

The technologist will get no argument from the inventor in another facet of their respective roles: protecting proprietary rights. The technologist must try to make a product easy to build, operate, and fix but must also make it difficult for others to copy or steal the idea. There are several weapons in the arsenal, including patent protection, trade secrets, and continuing updates.

Interested in Cost Optimization   Inventors/innovators often are poor estimators of what it will cost to bring an idea into practice. In part, this is because inventors believe that their ideas are the best thing since sliced bread and that the value is so obvious that commercialization will flow smoothly. Hence, the technologist is the personality that has to bring budget realism to the commercialization process. They must understand the basis of the concept in detail and have an unbiased view of what it will cost to commercialize. This includes making estimates of costs for technology assessment and evaluation, prototype development (bench scale, beta tests, pilot plants, semiworks, and other development stages), and full-scale production.[29]

Commensurate with their role as cost estimators, technologists are the primary planners of how to step through each of the stages enumerated above that comprise the various phases of development and commercialization. They need to be good communicators (in lay terms) of the implications of each stage. Additionally, they are the best arbiters and liaisons among the innovation team members because they are the ones who are obliged to remain the most objective in decision making.[30] To ensure that technologists behave objectively, the team could place monetary incentives on them to encourage this conduct.

Training-Oriented   As commercialization progresses, new people will be hired to perform a broad variety of assignments. For them to do their jobs well, they have to be trained properly. Clearly, the technologist is best suited for this role.

---

[29]Although primary responsibility for marketing, sales, advertising, staffing, and related management functions is that of the entrepreneur, all other members of the innovation team, including technologists, must be consulted on establishing these budgetary items.

[30]This is the ideal situation, but just like everyone else, technologists get very emotional when things don't go their way.

Focused on Operations and Maintenance   Although inventors can be valuable resources in designing and implementing operations and maintenance procedures, ultimate responsibility for establishing, executing, and monitoring these procedures resides with the technologist.

Bringing It All Together:
Charles Steinmetz the Technologist

As self-described technologists, the authors look across the panorama of history and see many talented and innovative people who are excellent examples of technologists, but perhaps the first and arguably the best modern-day technologist was Charles Proteus Steinmetz. Most famous for inventing the alternating-current motor, Steinmetz was a multifaceted

FIGURE 1.4   Charles Steinmetz (right) and Thomas Edison at Steinmetz's laboratory at the General Electric Company in 1922. (Courtesy of the American Institute of Physics—*Emilio Segré Visual Archives.*)

genius whose contributions to the field of electrical engineering redefined the study of electricity and powered the world.

Steinmetz was a brilliant engineer who readily demonstrated the attributes we believe are intrinsic to technologists. Steinmetz was focused on new technologies and attracted to new inventions. For example, shortly after emigrating to the United States in 1889, Steinmetz found work under Rudolph Eickenmeyer, a Yonkers-based hat manufacturer who wanted to expand his business into electrical generators and motors. When Otis needed a more powerful motor to lift his elevator to higher floors, Steinmetz designed the motor. When Stephen Field, nephew of Cyrus Field of Atlantic Cable fame, approached Eickenmeyer with a proposal to run trolley cars by electricity using alternating current, Steinmetz was called upon. When the transfer from direct current to alternating current was made, there was a slight delay: slight, but long enough to cause motors to overheat. Working in Eickenmeyer's laboratory and at his residence at 124 Waverly Street in Yonkers, Steinmetz solved the problem mathematically and his solution became known as the law of hysteresis or Steinmetz's law. This now-famous discovery remains one of the bedrocks of electrical engineering study.[31]

Steinmetz was also a practical man—another hallmark of the technologist. For him, discovering new technologies wasn't good enough; they had to be useful and cost-effective. Continuing his investigation into electricity generation, Steinmetz discovered a practical means of calculating alternating-current circuits so that the performance of the system could be predicted in advance (without having to build the system and then go through expensive testing and modification). This discovery fueled rapid development and fielding of an electrical infrastructure that is considered one of the bedrocks of modern society. Steinmetz considered this one of his most profound contributions to science.[32]

Technically brilliant on a wide range of subjects, Steinmetz was called upon to fix or improve other designs. Hired at General Electric by Thomas Edison, he was instrumental in creating the company's proposal to develop generators at the new Niagara Falls power station. Steinmetz was made head of GE's Schenectady, New York calculating department, where his work led to the development of numerous transformational capabilities, including devices to protect high-power lines from lightning strikes,

---

[31]http://en.wikipedia.org/wiki/Charles_Proteus_Steinmetz. Also see a superior description of the development of Steinmetz's law at http://www.yonkershistory.org/stein.html.
[32]www.geocities.com/bioelectrochemistry.com/index.htm and search for Steinmetz. There are many other sources that give similar descriptions of Steinmetz's accomplishments, including http://www.encyclopedia.com/doc/1E1-Steinmetz.html.

high-powered traveling-wave tubes (which enabled later development of modern devices such as radar and microwave ovens), and arc lighting.

Recipient of nearly 200 patents, Steinmetz's prowess as a technologist is legendary, but one story stands out and is worth retelling. Told by Charles M. Vest, president of the Massachusetts Institute of Technology, during commencement on June 4, 1999, it showcases one attribute of a technologist.

I want to tell you a story about an incident in the career of Charles Proteus Steinmetz, the great electrical engineer. In the early years of this century, Steinmetz was brought to General Electric's facilities in Schenectady, New York. GE had encountered a performance problem with one of their huge electrical generators and had been absolutely unable to correct it. Steinmetz, a genius in his understanding of electromagnetic phenomena, was brought in as a consultant—not a very common occurrence in those days, as it would be now. Steinmetz also found the problem difficult to diagnose, but for some days he closeted himself with the generator, its engineering drawings, paper and pencil. At the end of this period, he emerged, confident that he knew how to correct the problem. After he departed, GE's engineers found a large "X" marked with chalk on the side of the generator casing. There also was a note instructing them to cut the casing open at that location and remove so many turns of wire from the stator. The generator would then function properly. And indeed it did. Steinmetz was asked what his fee would be. Having no idea in the world what was appropriate, he replied with the absolutely unheard of answer that his fee was $1000. Stunned, the GE bureaucracy then required him to submit a formally itemized invoice. They soon received it. It included two items: 1. Marking chalk "X" on side of generator: $1. 2. Knowing where to mark chalk "X": $999.[33]

1.2.4   The Entrepreneur

The entrepreneur is the quarterback on the innovation team: the glue that holds the team together and inspires the members to achieve success. Entrepreneurs are the motivators and the people who make the whole thing happen. Often, the entrepreneur starts out in one of the other roles, eventually morphing into the force that the team relies on to move toward commercialization. Sometimes an entrepreneur will attempt to keep the other role at the same time, but in our experience, assuming two jobs at the same time doesn't work. Another analogy is that entrepreneurs

---

[33] Ibid. See also http://inventors.about.com/od/astartinventions/a/Steinmetz.htm for a similar description.

are like orchestra conductors. True maestros extract the best from skilled musicians, converting creative compositions into beautiful music.

Success-Oriented Just as with all of the other innovation team members, entrepreneurs are a different breed. They are single-minded and driven people, characterized by high energy levels, eclectic intellectual tastes, and most of all, the quest for success. For them, success is defined very individualistically. A common definition is that success = achievement = recognition. Sometimes power is more important than recognition, and more rarely, money is the ultimate goal of their achievement, but in our experience, not often. In short, "winning the game" frequently is the reward the entrepreneur seeks, with riches being a welcome benefit. A complementary characteristic of this success-driven personality is sociability. Entrepreneurs are gregarious and like to interact with others. This is what makes them good quarterbacks and great salespeople, without whom commercialization simply cannot happen.

Blends Other Perspectives Entrepreneurs are good at helping an innovation team to work together because they have the ability to blend the roles and duties of the other players. Moreover, the really good ones can even assume one or more of the other roles. But it is highly unlikely that entrepreneurs will be successful if they try to do too much themselves. The best entrepreneurs understand thoroughly the personalities, strengths, duties, and responsibilities of other team members, know who the outside experts are, and know when to use these experts to reach the commercialization process goals. This means that they cannot have a superficial understanding of any aspects of the idea or concept or of commercialization. They must have in-depth knowledge of how a concept works and how to sell it.

Keeps Focused Chances are that the entrepreneur has been successful before, so this idea will not be the person's only shot at success. In fact, being successful before probably is one of the reasons that he or she continues to gravitate toward this role. Prior experience helps the process, but it also prompts weakness. Once the person is convinced that the plan is sound and that the right team is in place, he or she may get eager to move on to the next idea. This can be a blessing or a curse. Entrepreneurs tend not to micromanage (good), but sometimes they become inattentive (bad). Keeping entrepreneurs focused clearly is a big challenge for the other players. Remember, we said that the commercialization process needs a great salesperson, and if the entrepreneur begins to believe that the idea will sell itself, trouble is brewing.

Money Isn't Everything   We alluded to it earlier: Most entrepreneurs don't get their kicks by making money. Because of this characteristic and their success orientation and the fact that they define success in varied ways, entrepreneurs need to be backed up by a good and persistent accountant. Even though entrepreneurs understand the need for fiscal responsibility, they often need a strong reminder. Usually, this reminder comes from the investor, who probably chose the accountant in the first place. We said it earlier—money is not the only measure of success, but it is the best and most objective way to keep score and track of where we are along the way.

Rebel with a Cause:
Steve Jobs the Entrepreneur

Few people have such a profound impact on society that people around the globe change the way they do things completely without thinking about it. As I sit here typing on my portable computer listening to my iPod after watching a movie rife with computer-generated animation, I cannot help but marvel at the development of these devices during my lifetime. But upon reflection, I realize that these devices weren't developed during the course of my lifetime. In fact, they are relatively recent developments spurred by the energy and determination of a focused entrepreneur. Steve Jobs has changed the world through his relentless pursuit of valued technology in the hands of the masses.

Like technical wizard and fellow entrepreneur Bill Gates, Jobs is a college dropout whose impatience with academics led to a broader life journey. A high school computer junkie, after leaving college he traveled to India on a journey of self-discovery only to return several months later fueled with a passion to develop and market affordable and functional computers for widespread use.

While still a high school student, he worked as a programmer at Hewlett-Packard, where he met and befriended Steve Wozniak, a technical genius. After an unsatisfying semester at Reed College in Oregon, Jobs returned to California and reunited with Wozniak at Atari, where they worked together as programmers. Soon Jobs realized that the two could do better on their own. Armed with Wozniak's ability to design and build computers and his own superior computer programming and business savvy, Jobs and Wozniak left Atari and formed the Apple Computer Company.[34] Soon the Apple computer splashed onto the world market with

[34]http://en.wikipedia.org/wiki/Steve_Jobs.

such innovations as the mouse pointing device and the point-and-click window presentation. Were these truly innovations? No. Invented elsewhere, they were integrated by Wozniak into a unique and easy-to-use platform, and Jobs brilliantly built a team to manufacture and market them around the globe.

With Wozniak quietly leading technical development, the success-oriented Jobs rapidly grew the ground-breaking computer business, matching it against industry juggernauts such as IBM. The Apple was a success on many levels and the company grew quickly. Jobs, realizing that he lacked experience managing such a large company, brought in John Sculley, an experienced Pepsico executive, as chief operating officer. Following the initial success of the Apple, the company followed with the Macintosh, with the brash Jobs pushing to expand the company's development efforts into other product lines. His blunt and aggressive approach, combined with sales figures that did not meet levels forecast, soon brought him into conflict with members of his board. Soon, the board forced him from the company and he left to create his own computer company, called NeXT.[35]

While at NeXT, Jobs sought to create powerful computers that featured creative capabilities not available in his competitors' systems. Although not a widespread commercial success in terms of sales volume, NeXT computers are regarded as one of the most capable and dynamic desktop devices ever built. Even though NeXT systems were the face of Steve Jobs' product line, Jobs was building a dynamo that would forever change the way we view entertainment.

Jobs' brilliance as an entrepreneur is highlighted by his ability to blend differing perspectives and fuse them into winning teams. During his period at NeXT, the company acquired a computer animation spin-off from *Star Wars'* creator George Lucas's studios and renamed it Pixar Animation Studios: creators of animated movies such as *Toy Story*, *A Bug's Life*, *Finding Nemo*, and *Cars*, and affiliated with the huge Disney entertainment empire. This transformation launched Jobs into the entertainment market with an enormous bang. When NeXT was acquired by Apple, Jobs found himself back at the company he founded, and he resurrected it. He led development of the iPod portable music system and the iTunes Internet-based digital music store, which forever transformed how the world acquires and listens to music.

An entrepreneur is defined as a person who organizes and manages any enterprise, especially a business, usually with considerable initiative and risk.[36] Steve Jobs has demonstrated—and continues to demonstrate—the

[35] http://ei.cs.vt.edu/~history/Jobs.html.
[36] http://dictionary.reference.com/search?r = 2&q = Entrepreneur.

attributes the authors believe epitomize those of an entrepreneur. However you view him, he is an American classic!

1.2.5   Managing Innovation Team Interactions

Forming a team of headstrong, intelligent, ambitious, and driven individual members who have diverse experiences, educations, and backgrounds is a daunting task. But the key factor that will bind them and hold them together is what they all hate most. They hate to lose, and unless they agree upon certain "rules of engagement," they indeed will lose. Here are some rules that the team should consider seriously.

- The entrepreneur should be the chief operating officer. For day-to-day decisions, the entrepreneur is in charge and other team members should accept the entrepreneur's direction and leadership.
- The investor (or designated lead investor, if there are many) should be chairman of the board. In the event that a final decision must be made on a critical matter where the team does not reach consensus, the lead investor is the final authority. He or she is the ultimate boss, for the obvious reason that he or she is funding the enterprise.
- No money should be spent without the knowledge and concurrence of the entire innovation team. Authority can be granted in advance for certain ordinary expenses, but the team needs to meet for decisions regarding really large expenditures.
- Formal agreements should be in place for each team member so that there is a clear understanding of what happens if one member needs to be replaced or if the team needs to be dissolved.
- Secrecy and confidentiality agreements are essential and must be required of each team member. Moreover, these agreements must be strictly enforced.
- Contracts and agreements taken together should be regarded as a "covenant": both legally and morally.

Recognize that innovation team boundaries, particularly when first seeing a new concept, tend to be fuzzy. Measures should be taken to create rules that help to foster the creativity that emanates from this fuzziness rather than to build bureaucracy that strangles the enthusiasm of people who work better as friends than as competitors.

1.3   THE IMPORTANCE OF FLEXIBILITY

In the U.S. Air Force (USAF), one of the doctrinal tenets is: "Flexibility is the key to airpower." Some jokingly say that it is also the sign of poor or incomplete planning. Nonetheless, the culture of the USAF incorporates flexibility as part of the planning process. Being prepared for multiple contingencies is an important part of planning for success. General Dwight D. Eisenhower said that "no plan survives first contact with the enemy." He was right. Flexibility gives you the strength to persevere and survive obstacles.

For this book we suggest the following cautionary remark: "To be successful in commercialization, stay loose, but be disciplined." When we say "stay loose," we mean remain flexible. Flexibility is necessary because the terrain of exploiting technology changes so quickly that the innovation team has to be in a position of deciding intelligently what to do next many times throughout the commercialization process, often in rapid succession. Thus, the team has to be prepared for change by anticipating it in their business plan and having alternative pathways identified for the various contingencies.

The need for flexibility depends on a number of factors:

- Timing
- Status of the idea
- Technical needs and requirements
- Financial needs and requirements
- Pace of progress
- Target audience or customer

We deal with each of these factors in this section and address most of them again later in the book.

1.3.1   Timing Is Everything

In his insightful editorial entitled, "The Rules of Innovation," Jason Pontin suggests the following rule of innovation: *"The first attempt to commercialize an invention almost never succeeds"*[37] (emphasis added). Pontin reports that this rule emanated from a luncheon discussion that he had with John McAfee, founder of the anti-virus company McAfee Associates. Pontin says: "There are two reasons for this. First, the innovator

---

[37] Jason Pontin, "From the Editor: The rules of innovation," *Technology Review*, May 2005, p. 12.

is often early: the really important market for the invention does not yet exist. Second (the point is related), the innovator doesn't know how to make money from the invention: the business model that will support the invention is imperfectly understood. Usually, therefore, another organization succeeds where the innovator failed. This is sometimes called the Second-Mover Advantage."[38,39]

Two critical points are implied: (1) timing is extremely important in the commercialization process, and (2) effective planning could reveal fatal flaws in constructing a business model to exploit the innovation. Fortunately, many inventors/innovators don't believe that the rule pertains to them, so they press on and successfully become part of an innovation team that is, for all intents and purposes, the second-mover. Thus, whereas the rule has currency if participants hew to a "go it alone" approach, arranging to associate with others and building an innovation team can overcome the pitfalls of being too early and not knowing how to commercialize the idea.

Nevertheless, it is possible to be too early. In the same editorial, Pontin articulates another rule of technological innovation: *"Any sufficiently radical invention seems ridiculous to most people when they first encounter it"* (emphasis added). Time has to be allowed to permit the innovation to gestate in the minds of both the inventor and the customer. But clearly, the inventor's job is to envision how to refine the idea into a marketable product before the concept can be sold to the customer or even to other members of the innovation team.

The issue of timing is tricky. Dawdling can be a greater sin than premature introduction of a good idea. Hence, balance has to be sought in exploiting the idea. That's why we are proponents of the innovation team approach. Each of the core members of the team (i.e., inventor/innovator, investor, technologist, and entrepreneur) will lend his or her expertise to assessing the impact that timing can have. Even very good teams can get ahead of themselves. An example of this is the huge and greatly underutilized fiber-optics network into which many high-tech companies

---

[38] Ibid.

[39] *Technology Review, MIT's Magazine of Innovation*, claims to be the oldest technology magazine in the world. "Founded in 1899, *Technology Review* describes emerging technologies and analyzes their commercial, economic, social, and political impact for an audience of senior executives, researchers, financiers, and policymakers, as well as for the MIT alumni. In addition, Technology Review, Inc. produces technologyreview.com, a Website that offers daily news and opinion on emerging technologies." We urge readers of this book to use this invaluable resource not only to assess technologies of particular interest to them, but also to learn how others have approached the process of commercialization. We have read the magazine for many years and have reflected the knowledge gained at many places throughout this book.

sunk immense capital in the middle to late 1990s. Occasionally, participants should slow down to permit technological horizons to come into view.

During the 1990s, facing the forecast of tremendous bandwidth demand in the inflated dot.com economy, several telecommunications companies invested heavily in the installation of massive fiber-optic cable networks around the United States. These fiber-optic builders were desperately afraid that their competitors would beat them to customers. The resulting mass installations yielded an incredibly robust fiber-optic capability in portions of the United States, but the market did not materialize as anticipated. As of this writing, much of the fiber remains "dark fiber," excess capacity that is not used and hence is not drawing revenue for investors.

One way to strike a reasonable and rational balance between haste and excessive deliberation is what we call the *bullpen*, *holding tank*, or *reserve box*.[40] If, in the process of evaluating ideas, the innovation team believes that a very good idea may be premature, it is put into a mode (i.e., the bullpen) where development of the idea moves forward, but at a more measured pace. In that way inventors and technologists don't forget about the idea completely and move on to other things. They remain in touch with the leading edge of the state of the art, continue to network with others in the field, and proceed with a more thoughtful and less frenetic pace of development. Should events come into better focus and dictate rapid ramping up, the team should be in a position to do so quickly. The entrepreneur, as quarterback and visionary, plays a key role in deciding the pace of development (see Section 1.3.5).

The ability to shift gears depends on a good, sound plan of action from the outset. The plan must be characterized by deliberate preparation and crisp decision making. We address the various elements of planning in later sections. But at this point we can summarize by saying that we can bring timing into control if we have a good idea, build an effective innovation team, and prepare and implement a thoughtful commercialization plan. The main reason for better control is that by having these elements in place, we are much less likely to be surprised.

In summary, here are the magic ingredients of knowing when and how fast to move forward with an idea: *timing, planning, insight*, and *luck*. Just a few words on luck; there are two great quotations on the subject that have special pertinence to our subject.

---

[40]One of the authors likes the term *bullpen* best. He says, "It is an idea that is still out there; all you have to do is warm it up." He makes an excellent point, and we will use that term.

"I find that the harder I work, the more luck I seem to have."—Thomas
   Jefferson

"Luck is the residue of design."—Branch Rickey

Together these quotes recognize the value of hard work and planning.
In the event that we are sluggish in exploiting an idea, we don't give up.
Because we have a plan, we can't be that far behind. So we don't give up,
we just work hard to recover ground lost and make up the difference by
improving on the quality and performance of the product. Finally, always
remember that other people can be lucky, too.

1.3.2   The Importance of Determining "Prime Time"

The intensity with which the innovation team reacts to a concept depends
to a large extent on how far along the idea is. If the idea is a barn-burner
but is still a concept on paper, you react one way. Conversely, if it's in
its fifth generation, you react in another way. The trick is in being able
quickly to tell the difference between the two. Clearly, the technologist
plays the most important role in making this determination.

   Learning the technical status of an idea is crucial to the entrepreneur
because the entrepreneur has to come up with the game plan for establishing an appropriate budget and schedule and the team has to make an
early "go–no go" decision. This is not meant to imply that we are forced
to shoot pennies out of the air, but it does mean that we have to match the
rigor of moving ahead with the status of the idea. Careful understanding
of the idea focuses on what's been done to date—both successes and failures. The innovation team, based on this understanding, basically decides
three things: (1) If we will move ahead with the idea (i.e., go–no go), (2)
how much we are going to have to spend, and (3) how long it will take
to meet the first milestone.

   In general, barn-burners generate a lot of enthusiasm, but there are a
couple of obvious problems. First, usually a lot less is known about the
idea. This is because hype and hope cloud the vision of those selling
the idea, and the inventors/innovators get ahead of the facts. This makes
the job of the technologist more difficult. Second, the enthusiasm could be
premature. Remember Pontin's "first rule of innovation" (Section 1.3.1).
Third, if it was all that great an idea and a lot is known about it, why is
it still on the street? So clearly, dealing with barn-burners entails lots of
risk, and caution must balance fervor. On the other hand, tired ideas that
have been beaten to death take a long time to bury. We still see ideas
that we passed up 35 years ago that somebody has reinvented and tried
to breathe new life into.

Ideas can range anywhere from a nascent airburst of an idea that a brilliant innovator had in the shower this morning to one that we characterize as "the walking dead." Obviously, ideas can fall anywhere in the spectrum between the two. Recognize where along the line we are and act accordingly.

1.3.3   Expanding the Innovation Team

Let's assume that the innovation team decides that the timing for exploiting a good idea is on the money (every pun intended)—that is, *now*! Moreover, also assume that the idea is far enough along so that there is a sound base of technical information; that is, the status of the concept is at the point where spending money for development is appropriate. Here's where the innovation team, in this case led by the technologist, earns its keep. It takes real talent and is a precursor for success to be able to assess accurately the status of a concept and (here's the hard part) then define the technical needs and requirements to make it happen.

Frequently, this means that an imperfectly understood concept requires the services of people who can understand every aspect of the idea. That, in turn, means that often the team has to look outside for the right experts. It's not easy for many team members to call in the right experts at the right time. That's because it's hard for their egos to accept that they don't know everything. Oddly enough, it usually isn't the technologist who is unwilling to seek expert help. Technologists are more accustomed than the inventor/innovator to working in a more collegial environment and feel comfortable getting validation of their "brilliant" insights from their buddies. As we said earlier, the inventor/innovator at times thinks that everybody else is stupid because they can't grasp the "obvious." But it's the investors and the entrepreneurs who have the biggest case of indigestion with "experts" or "consultants." Some of their concerns are legitimate.

One concern reflects on the technologist. "If you are so smart, how come we continually have to use outsiders?" The answer is simple. Even in specific areas, experienced technologists need to understand in greater detail nuances that sometimes mean the difference between success and failure. What seems like nitpicking to investors and entrepreneurs is crucial to the technologist. Remember that the technologist is a valued member of the team not because he or she knows everything, but rather, knows how to get things done. Thus, the ability to identify the need for outside help and to find the right people who can fill that need is a real key to success.

Investors and entrepreneurs are correct to be concerned about letting too many people in on an idea. There are several specific concerns. First, there is the potential for dilution of ownership, especially if the expert requires a piece of the action in addition to or in lieu of a fee. Second, revealing too much proprietary information puts the secrecy and confidentially of an idea at risk. Some team members can be particularly concerned if they regard the expert as a stranger. Third, what the innovation team doesn't need is another ego that will lead to personality clashes. Experience demonstrates that the person that the inventor likes least is an "outside consultant." Fourth, even if we've got a good consultant with whom everybody gets along and who is an effective resource, sometimes the person may leak insights to the concept that forces premature marketing and false starts.

One way to keep experts under control is to maintain a small stable of consultants and stick with that inner circle. If the scope of the concepts and ideas that the innovation team has chosen is not too broad-ranging, that approach may be possible. Another way is to trust in the innovation team's ability to work well with each other and their inherent talents, and not use outsiders. We prefer the former approach.

Despite the claims of the inventor, great ideas are not ready to walk at birth. They need a lot of refinement before they are ready for the marketplace. The process of determining the nature of that refinement is the essence of this section. Simply put, the ability to assess what the technical needs and requirements are that will make an idea or concept into a commercial success is absolutely crucial, and the talent to do so is managed initially by the technologist but ultimately depends on the genius of the entire innovation team.

Another excellent tactic that is used extensively today is *red teams*, peers to attack or look at our efforts from a different angle so that we can focus on the weaknesses in our position. It is a device that is used extensively to challenge and stretch opinions and work products. Keep in mind the need for confidentiality when picking a red team.

1.3.4   Determining How Much Money Is Needed

Once technical needs and requirements are determined, it's time to talk about money. It is essential that the innovation team toils carefully and collegially to make an accurate assessment of how long it will take and how much money it will cost to bring an idea into practice. We emphasize that the team has to undertake this effort with great focus and concentration because this step leads off the intensive planning and management regimen that makes the difference between success and failure.[41]

---

[41] Refer back to the list of key ingredients for successful commercialization.

All team members carry the same weight in this process.[42] Eventual resolution of budgets and schedules must be unanimous. There are many reasons why, but the main one is that in the course of commercialization, prolonged schedules and increased budgets are the norm. It's the nature of the beast that there will be changes and surprises. The last thing the team needs is somebody saying "I told you so!" Everybody on the innovation team must understand clearly that surprises (both good and bad) will occur and there will be a need to change the pathway. The ability to be flexible is absolutely essential to make an idea a commercial success. In summary, both the people and the plan they prepare must be flexible.

The real trick is to plan for change and to keep schedule and budget variances small. Time must be devoted to anticipating what the changes might be and developing alternatives to be implemented when these changes happen, as they invariably will. The alternatives should be viewed not as an addendum to the plan in case of trouble, but rather, as an integral part of the plan. In our experience (and we will say this more than once), the most unpleasant surprises occur when good things happen, not bad ones. That's because we often spend too much time figuring out what to do when things go wrong and not enough on what happens when we get lucky.

In addition, strong project discipline is necessary. It's a real challenge to stick to your knitting and proceed stepwise. The temptation at times to take shortcuts will be powerful, but in our experience, skipping over planned activities almost never works. Besides, it's stupid to expend time and effort to develop a detailed plan and then ignore it.

1.3.5 Maintaining a Reasonable Pace of Progress

The pace at which the commercialization process proceeds usually tests the tolerance of innovation team members to accept setbacks and delays. Their degree of flexibility or patience can vary considerably. That's no big surprise given the assorted perspectives that each team member brings to the project. For example, the investor wants to know how much more money will be needed. The entrepreneur wants to know how much longer it will take. The inventor wants to know when the technologist is going to stop fiddling and get moving ahead with dispatch, and the technologist wants everybody to stay calm and understand that progress is going along according to plan—more or less.

So what's the solution for keeping the team together without unduly challenging their patience? At the risk of being excessively repetitive, the

---

[42]Somebody has to lead this effort, and in this case as in most others, the entrepreneur will fulfill that role.

solution is the formulation of a solid, thoughtful, and flexible plan that anticipates deviations and takes them into account through development and inclusion of alternatives.

The innovation team should have formal progress reviews at regular intervals to keep everybody informed. If there are serious divergences not anticipated by alternatives in the plan, the plan must be updated. All team members have to play a part in these updates, just as they did in the original plan formulation. It is important to understand that these updates are needed periodically and must be addressed in a timely fashion.

1.3.6   Knowing the Customer

Typically, inventors/innovators, in their enthusiasm, believe that everyone wants what they have discovered. That can be a dangerous mind-set. iPods don't sell well to the hearing impaired, and some of us wouldn't play a videogame if you gave it to us. You have to know your market. The entrepreneur is the leader in keeping the team focused on the appropriate market, and sometimes development results can shift that focus dramatically.

One research and development project with which we were associated was charged with testing a naturally occurring ion-exchange mineral. Our project manager was distraught when he learned through experimentation that ion-exchange capacity was impaired severely by the presence of a competing ion commonly found in the solution he was testing. In an effort to calm him down, his office-mate asked about the process and why the interfering ion was able to decrease capacity. During the course of their discussion they came to the conclusion that they could make a lot more money by going after the competing ion than after their original target ions. Hence, they shifted gears and made a major positive impact on a wholly new market.

The point of this example is that the old mantra "know your customer" is extremely important, but sometimes opportunities will present themselves in a way that will cause you to see your technology from a completely different perspective. If you aren't flexible, you may miss the chance of a lifetime.

1.4   CAN ENTREPRENEURSHIP BE TAUGHT?

1.4.1   The Difference Between Talent and Skill

When we were writing this book, one of our extremely insightful friends raised the annoying question: Do you really believe that you can teach people how to be entrepreneurs? His theory is that like leaders, athletes, musicians, and artists, among others, entrepreneurs are inherently talented and cannot be taught because their gifts are innate. By raising this issue, he questioned the usefulness of our book. As we debated his thesis, we agreed that there is an immense difference between "talent" and "skill," but ultimately, we concluded that practice, discipline, and knowledge are essential attributes (in addition to those listed earlier: teamwork, planning, and perseverance) in perfecting the natural talents of these unique people.[43] Thus, by focusing on these attributes, we believe that we can help to hone the abilities of readers who want to commercialize innovative technology or to understand how it's done.

Moreover, in our discussions with our good friend, we acknowledged that teaching a subject for purposes of greater understanding is useful for full appreciation of the gifts of talented people. For example, teaching music, painting, and sculpture doesn't make a person a Mozart, Rembrandt, or Houdon, but it does permit us to recognize great talent and appreciate how such creativity enriches our lives. Therefore, we concluded that entrepreneurship indeed is an innate talent, but our book fulfills a definite need for those who are eager to understand how good ideas are put into practice and how people work hard to make it happen.

1.4.2   Entrepreneurship Programs at Major Universities

When we started this book, we had only a vague idea of the extent of formal educational programs focused on entrepreneurship. We knew of the outstanding programs at MIT and Stanford but did not have a full appreciation of the breadth and depth of academic programs across the United States and globally. Clearly, the scope of university programs is important to us because it extends our prospective audience to a potentially large body of faculty and students interested in the commercialization of innovative technology.

We decided that we would explore how many of the leading graduate schools of engineering and business had formal programs devoted specifically to the subject of entrepreneurship. We used three lists of top schools to conduct our exploration: (1) *U.S. News and World Report's* (*USNWR*) "America's Best Graduate Schools 2007, Top Engineering Schools"; (2) *USNWR*, "Top Business Schools"; and (3) The *Wall Street Journal*, "Back on Top," September 21, 2005, a list of the world's top business schools. Then we chose the top 10 from each list; understandably, there were many

---

[43]Think of how important practice, discipline, and knowledge are to the fabulous golfer, Tiger Woods.

duplications. We added Rensselaer Polytechnic Institute to the list of engineering schools because the senior author spent more than 20 years on that institution's various advisory boards and councils, giving us unique insight into that university's capabilities. Because of limitations of time and space, we chose to confine the list to universities in the United States. Obviously, there are many great universities in other countries that have similar programs, and we don't mean to neglect them. We looked at four: IMD, Lausanne, Switzerland; ESADE, Barcelona, Spain: IPADE, Mexico City, Mexico; and University of Western Ontario, London, Canada. Each had intensive and thoughtful programs that promote the education of eager entrepreneurs.

Table 1.2 catalogs the U.S. universities that we investigated using the three lists above to learn what vehicles (centers) they had established for the study of entrepreneurship and innovation and to get a feel for the types of courses that are offered. Interestingly, of the 20 universities cited in Table 1.2, all but one had a formally designated center of excellence devoted to entrepreneurship, and all have strong programs in technology, innovation, and the management of new enterprises. Table 1.3 provides details on centers of entrepreneurship and courses taught on the subject.

Clearly, the best universities in the United States are seriously committed to educating budding entrepreneurs and to building awareness of the importance of launching new enterprises for the economic health of the nation. Thus, we conclude that there are many more programs than those that we identified in Tables 1.2 and 1.3. We conclude further that most of the programs are centered in graduate schools of business, although many business schools have included or are affiliated with engineering schools in some way.

The Ewing Marion Kauffman Foundation in Kansas City, Missouri, is dedicated to promoting entrepreneurship education. The foundation has published the *Census of the Status of Entrepreneurship in American Higher Education: 2006*. An article by Frank[44] summarizes some of the data from the *Census*.

- Entrepreneurship education is the fastest-growing field of study in 2006.
- During 2006, at least 300 four-year higher education institutions offered entrepreneurship courses designed for students *not* enrolled in business schools.
- More than 1600 colleges offered courses in entrepreneurship in 2006.

[44]J. A. Frank, "Ideas in action," *Rensselaer*, Fall 2006, pp. 18–23.

TABLE 1.2 Programs in Entrepreneurship at Top Universities in Engineering and Business

University	USNWR Engineering Rank	USNWR Business School Rank	WSJ Business School Rank
Cal-Berkeley	3	7	7
Cal Tech	10		
Carnegie Mellon	8		3
Chicago		6	
Columbia		7	8
Dartmouth		9	1
Georgia Tech	4		
Harvard		1	
Illinois	5		
Michigan	7		2
MIT	1	4	
North Carolina			9
Northwestern		4	4
Penn		3	6
Purdue	6		
Rensselaer	37		
Stanford	2	2	
UCLA		10	
USC	9		10
Yale			5

- About 1050 colleges offered entrepreneurship courses in the early 1990s.
- About 300 colleges offered entrepreneurship courses in the 1980s.

Thus, our conclusion about the scope of entrepreneurship education appears to be right on the mark: in fact, the data from the Kauffman *Census* came as a bit of a surprise, even to us. The enthusiasm of the academic community was confirmed during our recent participation in a National Science Foundation environmental engineering education workshop, where the professors attending were particularly vocal in their support of stimulating and implementing innovation in their curricula.[45]

---

[45]C. J. Touhill, "Entrepreneurship and technology commercialization," presented at the Workshop on Frontiers in Environmental Engineering Education, January 10, 2007, Tempe, Arizona. Sponsored by The National Science Foundation, the American Academy of Environmental Engineers, and the Association of Environmental Engineering and Science Professors.

TABLE 1.3 University Centers Are Courses in Entrepreneurship

University	Program/Center	Selected Courses	Notes
MIT	Deshpande Center for Technological Innovation and the MIT Entrepreneurship Center	Law for the Entrepreneur and Manager Managing the Innovation Process Managing Innovation: Emerging Trends Product Design and Development How to Develop "Breakthrough" Products and Services Global Entrepreneurship Lab Designing and Leading the Entrepreneurial Organization Entrepreneurial Finance Patents, Copyrights, and the Law of Intellectual Property Developmental Entrepreneurship Social Entrepreneurship Entrepreneurship/Venture Capital Without Borders Technology and Entrepreneurial Strategy	Courses offered through the Sloan School of Management

(Continued)

TABLE 1.3 (*Continued*)

University	Program/Center	Selected Courses	Notes
Stanford	Center for Entrepreneurial Studies	Investment Management and Entrepreneurial Finance Environmental Entrepreneurship Strategies and Practices of Family and Closely-Held Companies Entrepreneurial Design for Extreme Affordability Intellectual Property and Its Effect on Business Entrepreneurship: Formation of New Ventures Entrepreneurship and Venture Capital Evaluating Entrepreneurial Opportunities Social Entrepreneurship Strategic Management of Technology and Innovation	Courses offered through the Graduate School of Business

University	Center/Program	Courses	Description
University of California–Berkeley	Center for Entrepreneurship and Technology	Engineering Entrepreneurship Entrepreneurial Marketing and Finance Distinguished Innovator Lecture Series	Associated with the College of Engineering; The College of Engineering offers a program that awards a Certificate in Management of Engineering and Innovation
	Lester Center for Entrepreneurship and Innovation	Organizational Leadership (multidisciplinary curriculum)	Associated with the Haas School of Business
Georgia Tech	**TI:GER** (Technological Innovation: Generating Economic Results)	Fundamentals of Innovation I & II Special Topics in Technology Commercialization Entrepreneurial Finance Innovation of Entrepreneur Behavior Venture Creation Corporate Entrepreneurship Legal Issues in Technology Transfer	College of Management offers a "Program for Engineering Entrepreneurship" leading to a Certificate in Engineering Entrepreneurship
University of Illinois–Champaign/Urbana	Office of Business Innovation and Entrepreneurship	Small Business Consulting Entrepreneurship: Small Business Formation Financing Small Business Development	The College of Business offers concentration in entrepreneurship at the undergraduate level focusing on small business

(Continued)

TABLE 1.3 (*Continued*)

University	Program/Center	Selected Courses	Notes
Purdue	Burton D. Morgan Center for Entrepreneurship	Introduction to Entrepreneurship and Innovation Entrepreneurship and Innovation II	The Center offers undergraduate students in any major the opportunity to earn an Entrepreneurship and Innovation Certificate
University of Michigan–AnnArbor	Sam Zell and Robert H. Lurie Institute for Entrepreneurial Studies	Entrepreneurial Management Entrepreneurship via Management Venture Capital, Private Equity I & II Managing the Growth of New Ventures Marketing for Entrepreneurs Entrepreneurial Turnaround Management Legal Aspects of Entrepreneurship Writing Fundamentals for Entrepreneurs	Program is in the Ross School of Business

Carnegie Mellon	Ph.D. program in strategy, entrepreneurship, and technological change	Economics of Entrepreneurship Economics of Technological Change Courses in entrepreneurship, firm startups, and financing of new ventures Courses in engineering pertaining to innovation and technology Courses in technology policy and innovation	Joint program of the Social and Decision Sciences Department, Tepper School of Business, Heinz School of Public Policy and Management, and the Engineering and Public Policy Department
	Donald H. Jones Center for Entrepreneurship	Introduction to Entrepreneurship Entrepreneurial Thought and Action Funding Early Stage Ventures Commercialization of Technology in Entrepreneurial Companies Entrepreneurial Business Planning Entrepreneurial Management	Program is in the Tepper School of Business

(Continued)

TABLE 1.3 *(Continued)*

University	Program/Center	Selected Courses	Notes
University of Southern California	Lloyd Greif Center for Entrepreneurial Studies	Technology Feasibility Technology Commercialization Investing in New Ventures Management of Rapidly Growing Ventures Engineering Project Management Invention and Technology Development Strategic Management of Technology Strategies in High-Tech Businesses	Graduate Certificate in Technology Commercialization in the Marshall School of Business
Cal Tech		Engineering Entrepreneurship Management of Technology	No formal programs explicitly directed toward entrepreneurship or technology commercialization, but many opportunities to participate in new venture workshops and seminars in the Division of Engineering and Applied Science

50

University	Center	Courses	Notes
Rensselaer	Severino Center for Technological Entrepreneurship	Entrepreneurial Finance Invention, Innovation, and Entrepreneurship Starting a New Venture Corporate Entrepreneurship Marketing High Tech Products R & D Management	Program is in the Lally School of Management and Technology
Harvard	Technology and Entrepreneurship Center at Harvard	Biotechnology Startup Introduction to Biotechnology Innovation in Science and Engineering: Conference Course	
	Arthur Rock Center for Entrepreneurship	The Entrepreneurial Manager Entrepreneurial Finance Entrepreneurial Marketing Managing for Creativity Building and Sustaining a Successful Enterprise Leading Innovation, Change and Organizational Renewal Entrepreneurship and Global Capitalism International Entrepreneurship Managing Innovation and Product Development Commercializing Science and High Technology Evaluating the Entrepreneurial Opportunity	Center at Harvard Business School (partial list of courses)

(Continued)

TABLE 1.3 (Continued)

University	Program/Center	Selected Courses	Notes
Penn	Sol C. Snider Entrepreneurial Research Center	—	Home of research for Wharton Entrepreneurial Programs, it is the first center dedicated to the study of entrepreneurship
	Goergen Entrepreneurial Management Program	Technology Strategy Entrepreneurship Change, Innovation and Entrepreneurship Venture Capital and Entrepreneurial Management Formation and Implementation of Entrepreneurial Ventures Private Equity in Emerging Markets Entrepreneurship Through Acquisitions	Wharton School of Business
	Minor in Engineering Entrepreneurship	Engineering Entrepreneurship I and II High-Tech Venture Development Ideas to Assets From Laboratory to Marketplace	Offered in the School of Engineering and Applied Science

Northwestern	Larry and Carol Levy Institute for Entrepreneurial Practice	Successful Entrepreneurship Entrepreneurship and New Venture Formulation Entrepreneurial Selling Understanding and Managing Risk Entrepreneurial Finance Managing Technology Technology Marketing Internet Marketing	Offered at the Kellogg School Entrepreneurship and Innovation Program
Chicago	Polsky Center for Entrepreneurship	Entrepreneurial Finance and Private Equity New Venture Strategy Building the New Venture Commercializing Innovation Developing New Products and Services Technology Strategy Structuring Venture Capital and Entrepreneurial Transactions Statistical Insight into Marketing Consulting and Entrepreneurship	Offered in the Graduate School of Business
Dartmouth	Center for Private Equity and Entrepreneurship	Introduction to Entrepreneurship Private Equity Finance Advanced Entrepreneurship Entrepreneurial Management Growth Strategies of Emerging Enterprises	Offered in the Tuck School of Business

(Continued)

TABLE 1.3 (*Continued*)

University	Program/Center	Selected Courses	Notes
UCLA	Harold Price Center for Entrepreneurial Studies	Managing Entrepreneurial Operations Managing Finance and Financing the Emerging Enterprise Law for Entrepreneurs Technology Management	Offered in the Anderson School of Management
Yale	(No formal center)	Entrepreneurial Business Planning Venture Capital and Private Equity Investment SynThesis: Product Design for Entrepreneurial Teams	Offered in the Yale School of Management
Columbia	Eugene M. Lang Center for Entrepreneurship	Introduction to Venturing Entrepreneurial Finance Launching New Ventures Entrepreneurship and Private Equity in Emerging Markets Technology Strategy Business Technology and Innovation Entrepreneurial Selling High Technology Marketing and Entrepreneurship New Product Development Law for Managers and Entrepreneurs	Offered in the Columbia Business School

North Carolina	Center for Entrepreneurial Studies	Introduction to Entrepreneurship Business Plan Creation Venture Capital Management Entrepreneurial Marketing Innovation and Product Development Managing in the High Tech Sector VC Valuation and Deal Structure Acquiring Proprietary Technology Launching the Venture I & II Mergers and Acquisitions	Offered in the Kenan–Flagler Business School

55

1.4.3   Corporate Research and Development Programs

People who sell computers, pharmaceuticals, medical devices, automobiles, and razor blades spend billions of dollars every year to find innovations that will keep their companies growing and profitable. Is this spending comparable to the commercialization process we describe in this book? The answer is generally "no." Virtually all of these companies are large, with significant research and development budgets that support laboratories dedicated to a disciplined process of extending and expanding the scope of company products. Commercialization is built in at each stage of product development. So whereas there are aspects of corporate research and development (R&D) that could be helpful to budding entrepreneurs, reading up on drug company R&D isn't going to help Johnnie Inventor sell his new light bulb that will last forever. But we like to believe that our book can be a significant help.

Before we leave this topic, we'd like to mention a couple of ways that some companies that have "formal" research/commercialization programs get into trouble. First, in an effort to stimulate creative employees to come up with innovative ideas, companies establish budgets to encourage and fund such endeavors. In many cases, managers have good employees who aren't fully billable at the moment, so the R&D fund becomes a "slush fund" and is used to tide the employee over until a real project comes along.

Second, one of the world's leading research contractors many years ago provided an early investment into an innovation that became a booming success. In an effort to reproduce this great achievement, they formed a subsidiary organization with profits made in the original success. The intent was to attract outside inventors and in-house scientists and engineers who would develop new ideas and share in the commercial success with the research contractor. Unfortunately, for over 60 years they have been unable even to come close to the original boon. There are several problems: They failed to acknowledge that their first find was lucky, and they never set up a system that would work. The system they used was very bureaucratic. They wanted too much ownership in the eyes of internal and outside inventors,[46] and it eventually degraded into a sort of slush fund, as described above.

Finally, those of us who have served on SBIR/STTR review panels have learned pretty quickly that there are many proposers whose names turn up time after time. These are proposal mills, whose primary *raison d'être* is cranking out SBIR/STTR proposals, not necessarily the commercialization

---

[46]The system was so bad and burdensome for insiders that anybody who had a really good idea simply quit and sought his or her own investor capital.

of good ideas. A characteristic of such companies are jazzy proposals on such hot topics as nanotechnology, biotechnology, and homeland security. Their proposals often are very well done, and their boilerplate on the subject of commercialization is satisfactory, if vague, but if their record of commercializing previous innovations is a measure of success, they don't do very well. The problem is that they are really more interested in SBIR/STTR funding than they are in the commercialization of new technology.

1.5   KEY POINTS

- This book is intended to provide insight for those who are eager to commercialize good ideas and concepts. It can serve as an inventor/innovator manual, a university textbook, an SBIR/STTR reference, or a technology investment handbook. It will also be helpful to business executives and management students in explaining the life cycle of product innovation and the dynamics of bringing good ideas to the marketplace.
- The four key ingredients that make commercialization of good ideas successful are teamwork, planning, discipline, and perseverance.
- Building an innovation team is crucial to the process of bringing good ideas into practice. The innovation team best equipped to commercialize technology is one comprised of four distinct personalities: inventor/innovator, investor, technologist, and entrepreneur.
- To build a successful innovation team, the mind-set of each personality or role must be thoroughly understood.
- Profiles of famous people who embody the best characteristics of the roles of inventor/innovator, investor, technologist, and entrepreneur are included in this chapter as brief vignettes.
- Flexibility is crucial because the terrain of exploiting technology changes quickly. To prepare for change, the innovation team has to anticipate it in the business plan and have alternative pathways identified for various contingencies. The need for flexibility depends on a number of factors: timing, status of the idea, technical needs and requirements, financial needs and requirements, pace of progress, and target audience or customer.
- Virtually every major technological university and business school has a formal center and academic program that promotes and teaches entrepreneurship.

2

OUR PERSPECTIVE

To provide readers with a realistic view of the commercialization process, we believe that the subsequent narrative in this book will be most meaningful if we reveal our perspective at the outset. If we don't, we fear that our message will be vague and theoretical rather than the practical step-by-step guide that we intend. Our experience and thus our bias is that of technologists, and we present our ideas and advice from that viewpoint. Being aware of our perspective should help readers to understand our motivations and partialities better. We believe that this does not dilute the roles of the other members of the innovation team in our mind or in the text. To the contrary, we think it helps to show how team interrelationships are crucial to success.

For purposes of this book, we presume that the underpinning strategy of the innovation team is to search for multiple candidate technologies in a specific and focused area of interest for purposes of building a stable (portfolio) of related businesses.[1] The rationale for adopting this strategy will become apparent as the book proceeds, but to begin with, here are a few of the central reasons:

[1]Typical categories of interest can be seen in Table 2.1. For our purposes, any of these categories are good examples of current leading-edge technology. In selecting our area of interest, we try not to be too broad-ranging; otherwise, we will soon learn that we have many more potentially good ideas than we can manage reasonably.

Commercialization of Innovative Technologies: Bringing Good Ideas to the Marketplace, By C. Joseph Touhill, Gregory J. Touhill, and Thomas A. O'Riordan Copyright © 2008 John Wiley & Sons, Inc.

1. Our perspective as technologists lends itself to the discovery, improvement, and exploitation of multiple ideas, not just a single idea. If we are good at what we do, we want to play for the entire season, not in just one game. In fact, most brilliant inventors/innovators are not content to find only one gem of an idea and retire to Hawaii; they continue to explore other vehicles to fill needs and satisfy their power of imagination. Similar characteristics are shared by investors and entrepreneurs.

2. Not all ideas and concepts succeed. Investing in technological innovation is just like other types of investing—diversity is an important component of success.

3. Broader vision and scope (within the category of interest, of course) leads to uncovering more opportunities. It is very rare that an innovation team is assembled to commercialize a single idea. We show how risk spreading plays a major role in managing our commercialization strategy.

4. Investors understand that not all ideas pan out. So it's rare that they will want to sink all their venture capital into just one idea or concept. As a matter of fact, the idea of investing in a stable or portfolio of ideas gives them greater confidence in the team's ability to produce and reduces their risk. This will help to make them open their wallets faster.

5. Because a portfolio that contains more than one good idea will have various stages of research, development, and demonstration going on simultaneously, the likelihood that innovation team members will be kept energized and attentive by the breadth and pace of activities is increased.

In the remainder of the chapter we focus on the basics regarding how a team moves ahead in choosing a strategy and preparing to select appropriate ideas and concepts.

2.1 STRATEGY DEVELOPMENT

In line with our saying that investing in technological innovation is just like other types of investing, we begin this section by identifying rules for investing borrowed from many successful investors who have risked their fortunes in stocks, bonds, currencies, real estate, commodities, and other assets. Our rules generally apply to almost all forms of investing. Next, we show what the informed public currently believes to be lucrative areas of interest for technology commercialization. Then we discuss the concept of risk, and finally, we reemphasize the need for flexibility in executing the strategic plan.

2.1.1 Rules for Investing

Most successful people are quite willing (if not eager) to share their formulas for winning investment strategies. These may be found in all types of publications, on the Internet, and even in that relatively recent phenomenon, the blog. We have taken advantage of these resources and cherry-picked the best thoughts from multiple places to try to encapsulate the wisdom of successful investors and entrepreneurs. What follows is our take on consensus rules for investing. We believe that the rules are self-evident and really don't need further comment here. On the other hand, we address these rules more completely in subsequent chapters, if sometimes obliquely.

Rules for Investing in Good Ideas[2]

1. Define your goals.
2. Know your risk profile.
3. Invest in things you know.
4. Diversify in terms of type of technological innovation, time horizon, financial capabilities, and risk tolerance.
5. Have sufficient capital to reach your goals.
6. Get the best professional advice that you can.
7. Beware of fads.
8. Don't pay too much for a good thing.
9. Have a schedule, a budget, and manage costs.
10. Be disciplined.
11. Be attentive.
12. Be patient.
13. Be ruled by knowledge and not by emotions.
14. Hold onto your winners and sell your losers.
15. Take your losses quickly and your profits slowly.
16. Stick to your plan.

---

[2]The rules for investing presume that the participants are current in technological understanding and keep up with the state of the art through active inquiry and continuing education.

17. Rebalance your portfolio.
18. The object is not to be right all the time, but to make money when you are right.

2.1.2 Areas of Interest

That great American philosopher Yogi Berra has been accused of saying, "If you don't know where you are going, you'll probably never get there!" For any of us to be successful, it is necessary that we have a very clear idea of what we are doing and how we are going to do it. Table 2.1 summarizes the *Wall Street Journal's* Technology Innovation Awards for the years 2004, 2005, and 2006. We call attention to this table for a number of reasons: It provides some idea of the categories of technological innovation that currently interest the investing community, it shows where the ideas are coming from in terms of types and sizes of innovating companies and their national origin, and it provides general information on the types of ideas that the *Wall Street Journal* award panel thought deserved this prestigious and closely followed award.

For our purposes, the target area of interest will be dictated by the people who assemble and comprise the innovation team. Because our perspective focuses on developing a stable of companies (a portfolio) that are related, we do not approach commercialization from the viewpoint of the inventor who wants only his or her concept to be a smashing success (although if the inventor is on our team, we will do everything we can to help meet his or her expectations). Rather, we want to concentrate on that family of ideas that plays to the strengths of the innovation team. Although it's good to be diversified, it's not good to be diverted by ideas that don't fit the overall strategy.[3]

During September 2006, the *Wall Street Journal* published an article that gave an update of the status of a few of the previous winners of the Innovation Awards.[4] Here's what they found.

- *Witten Technologies* (Software Winner, 2004) finished technology trials; trying to get venture capital but having trouble getting investors; has only one licensee, the Florida Department of Transportation.
- *Poseidon Technologies* (Innovation Award Winner, 2001) has installed 150 systems of its drowning detection technology, up from six in 2001; in 2006 received biggest contract, to outfit 20 Atlanta-area

---

[3]In a later chapter we talk about what we do with good ideas that are very attractive but don't fit easily into the overall strategy.
[4]Ryan, Chittum, "Where are they now?" *The Wall Street Journal Online*, Sep. 11, 2006.

TABLE 2.1 *Wall Street Journal* **Innovation Award Winners**

Category	Company	Country	Innovation
Biotech–medical			
2004	Given Imaging Ltd.	Israel	Pill-shaped videocamera screens the esophagus for disorders
2005	454 Life Sciences (Gold Medal)	U.S.	Low-cost gene sequencing
2006	Pfizer/Nektar Therapeutics, Inc.	U.S.	Exubera, a powdered inhalable insulin for the treatment of diabetes
Consumer electronics, 2006	Sonos	U.S.	System for broadcasting music around a home over a wireless network
E-commerce, 2004	Galp Energia SGPS SA	Portugal	Gas stations use a biometric payment system, where customers press a thumb against a glass pad
Energy and power			
2005	Solar Integrated Technologies	U.S.	Solar roof system using a single-ply roofing membrane
2006	Helio Volt	U.S.	Process for making ultrathin solar-powered materials
Environment			
2004	Ferrate Treatment Technologies LLC	U.S.	Wastewater and industrial effluent treatment without toxic by-products
2005	MIT/Environment and Public Health Organization	U.S. and Nepal	Inexpensive water filtration system
2006	ET Water Systems	U.S.	System that uses weather data and Web technology to automate the irrigation of plants
IT security and privacy, 2006	AuthenTec	U.S.	Technology that reads below the surface of a fingerprint, eliminating the need for passwords and PINs for electronic devices

(Continued)

TABLE 2.1 *(Continued)*

Category	Company	Country	Innovation
Materials and other base technologies			
2004	Startech Environmental Corporation	U.S.	Recycling system that destroys wastes by subjecting them to superheated ionized gases
2005	Ecology Coatings	U.S.	Environmentally friendly coatings
2006	Eikos	U.S.	A transparent, electrically conductive coating that can be used to make displays that are less prone to dead spots
Medical devices			
2005	Optimyst Systems Inc.	U.S.	Eye-medication device that emits a fine mist, which is more efficient than eyedrops
2006	Incisive Surgical	U.S.	Mechanical skin stapler that places absorbable staples underneath the skin
Multimedia, 2004	International Business Machines Corporation	U.S.	System for searching multimedia content using technology that analyzes audio, visual, and text components
Network–internet technologies, 2004	Flarion Technologies Inc.	U.S.	New approach to mobile broadband networks, based on Internet protocol
Network–broadband–internet, 2005	Riverbed Technology	U.S.	Network appliances that speed data transfer between remote offices and central servers
Security (facilities)			
2004	Nomadics Inc.	U.S.	Handheld portable explosive detector
2005	ObjectVideo	U.S.	Software that monitors multiple feeds from videocameras and can detect potential threats
2006	axonX	U.S.	Security camera system that uses artificial-intelligence software to detect smoke and fire

TABLE 2.1   *(Continued)*

Category	Company	Country	Innovation
Security (network)			
2004	Sana Security Inc.	U.S.	Antihacker products based on the ways that the human body repels invaders
2005	Fujitsu Laboratories	Japan	Device that can read the veins in the palm of a person's hand
Semiconductors– Electronics, 2004	Sun Microsystems Laboratories (Gold Medal)	U.S.	New method for chips to transmit data inside a computer up to 100 times faster than today's top speed
Semiconductors			
2005	Allen Technology	U.S.	Manufacturing process that reduces the cost of RFID tags
2006	Semprius	U.S.	Process for making electronic circuits that can be applied to any surface
Software			
2004	Witten Technologies Inc.	U.S.	Technology that creates detailed images of conditions underground
2005	Agitar Software	U.S.	Tool that helps software developers find and fix bugs when writing new programs
2006	Sun Microsystems (Gold Medal)	U.S.	D-Trace open-source software that troubleshoots problems in real time
Technology design, 2006	Seagate Technology	U.S.	Perpendicular recording technology on hard disks, resulting in greater storage capacity
Transportation			
2004	Toyota Motor Corporation	Japan	Hybrid Synergy Drive, the newest version of the gasoline–electric hybrid power train used in Toyota's Prius model
2005	QinetiQ	U.K.	Airport radar system for detecting runway debris

(Continued)

TABLE 2.1   *(Continued)*

Category	Company	Country	Innovation
Wireless			
2004	Mesh Networks Inc.	U.S.	Command system enabling real-time tracking of firefighters and other emergency personnel in buildings, tunnels, etc.
2005	Freescale Semi-conductor	U.S.	Development of ultrawideband wireless technology
2006	Zensys	U.S.	Wireless technology for controlling home lighting, entertainment, and security systems

Source: "Technology innovation winners," *The Wall Street Journal Online*, Nov. 15, 2004. Michael, Totty, "Innovation awards: a better idea," *The Wall Street Journal Online*, Oct. 24, 2005. Michael, Totty, "Innovation awards: the winners are …," *The Wall Street Journal Online*, Sep. 11, 2006.

YMCA pools; company representative believes that slow sales are due to the high price that investors require to recoup their investment; working with French legislators to have a law passed that will require drowning-detection systems in all public swimming pools.

- *454 Life Sciences Corporation* (Gold Medal Winner, 2005)   increased workforce by 50%, to 150 during 2006; had revenue of about $30 million from fall 2005 to fall 2006; most sales have been to big genetic research institutions and biotechnology companies.
- *Optimyst Systems Inc.* (Medical Devices Winner, 2005)   still seeking regulatory approval; continues to work from angel investor funding; seeking another round of investment.
- *Ecology Coatings* (Materials and Other Base Technologies Winner, 2005)   entered into licensee agreements with DuPont; in the process of consummating a reverse merger.[5]

The *Wall Street Journal* Technology Innovation Awards represent ideas that are in or very close to the marketplace. Perhaps it would be a good idea if the innovation team focused on innovations that are one step ahead: what's commonly referred to as *emerging technologies*. Each year *Technology Review* magazine identifies 10 technologies that they believe are "worth keeping an eye on." Table 2.2 shows the 10 technologies selected for 2006 and 2007.

[5]The nature of the reverse merger was not defined or described in the article.

TABLE 2.2 *Technology Review's* **10 Emerging Technologies for 2006 and 2007**

Technology	Description
2006	
Comparative interactomics	Visualizing and mapping the body's complexity
Nanomedicine	Guiding drugs to precise locations
Nanobiomechanics	Measuring tiny forces acting on cells
Epigenetics	Determining ways that chemical compounds influence DNA
Cognitive radio	Exploiting unused radio spectrum
Nuclear reprogramming	Devising ethical derivation of stem cells
Diffusion tensor imaging	Developing novel brain imaging
Universal authentication	Creating a privacy-protecting online ID system
Pervasive wireless	Consolidating wireless gadgets
Stretchable silicon	Making flexible electronic chips
2007	
Peer-to-peer video	Enhancing Internet efficiency and saving bandwidth
Quantum-dot solar power	Boosting output in cheap photovoltaics
Neuron control	Turning selected parts of the brain on and off
Nanohealing	Stopping bleeding and aiding recovery from brain injury
Mobile augmented reality	Using sensor data to locate any object
Metamaterials	Building "invisibility shields"
Compressive sensing	Revamping digital imaging systems in cameras and medical scanners
Personalized medical monitors	Using computers to automate diagnostics
Optical antennas	Making high-capacity DVDs, more powerful computer chips, and higher-resolution optical microscopes
Single-cell analysis	Detecting minute differences between individual cells to improve medical tests and treatments

Source: "10 Emerging technologies," *Technology Review*, Mar.–Apr. 2006, p. 55; "Emerging technologies 2007," *Technology Review*, Mar.–Apr. 2007, p. 45.

Obviously, there are other places where we can identify emerging technologies, but the point is that the innovation team must be aware of what's happening. Moreover, the team has to be able to anticipate where there's a need and how to satisfy that need using appropriate technology. The category of interest selected usually emerges because the creator of the innovation team has a track record in that business. In our case, most often the creator could be the technologist, investor, or entrepreneur who formulates the innovation team, not the inventor/innovator. The reason, of course, is that generally the inventor is a single-minded person whose personality we described in some detail in Chapter 1. There are occasional exceptions, where a prolific inventor sees the value of diversification and constitutes a team to exploit more than one of their ideas, but that's a rarity.

Creation of an innovation team generally happens when a good idea comes to the attention of a person who decides to commercialize the idea. Clearly, the team creator wants to move ahead because he or she sees substantial merit in the idea based on their experience. The technologist will want to go forward due to the promise of the technology, whereas the investor and the entrepreneur usually see merit because the inventor/innovator has a proven track record of success. If the team is searching for ideas to fill a hole in an existing portfolio, the hole may be filled by finding an idea that complements one or more of their existing technologies, or they may be looking for a good idea in an area that they believe will become "hot." Being an active and knowledgeable player in technology development helps an innovation team choose hot topics on the basis of sound scientific and business acumen rather than emotion. For example, nanotechnology is a category that's crammed with people eager to get into the field who haven't a clue what the science is all about.

In sum, pick an area of interest that the team understands thoroughly and in which they jointly have strong experience, and keep focus and project discipline throughout the commercialization process.

2.1.3   Risk

The team has now chosen a particular area of interest in order to assemble a stable or portfolio of good ideas that should be explored for potential commercialization. The next question is: "How much risk should we take?" In our experience, larger organizations don't take enough risk unless it is built formally into a very large research and development budget in a centralized and planned way. Risk for smaller entities is controlled by the availability of investment capital. Paradoxically, our experience suggests that smaller entities tend to be much more conservative because they find that the consequences of failure are more devastating. That's one major reason why inventors/innovators turn to investors earlier than they would like; they reluctantly accept that it's better to share than to fail.

The reason that judgments on risk are so important is because risk is what influences all major decisions in moving forward with an idea. We found an interesting view of risk in what we first thought to be an unusual setting. Lee Smolin, theoretical physicist at the Perimeter Institute for Theoretical Physics in Waterloo, Ontario, Canada, wrote a journal article on creativity in science and physics in particular.[6] The article stimulated

---

[6]Lee Smolin, "Why no 'new Einstein'?" *Physics Today*, June 2005, p. 56.

considerable comment, pro and con, in the Letters to the Editor section of a subsequent issue.[7] In his reply to the letters, Smolin comments on the relationship of risk and rate of progress for cutting-edge technological innovation and biomedical research. His response is especially interesting: "I once asked a very successful venture capitalist how his firm decided what level of risk to take on. He said, 'If more than 10 percent of the companies we help start up are making money after five years, we know we are not taking enough risk to maximize return on our investment.' "

We are not certain that we agree with Smolin's venture capitalist, but he isn't too far wrong. Remember that investing in technological innovation is just like other types of investing. One of the first things that investment advisors counsel is that we have to understand the concept of risk in investing. The reason that Smolin's venture capitalist chose the number he did was because he had a basis of experience that permitted calculation of the level of return on investment that he found acceptable for the risk he was taking. The numbers indicate that payoffs have been pretty good for this person.

Recently, one of the authors of this book and his boss were visiting with the chief executive officer (CEO) of a Fortune 100 company engaged in high technology. During the course of conducting our business with this well-known CEO, we asked the following question: "Given your strategic planning construct, how do you assess and manage your risk?" The CEO, known for his gift of incisiveness, quickly responded with what we think is a superb answer: "Great question! There is no definitive way to assess risk, because there are many different kinds of risk. That said, we look at legal risk: Can the issue get us into trouble? We look at financial risk, which is so obvious: Is this something that will make us money? Is it worth doing? We also look at operational risk: Will it work? Will it integrate into our platforms? Finally, we've included in our risk assessment a review of strategic risk: For example, will this enhance or harm the reputation of our company?"

We believe that in his answer to our question, the CEO encapsulated succinctly the various types of risk that must be considered in assessing whether or not to move forward with innovative ideas:

- Legal risk
- Financial risk
- Operational risk
- Strategic risk

The answer validated our already high opinion of this person's superior leadership capabilities.

[7]Letters, "Mixed reactions to 'No new Einstein,'" *Physics Today*, Jan. 2006, p. 13.

In our strategy, we estimate that we can expect to see the following levels of percentages for our portfolio: 10 percent of ideas will be barn-burners (huge successes); 20 percent will be good solid moneymakers with reasonable potential for capturing significant market share or entry into an untapped market; 40 percent will be fair-to-middling and will be candidates for sale and spin-off; 20 percent will not live up to expectations and will be abandoned; and 10 percent will be unmitigated disasters. Thus, in the long term we expect to keep only 30 percent of the ideas in our portfolio in one form or another.[8] Actually, 30 percent is a pretty good number. For many entrepreneurs the number is far lower. In our case, we are presuming that we have a good strategy, a solid and compatible innovation team, tight management, and capable professional advisors. We cannot emphasize too strongly that commercialization of technology is an inherently risky business and that even when we have a terrific idea, a great plan, and good people, lots can go wrong.

2.1.4   Flexibility

Recall that we emphasized the need for flexibility in executing a commercialization plan. Deciding on a particular strategy doesn't mean that we can't change our minds along the way. However, after we have decided on a strategy, we must make certain that if we deviate from the original plan, it's our choice and not one dictated by serendipity. For example, it may have been our original intent to demonstrate a technology and then sell the company. But consider what happens if our results are so good that we believe moving into production on our own is a far better way to go. There is no problem if we have accounted for this eventuality in strategy development and formulation of the strategic plan. Having a lot of alternatives that anticipate bends in the road and detours is a good thing. It saves time and money and gives us a much better chance to succeed.

Here is a key thought that we want readers to remember when formulating a strategic plan: *Nobody ever succeeded by visualizing failure*. We fear that too many people fail in their effort to commercialize good ideas because they focus too much on what can go wrong rather than planning on what to do if everything goes better than expected.[9]

---

[8]The manner in which we retain successful ideas and concepts in our commercialization portfolio is discussed in greater detail in Chapter 3.

[9]Lawyers are extremely valuable allies in permitting the innovation team to make key business decisions that facilitate the commercialization process. Just remember that it's their job to anticipate and surmount stumbling blocks. It's what we pay them to do. We don't expect them to take the intellectual risks necessary to recognize and capitalize on technological breakthroughs.

2.1.5 Experience of Others

In his book *The Chasm Companion*,[10] Wiefels summarizes many of the lessons he learned personally and from his colleagues in developing, managing, and marketing innovative high technology over a period of several decades. We believe that Wiefels' lessons are germane to our strategy development and are valuable insights that we quote below.

- Making strategy decisions in high-technology markets is a high-stakes, low-data game. Successful pattern recognition of market dynamics is hugely important. To quote John Maynard Keynes, "I'd rather be vaguely right than precisely wrong."
- A company's competitive advantages in sum can be sustainable over time. The parts that make up these advantages, taken singularly, are not sustainable.
- If strategies are to be implemented successfully, they must be understood and committed to by many different organizations. As such, marketing and/or strategy groups may lead this exercise, but they are not solely responsible for the outcome.
- The need for rapid and decisive responses to a shifting and ambiguous marketplace—and the need to gain teamwide commitment to these responses on a sustainable basis—requires rapid and repeatable strategy creation alternatives.
- To win, the strategy must be *executed* based on the key assumptions underpinning the strategy. Poor execution kills brilliant strategy. Brilliant execution can make up for mediocre or uninspired strategy.
- Finally, never let a strategy get in the way of a big idea. But you must recognize what is truly big, and what masquerades or is sold as such.

2.2 TECHNOLOGY ASSESSMENT

After the innovation team has completed strategy development and planning, the fun begins. We gather ideas and concepts for evaluation. The objective of the evaluation is a complete and unvarnished understanding of what an idea or concept is all about. An unwritten rule of investing is "keep it simple." In our view, if we don't understand the idea well enough to explain it in simple terms to a bright teenager, then we need more study or the idea stinks.

[10]Paul, Wiefels, *The Chasm Companion*, HarperCollins (HarperBusiness), New York, 2002, p. 279.

2.2.1 Discovery

The process of discovery is a touchy thing. Even when they know people on the innovation team well, inventors/innovators find it very hard to reveal their idea completely. Trust is a critical issue, but it often goes deeper than that because of all the effort that went into the conception and early development of the idea. Notwithstanding this prior history, the innovation team must insist that the inventors/innovators tell them everything. In return, the team has to promise to maintain confidentiality and to work diligently in structuring agreements that will satisfy the inventors/innovators.

If the inventors/innovators still are uncomfortable in being forthcoming during the technology assessment, we may want to use a technological trustee. This can prove to be a good way to bridge the gap between inventors and the innovation team. We described the role of the trustee in Chapter 1 and could summarize it briefly as follows: Both parties (e.g., inventor and innovation team) will agree that a third party will be the repository for details of an idea or concept. The inventor will reveal all details of how and why the idea works to the third party, the technological trustee, who is judged to be an expert in the area of application. By thorough probing, the trustee will form an overall opinion of the idea and will share this opinion with the team. Thus, the inventor trusts the trustee to retain the idea and keep all details in secret, and the innovation team trusts the technological opinion of the trustee sufficiently to lend money for development of the idea. If the confidentiality agreement and technological trustee approaches are rejected by the inventor and he or she continues to refuse to permit complete discovery, we don't waste our time — we just walk away.

2.2.2 Evaluation

We make certain that the innovation team has the ability and tools to decide if an idea is a good one. The team looks to the technologist to make a sound and timely evaluation of the idea. If to complete the evaluation, the technologist needs outside help, the technologist should work with the inventor/innovator to get someone the inventor trusts to provide that help. There's an upside and a downside to this approach. The upside is that the inventor probably has very good knowledge of the technical experts in the area of research and development related to the concept. The downside is that the experts trusted and recommended by the inventor probably agree with the inventor. Remember that to an inventor, "trust" = "concurrence." The best way to handle the use of outside experts is for the technologist to have the inventor suggest three names, with the technologist interviewing them and choosing either one of them or a third party known and respected by those three. After awhile it's pretty easy for the technologist to make a choice because we get to know who the real experts are in the area of interest.

Some ideas require laboratory and/or testing facilities to prove the concept. The simplest way of handling this is to use the inventor's facility if one exists. If that facility is not capable of making the evaluation required, there are other avenues. For example, some universities will permit their laboratories to be used on a contract basis. The difficulty with this approach is that universities may require use of students and faculty to complete the testing. This adds time and cost that may not be necessary and raises confidentiality concerns. A few universities recognize these concerns and are taking measures to alleviate them.

Another avenue is the use of contract research and development laboratories such as Battelle, Midwest Research, and SRI. The problem here is cost. These laboratories have high overhead costs that must be passed on to their clients. Such places should be used only where the equipment needed to conduct experiments is unique and can't be obtained in any other way.

Yet another alternative is to develop our own testing facility. If the innovation team believes that there will be enough testing over a reasonable time frame to justify the cost of such a facility, this is a viable option. From the standpoint of the technologist, this is often the best option, as it gives the team the most security and control over the ideas as well as flexibility over their development. Investors invariably hate the suggestion because they try to avoid fixed costs whenever possible.

Let's consider the point of view of inventors/innovators. They want to reveal as little as possible about the idea because from their standpoint, one of the worst things that can happen is that they reveal everything and then the innovation team decides that the idea somehow doesn't match their plans or doesn't meet their expectations. Even worse is when an initial evaluation is positive and the innovation team backs off after getting more knowledge. The inventor must anticipate this and structure stiff penalties if that situation occurs; for example, the inventor could demand a steep "walkaway" fee. Both sides must be aware of the inherent risk in commercialization, but agreements must reflect fair and equitable arrangements for terminating contracts. All parties should be careful from the beginning and do it right the first time.

2.3 TECHNOLOGY DEVELOPMENT

Let us presume that we have now selected an area of interest, assembled an innovation team, found good ideas, learned that they do work, and have real potential. What happens next? In our perspective of building a portfolio of ideas, we move to the next step: technology development. Some venture capitalists simply perform a proof-of-concept evaluation and then sell the proven concept to others, who pursue the development phase. There is nothing wrong with that approach if it fits the strategic plan, but it doesn't correspond with where we are headed. We believe that selling too hastily is a low-risk, low-return proposition that rarely leads to the whopping returns that justify investing in the evaluation and development of multiple opportunities. Besides, this stingy, "safe" approach takes all the joy out of the commercialization process.

The details of technology development are left for later chapters. Our intent in this section is to provide observations on some of the relationships involved in the development process. The key to making this crucial phase go smoothly is a solid relationship between the inventor/innovator and the technologist. Mutual respect is the foundation for a solid relationship. If cooperation is good, it will help the inventor quickly to visualize that improvements proposed by the technologist are positive and promote commercialization and are not a personal attack (as often happens). On the other hand, the innovation team must be cautious that inventors and technologists don't jointly become too enamored of the development efforts and turn the association into a mutual admiration society. Such love fests cloud their judgment and decision making when objectivity is a must.

As technology development proceeds, interactions with others expand: those on the innovation team, the supporting cast (lawyers, accountants, suppliers), and outside consultants. Care must be taken as to how much and what kind of information should be shared. This determination should be made in advance of the time when outsiders are encountered.

2.4   TECHNOLOGY MANAGEMENT

In our case, management of the commercialization process will be controlled by the innovation team, comprised of the core members indicated earlier: inventor/innovator, investor, technologist, and entrepreneur. As we indicated in Chapter 1, the entrepreneur will be the quarterback or chief operating officer of the team and will manage the day-to-day efforts and chair all operating meetings. The lead investor will be chairman of the board and will chair all strategy and policymaking meetings. Obviously, the board is congruent with the innovation team. Remember the old rule about the relationship between boards and management: Boards of directors *direct* and managers *manage*. The prerogatives of each should not be preempted.

For technology management to be effective in commercialization, care must be taken to organize appropriately. This means that professional project management techniques must be used, and the need for professional services (i.e., accounting, legal, sales, marketing) must be recognized. The temptation to deal with technology as a research and development program must be resisted assiduously. This is a business and must be run like one.

2.5 KEY POINTS

- Our perspective presumes that the underpinning strategy of the innovation team is to search for multiple candidate technologies in a specific and focused area of interest for the purposes of building a portfolio of related businesses.
- Investing in technological innovation is just like other types of investing—diversity is an important component of success. Targeting multiple technologies spreads risk, uncovers more opportunities, and maintains the focus of the innovation team.
- Rules for investing generally apply to almost all forms of investing, including good technological ideas. We suggest 18 rules for investing that are ignored at the peril of those who would commercialize such ideas.
- The portfolio area of interest should reflect the knowledge and experience of all members of the innovation team.
- Areas of risk that must be explored in assessing good ideas include legal, financial, operational, and strategic risk.
- Based on the risk profile expected, our portfolio anticipates retaining about 30 percent of the ideas evaluated.
- A key thought to remember when formulating our strategic plan is: *Nobody ever succeeded by visualizing failure*.
- We reproduced some valuable lessons about strategy development as expounded by Paul Wiefels in his book *The Chasm Companion*.
- Technology assessment and development require close cooperative relationships with all team members, especially between the inventor and the technologist.
- The most effective results are expected when professional management techniques are employed in the commercialization process.

3

DEVELOPING AN ENDGAME

In this chapter we lay the groundwork for the rest of the book by discussing, in general, alternative endgames: how to know when we are finished (i.e., when we've achieved our objective), what actions to take upon reaching the goal, and how to manage an idea to make the commercialization process work. In addition, we describe some examples of how people approached endgame situations and the ultimate outcomes. We also give the reader insight into an emerging new technology so that they can follow the progress of an early innovator.

3.1 ALTERNATIVE ENDGAMES

It's extremely important to have a tentative goal (or endgame) in mind when taking on a technology for assessment. Clearly, not every idea will turn out to be a Xerox or a Google, but when we first encounter an idea, unless we see it as having strong commercialization potential, we shouldn't expend valuable resources on it.[1] Several times in this book we emphasize the following two points:

[1]Remember that money is only one resource. Sometimes the far more important resource is time.

Commercialization of Innovative Technologies: Bringing Good Ideas to the Marketplace, By C. Joseph Touhill, Gregory J. Touhill, and Thomas A. O'Riordan Copyright © 2008 John Wiley & Sons, Inc.

1. Conduct all our activities by visualizing that the technology will be a booming success.[2]
2. Know in advance what we will do if all these activities go better than our wildest dreams. Opportunities are lost when we focus instead on what can go wrong.

Thus, we must anticipate what to do when we believe that we have a success, which means that we need an endgame strategy when we bring each new technology into our portfolio, including those that are barn-burners, those that turn out to be turkeys, and everything in between. We are neither lawyers nor investment bankers, so our discussion of alternative endgames focuses on what we would like the outcome to be, and we leave the nuts-and-bolts details of how to do it to the professionals that we hire (e.g., lawyers, and investment bankers).[3]

The endgame depends to some extent on the interests and capabilities of the innovation team. For example, if the lead technologist is a world-renown mechanical engineer with in-depth experience on a machine similar to the one being evaluated, we may want to go directly to product manufacture ourselves rather than licensing or selling the idea. On the other hand, some innovation teams may feel more comfortable avoiding development activities altogether and simply confine their activities to brokering intellectual property.

A couple of things happen when we have an endgame objective clearly in mind. First, it helps provide focus and discipline to the assessment and evaluation process. Second, it helps to structure the idea for the next step. For instance, if our endgame involves selling the idea after proof of concept, we will want the assessment and evaluation history to be clear and associated documentation geared toward sale to a targeted buyer. The commentary that follows describes a number of endgame strategies that may be appropriate.[4]

3.1.1 Growing a Company to Maturity

Inventors with great ideas like to see themselves as being the future Michael S. Dell, founder of Dell Inc. That's not a bad model because

---

[2]One of the present authors coaches his employees to "start small, think big, and scale fast" when planning and implementing major projects. We have found that this approach works extremely well for complex technical projects.

[3]Investors who are part of the innovation team usually have strong connections with investment bankers, who are familiar with strategies for maximizing returns based on the endgames chosen.

[4]The endgame strategies suggested in this chapter are only a sample of the range of possible alternatives. New strategies continue to emerge, and some may involve combinations of those articulated here.

in 1984, Dell started a computer company called PC's Limited in his dormitory room at the University of Texas at Austin. The company became successful enough that with the help of a loan from his grandparents, Dell dropped out of college at the age of 19 to run the business full-time. Dell Inc. is now the most profitable PC manufacturer in the world, with sales of $57 billion and profits of $2.6 billion in the year ending February 2007, making Dell one of the richest men in the United States. Despite the fact that the recent history of Dell Inc. has included acquisitions and expansion into other areas (e.g., plasma television sets), Dell oversaw growth of his nascent idea into the computer behemoth it became.

Dell's success sprung not from a device but from a concept: assembling customized personal computers from components after orders were placed. Obviously, the concept was a good one. Dell didn't need an innovation team because his grandparents and his savings provided the needed capital, and he was the innovator and entrepreneur (a very, very good one). As the entrepreneur, he hired technology experts to keep him abreast of state-of-the-art developments rather than getting deeply involved himself.

Dell is the latest in a long line of successful people who in their single-minded way took a technology and grew it into a large and mature corporation. A few other examples are Eleuthère Irénée du Pont of DuPont, Thomas Edison of General Electric and other companies, Henry Ford of Ford Motor Company, and Bill Gates of Microsoft. Note carefully that in each case, once the company reached maturity based on the initial concept, it continued expansion through acquisition, merger, and diversification into other, usually related strategic areas.

These companies share a number of similar characteristics. First, in the early stages of the companies, the founders toiled at the bench either by themselves or with a tight-knit cadre of associates. Second, what caused growth to occur was primarily their talent as entrepreneurs and as motivators of people, and their business acumen. Third, they surrounded themselves with highly qualified people who they trained and paid very well. Fourth, they knew how and when to reconstitute the innovation team and their personal role in it.

For our portfolio we reserve this endgame (i.e., growth to maturity) for great ideas that appeal to a very large market. Moreover, the market has to be ripe for development, consistent with the timing of emergence from the technology development phase, and we have to be able to envision a market that will last for decades. We may uncover more spectacular ideas scientifically, but lack of a sizable market and inappropriate timing may dictate that we choose a different endgame for such ideas.

Even though it's the dream of all innovation teams to grow an idea into a corporate icon, be aware that this alternative isn't achieved very often;

in fact, it rarely is. But there is no harm in trying to grow to maturity, because if events demonstrate that it will not happen as desired, it is still possible to execute one of the other alternatives: IPO (initial public offering), spin-off, or merger and acquisition.

3.1.2 Growing a Company to a Target Point

This endgame anticipates that we set a distinct goal or target for exiting the venture in whole or in part. We may also want to buy out a partner, which could mean that we have shifted our focus to another endgame strategy not shared by the entire innovation team. In the sections that follow we discuss a few of the possibilities for ownership transition. We defer to legal and investment banking experts for the details and variations available.

Acquisition by Others   This is a popular alternative for those wishing to cash in on a commercialization effort. The sale can be for cash or stock or a combination of the two. The price may anticipate taking out the principals entirely or leaving founding management with a minority ownership position. It's up to the innovation team whether they want to have any ownership and to what degree. It depends on how much they need the money for other idea development, the extent to which they believe that they can influence the new ownership, and their vision of the prospects of the new company under the changed ownership.

If some of the people in the founding innovation team expect to remain with the new company, there are a couple of points to bear in mind. First, remember that the founders are no longer in charge. For innovation teams that are particularly attached to an idea emotionally, this is a difficult position to be in, especially when somebody is fiddling with our baby. It's also tough on the ego. Second, it is not uncommon for those who stay with the acquiring company to have to sign contracts promising a prescribed service term, including noncompete agreements.[5] Be careful to specify the conditions of severance in these agreements because in many cases, relationships become strained between the new and old owners. Conversely, the new owners have to be careful that the old owners don't treat the acquisition as a high-class retirement plan.

For our purposes, we believe that the optimal arrangement is to take a combination of cash and stock: mostly cash, with just enough stock to assure a seat on the board of directors, but no more. In addition, innovation team members should not continue as employees of the new company,

---

[5]For core members of the innovation team, noncompete agreements could cause very big problems, due to constraints that may flow to other parts of their technological portfolio. Thus, great care must be exercised in constructing noncompete agreements.

but rather, should serve as outside consultants for a fixed term with a guaranteed minimum level of fee or retainer for a defined period. In our opinion, this creates the least potential for conflict and is the most flexible arrangement for both parties.

In a consolidation acquisition, the shares of one or more members of the innovation team (i.e., one or more of the investors, the inventor/innovator, or the technologist) are sought. It's rare that the entrepreneur would want to be bought out. In fact, it's usually the entrepreneur who leads the consolidation acquisition. A common reason for such an acquisition is that one or more members of the team want the idea to be the centerpiece of their own portfolio at a time when others simply want to liquidate their involvement.

IPO (Initial Public Offering)   Offering shares of a developed idea to the public to create a new company is often regarded as an intermediate step toward the real endgame rather than as an end in itself. The main reason for this step is twofold: first, to establish a market value for the new company, and second, to permit the owners to sell their shares of the company more gradually and probably at a higher value than if the company were privately held. Conversely, if the company becomes increasingly successful, they can hang onto the stock and enjoy the run-up until they decide to sell on the open market.

Recognize that IPOs have a downside. Public companies have to comply with a myriad of governmental rules and regulations. In addition to the constraints and restrictions that this implies, it also means that the company must have considerably more legal, accounting, and government relations assistance than if the company had remained private. This leads to increased overhead costs.

In the past, going public using an IPO often meant that the objective was to sell the company eventually to a much larger entity unless the newly formed company had an obvious strategic goal of "growth to maturity." Because of recent legislation designed to protect the investing public, it appears that at present, companies are easier to sell without an IPO.

Professional Management   In earlier discussions we didn't mean to imply that members of the innovation team are all supermen or superwomen. To the contrary, they usually are like you and me and have their own strengths and weaknesses. Often, the best way to get optimal results from a budding company is to turn it over to professional managers. This may come about because the innovation team is busy with other opportunities and there isn't anybody who can be shaken loose to run the company, giving it the attention it deserves. It simply may be that nobody on the team is qualified to manage exploitation of the idea, or there is an outsider who is eminently qualified and would do a fantastic job. Another reason to turn to professional management is when the company grows to a size beyond which the original innovation team doesn't have the skills or experience to manage booming growth. A good example is when Dave Thomas of Wendy's turned to a management group that had the capability to accomplish what he believed he couldn't himself.[6] It takes guts to allow somebody from outside to run "our baby"; it also takes wisdom to know when to do it.

Liquidated Partnership   This is a peculiar endgame because it isn't done very often, but it does make sense in certain situations. Effectively, what happens is this. At the outset of establishing the strategic plan, a definitive target endpoint is established which has very specific conditions. When these well-defined conditions are met, the partnership is liquidated. The manner of liquidation need not be specified in advance, although it can be. In fact, members of the partnership can demand first right of refusal to buy the partnership's assets. The difficulty with doing so is finding an equitable method of valuation. It's easier to get outsiders to place fair market value on the partnership than to get insiders to do so. Why would we want to do this? This endgame makes the most sense when the innovation team members are focused only on a particular idea or have a limited portfolio, and just want to complete development of the idea, then move on to other things.

Spin-off   Spin-off as a subsidiary is a popular endgame. In this endgame, one innovation team member or a newly hired professional manager runs the company, either as a privately held entity or as a public company controlled by the team. In both cases, the team acts as the board of directors and the company effectively is a subsidiary. This is a very comfortable vehicle for several reasons:

- The company gets focused attention from an interested professional manager.
- There is a better degree of control.
- Risk is moderated.
- It buys time to let the commercialization process develop.

One disadvantage of this approach is that one of the best team members may be sidetracked from other duties important to growing the overall portfolio.

[6]Remember that Dave Thomas didn't leave the company altogether, he became an outstanding advertising star for Wendy's until his death.

3.1.3   Selling a Patent or Trade Secret

Some innovation teams decide at birth that their goal is to invest in intellectual property only and to avoid getting too far into technology development. Others, for reasons of risk or modest interest, may decide not to expend development money to pursue an idea. Even though the idea may have considerable potential, they choose to move on. In such a case, the idea is put up for sale by selling a patent or trade secret. Relative to trade secrets, it is extremely hard to keep one confidential. Today's analytical equipment and reverse engineering tools have become sophisticated to the point where it is virtually impossible to maintain a trade secret. Hence, we do not dwell on trade secrets further other than to acknowledge that they are intellectual property and have a place in technological innovation.

If development efforts are skipped and if a patent is sold, it's hard to get full benefits from anticipated or projected success. The reasons are twofold:

1. When we shuffle off risk, we give up reward.
2. Without doing development work, it's impossible to gauge the full potential of an idea.

From the point of view of the buyer of a patent, it is a bad idea to share downstream benefits with the seller, because the buyer has accepted almost all of the risk of bringing the idea into practice. Deals where such an arrangement is suggested should be avoided.

3.1.4   Licensing a Patent or Trade Secret

Licensing a patent or trade secret can take place anywhere along the line of commercialization: after cursory assessment and evaluation, after development, or in the early stages of production. However, the most common point is either after assessment and evaluation or in the early stages of development. This requires the buyer to accept some degree of development work.

Licensing can be a lucrative arrangement, but it takes a lot of work to monitor and control.[7] Additionally, complicated contracts and monitoring create high administrative costs. Both buyers and sellers have to be cautious about managing license agreements. Licenses can be either exclusive or nonexclusive.

---

[7]It's unpleasant to acknowledge, but licensees sometimes cheat and don't report all revenue due to the licensor.

Exclusive Licenses   Exclusive licenses are much easier to sell, negotiate, and monitor. Because exclusive licensees have a unique right to the intellectual property, they should be expected to pay more than if the license is nonexclusive. In addition, contract documents are more straightforward because the contracts are unique and don't have to be structured for numerous organizations with different missions and characteristics. Since there will be either a single exclusive license or a very limited number, the monitoring effort will be manageable.

If multiple exclusive licenses are issued, there should be no potential for overlap in the areas (generally, geographical) covered by the licenses. If the areas are not well defined in the contract license documents, monitoring and legal nightmares are inevitable.

Nonexclusive Licenses   Given the potential for monitoring and legal entanglements alluded to above, why would anybody want to deal with nonexclusive licenses? The answer is that in some cases, especially for weaker ideas or one where defense of intellectual property rights is vulnerable, this may be a suitable arrangement for the buyer and seller. If the parties to the agreement are trusted and compatible partners, things could work out reasonably well. But in actual practice, there are not too many nonexclusive licenses in the field of high technology.

3.1.5   Developing a Technology, Then Selling the Patent or License

It's wonderful to contemplate that somebody will buy patent rights or a license without development work, but in reality most people want development work, and lots of it, before they buy. Hence, this is one of the most common endgames for innovation teams. Skeptics invariably demand a well-developed prototype or a thorough beta test (a test for a computer product prior to commercial release) before they will even consider talking with the team. Developers (members of the team) have to structure a reward profile so that the development costs can be recoverd and team members will be compensated for the risks taken in uncovering, assessing, and evaluating the technology. It may seem complicated to reach agreement with a potential buyer or licensee, but that's not the case—because we, as the developers, hold all the cards. We took the risks and should be rewarded accordingly.

Along with spin-offs to a subsidiary and IPOs, selling patent rights or licensing is one of the endgames preferred by strong innovation teams with lots of capital backing. Essentially, we get to pick and choose the pathway we want to follow with our portfolio of technologies. Realize that development phase results may not be as wonderful as expected, but also recognize that this is the risk we take and why diversification is an absolutely necessary element of a technology portfolio. In our experience, the development effort is worth both the cost and the risk. Innovation teams that take this tack invariably do better than those that are simply intellectual property brokers.

3.2 USING ACQUISITION TO FILL IN HOLES

Because keeping up with the state of the art is an essential element of the commercialization process, we can expect to come across some very good ideas that seem to fit well within the portfolio we are building. Hence, when on the path to being acquired, it is often wise to be the acquirer. One important way to decide whether acquisition is a good strategy is to estimate how much it would cost to acquire the technology versus the cost of developing it ourselves. Don't forget that time is a key element of the cost estimation. For example, if our acquisition target has the concept developed *now* and it would take us years to fill the hole through internal development, that well could be what tips the scale toward buying a company. An astute acquisition decision could be crucial in bringing a product or suite of products to market at precisely the right time.

In our experience, it's crucial to consider the quality of management of a target for acquisition. Frequently, getting experts in the desired technology to work for our team is even more important than the device or service being acquired. Try to remember that the intellectual property was generated by those running the company or venture. Similarly, acquisitions often are sources of considerable management talent that can help the entire portfolio to operate more smoothly and profitably.

3.3 SHOWSTOPPERS

The first company that the senior author founded was Touhill, Shuckrow and Associates, Inc., in 1977. We offered environmental engineering consulting in rapidly emerging areas of the profession: hazardous waste management, advanced wastewater treatment, physical–chemical treatment, and integrated environmental control. We believed that our timing was exceptional. One of our first contracts was with the U.S. Environmental Protection Agency (EPA): to identify suitable treatment technology for hazardous waste leachate. Within a few months after signing the contract, Love Canal became a *cause célèbre*. That was soon followed by numerous instances of legacy hazardous waste sites that captured national headlines. Public concern eventually led to the passage of legislation that came to be known as Superfund. So here we were at the crest of the wave in what was to prove to be one of the most lucrative engineering businesses of the time. How did we do? It turns out, not as well as we would like.

Our original endgame was to grow our consulting business to maturity and become as large as we could manage while still providing high-quality innovative services. We were well known for good work, respected by our clients and competitors (with whom we had very cordial relations, for the most part), and were regarded as well managed with very attractive overhead rates that made us tough competitors versus the "big boys." Despite all of these good things, in nearly four years we had grown to a firm of only seven people. During mid-1981 our firm was acquired by Michael Baker Corporation. Why?

There were several reasons, the two largest being undercapitalization and inadequate marketing. The enterprise was funded solely from the bank accounts of the two founders. In 1977, the senior author had four children lining up for college; the first (a coauthor of this book) started in 1979, followed by another in 1980, another in 1981, and the last in 1984. Thus, capital was tough to come by for the two founders, who started the company in their late 30s. But we were always profitable and we believed that we could build slowly but surely using current revenue combined with the understanding of our neighborhood bankers. Even our clients cooperated by paying promptly. Rarely was there a cash flow problem. But what we were doing in reality was working for somebody else and not building a business.

In retrospect we should have tried to identify an outside investor who would furnish the capital needed to truly develop and build the business. We needed aggressive marketing and more sophisticated tools to perform the work. We needed a better location in which to house our staff and do the work. Our side alley location did not portray the image of enthusiastic innovation that we wanted others to see. Our stubborn refusal to seek capital early was a mistake. We could have had a substantial share of a much bigger organization rather than all of a small one.

Accomplished entrepreneurs know that to succeed, you not only have to do great work, but also have to sell it fast enough so that when one project is completed, there's more than enough work to occupy everybody. Our problem was that the principals were doing the work and selling simultaneously. When there was a crunch to meet project deadlines, no marketing got done. So when projects began to wind down, marketing started in desperate earnest. Eventually, the hole became too big. The principals decided that the only answer was to pay attention to the companies that were interested in buying us. It was painful to go to work for somebody else again after being our own bosses—but remember those kids in college.

How did it turn out? As part of the sales agreement, we signed contracts that committed us to five years with the acquiring company. Shuckrow left after five years to head a division of a competitor. Touhill stayed on for nine years and grew the seven-person operation into a subsidiary with more than 300 employees that won a $100 million contract with the U.S. Navy shortly before he went off to become a group senior vice president for ICF Kaiser Engineers.

What are the lessons? Clearly, our stubborn adherence to 100 percent ownership was the defining mistake. It prevented us from taking advantage of the great technology and superb timing of our venture. If we shared our vision with an investor, we could have done even better than a 300-person subsidiary. In addition, we would have continued to have substantial control. Marketing was the key. Even though our timing was good, we never exploited the limited timing advantage that we had. The big boys caught up fast. Before we were acquired, customers believed that we were good, but they were not about to place complex hazardous waste cleanup in the hands of a seven-person firm. We had limited credibility. When we asked "Do you ever plan to give us business?", one prospective client said "I know that you are great technically, but if I give your large competitor a project and they fail, I tell my boss I gave it to one of the biggest and the best, so we will never use them again. But if I give it to you and you fail, my boss fires me."

Thus, the lessons are: (1) don't be undercapitalized; (2) have an aggressive marketing program; (3) don't fritter away timing advantages; (4) build credibility both technically and financially; and (5) learn to share to achieve the optimal end state.

3.4 ENDGAME OBJECTIVE REALIZED—SORT OF

"Be careful what you wish for, lest it come true." The origin of this famous quote is fuzzy and frequently attributed to an old Chinese proverb, but most people will agree that it sums up an important lesson in life. This vignette on endgames is a modest example of such a lesson—sort of. Although the name of the company and the major players are not revealed, it happened.

In the days of the dot.com craze, some bright young people developed a method for inserting advertising into streaming audio and video accessed through the Internet. The technology devised by the innovators initially was adopted by online radio stations as a way to generate online advertising revenue by replacing their "over-the-air" ads with advertising sold specifically for an online audience. This enabled stations to monetize their online streams legally because the broadcast ads were not cleared for online use, due to contractual terms with the commercial actors' guilds, which never contemplated online media. In exchange for this technological solution, the company negotiated rights to sell online advertising and share the revenue with the stations.

The early positive reaction from online radio stations led the innovator/entrepreneur, with the financial help of early investors, to put together a sizable sales staff to capture the "soon-to-boom" streaming audio market. Unfortunately, broadband Internet access developed much more slowly than the new venture anticipated. Revenue never caught up with expenses incurred to scale a business that never materialized. The tiny audience of online media listeners didn't reach the critical mass required to interest leading national advertisers, and margins for the audio ads sold held little promise for the longer term.

After burning through millions of dollars with the abortive audio thrust, the company regrouped. It became apparent to investors that the innovator/entrepreneur was a brilliant technologist but a deficient manager. As a result, they brought in a professional manager who they believed could move the broadband initiative ahead better and faster. The new CEO had experience as a venture capitalist, entrepreneur, and lawyer, with a track record of building a technological startup to profitability and managing its sale to a larger company.

This executive began by jettisoning the ad sales staff and refocusing the company as a technology solution provider, with an emphasis on serving the higher-margin video marketplace, rather than audio. New investors were added, including the investing arm of a large communications company (the largest investment share), a few smaller venture capital firms, a local well-fixed group of angels,[8] and a group of professors from a nearby graduate school of business.

The original endgame was to demonstrate the technology, be an early innovator, and establish a preeminent position as the technology leader, grow to profitability, and sell out to an Internet behemoth. The new investors agreed with this endgame vision and were joined enthusiastically by early investors who were eager to recover their initial investment and make a decent return.

As broadband penetration in U.S. households finally reached critical mass, the rejuvenated streaming video advertising venture was landing attractive new business with many leading media companies. The investors remained underwater financially, however, despite good future prospects for online video advertising. Finally, the investors who controlled the

---

[8]See Chapter 4 for a description of the characteristics of angel investors.

board of directors decided that despite the proven, valuable technology and the apparently bright prospects, emerging competition from larger, deep-pocketed technology firms presented a threat that they preferred not to face alone. They were tired and believed that selling the company would make everyone even financially and provide the organization with the financial and technical resources to remain competitive. The company was subsequently sold to an Internet giant. Financial details of the transaction were not made public, but rumors indicate that everybody got out whole and with just a little bit more. Therefore, the endgame was realized—sort of.

Here are some lessons:

- Timing was flawed at the beginning. The impact of broadband was not assessed properly.
- Too much money was spent on gearing up for an audio market that never materialized.
- Wrong choices were made in identifying the entrepreneur to lead the company.
- Investors, worn out by continuing losses, decided to recoup their investment despite good future prospects because they believed that shifting support to new ventures would offer more attractive returns sooner. (The final point is our speculation, because the investors still want the buyer to believe that they got a great deal and would be loathe to admit this reasoning.)

3.5 WHAT'S A WIDGET

It's not often that we get a chance to see an endgame in the making, but we have run across a great example. When people write books on innovative technology topics, sometimes things move so fast that by the time the book is published, events have made the authors' exposition stale and out of date. By the time you read this, everybody with an interest in technology will know what a *widget* is; however, at this moment (November 2006) it is an emerging (and a bit fuzzy) concept to be used in conjunction with Web log pages, personalized home pages, or social network pages as in MySpace.com.

Widgets have been described as "tiny computer programs that allow everyday people to incorporate professional-looking content into their personal Web pages or computer desktops."[9] Widgets are sometimes

---

[9]Emily, Steele, "Web-page clocks and other 'widgets' anchor new Internet strategy," *The Wall Street Journal Online*, Nov. 21, 2006.

referred to as *gadgets*. Typical examples include news feeds, clocks, calculators, and weather information. Yahoo and Google provide stock ticker and airline schedule gadgets that incorporate advertising as a promotional consideration. Widgets can be video, opinion polls, videogames; any content that can be presented on a Web page can be "widgetized." A key benefit of widgets is their ability to permit marketers to monitor user preferences directly.

In November 2006, the *Wall Street Journal* published an article that hinted at the potential importance of widgets.[10] The article described how the senior vice president of interactive marketing at Viacom used the next generation of advertising on the Web (widgets) to launch a new movie. The film, *Freedom Writers* stars Hilary Swank as a teacher who helps students to keep journals. Paramount Pictures worked with Freewebs, a company that provides free tools for consumers to use to build Web sites. By visiting the Freewebs site, visitors can upload a "toolkit" that includes many widgets that build on the movie's theme of self-expression.

The *Journal* article goes on to describe a highly successful weather widget that allows users to test Microsoft's Flight Simulator X for Xbox using live feed from the National Weather Service. For two months before the article was published, the widget was downloaded 150,000 times. Users spent an average of 23 minutes with the flight simulator. We speculate that Microsoft Flight Simulator X sales spurted because of this experience.

One month later (December 2006), *Newsweek* published an article that called 2007 the "Year of the Widget."[11] The article stated that 2006 was characterized by user-generated content à la MySpace, and that 2007 would see rapid progress toward customizing social networks using thousands of new widgets. Apparently, the concept has caught on like wildfire. Most widget users understand that the benefits they receive must be repaid by viewing advertising. We do not believe that they fully comprehend (at least at this point) that they are also permitting advertisers to collect specific and quantitative information about their online preferences. However, when that happens, we don't believe that it will slow down the exploding use of widgets and gadgets. It simply is too appealing for Johnnie and Janie, using simple tools that are easy and relatively intuitive, to look like big-time Web designers.

A few young companies have developed technologies that facilitate the creation, distribution, and tracking of widgets. The press release and blog that follow give the reader an idea of how one company believes that this

[10]Ibid.
[11]Brian, Braiker, "Tech: Welcome, year of the widget," *Newsweek*, Dec. 22, 2006.

new technology can be applied and the value they can provide to widget developers. After the press release and the blog, we address the issue of the endgame: what the initial aim was and what it is now.

NEWS RELEASE

VENTURE-BACKED CLEARSPRING TECHNOLOGIES INTRODUCES WIDGET SYNDICATION SERVICES

Platform, Tracking and Analytics Tools Enable Digital Content Providers

To Reach and Engage New Audiences

ARLINGTON, VA—November 6, 2006—Clearspring Technologies, a leading provider of widget syndication services, today announced the introduction of the company's hosted platform that enables content providers to easily deploy, track, and analyze content assets as widgets through a single point of management. Following an initial assessment phase with key partners, Clearspring will open this platform for developers.

Earlier this year Clearspring secured financing from Bethesda, MD–based Novak Biddle Venture Partners and a limited group of strategic investors. Accomplished technology veteran Miles Gilburne and Novak Biddle general partner Phil Bronner have joined Clearspring's board of directors.

Clearspring captures content and services in a framework that enables tracked widget distribution through social networks, blogs, start pages, personalized Web sites and more. A massively scalable data collection engine compiles information that provides perspective on the reach and impact of content accessible through Clearspring's easy-to-use reporting and analytics tools.

"Widget technology presents an enormous opportunity for content owners to unlock the value of their assets. Demand for personalized Web experiences is exploding and widgets are a new distribution mechanism to reach and engage new audiences," says Chris Marentis, CEO of Clearspring. "The Clearspring platform simplifies the publication and tracking of content and services to multiple channels, enabling content owners and publishers to capitalize on this massive shift in online consumer behavior."

Clearspring designed its robust services in collaboration with content providers and developers. Key benefits of the platform include:

- Ability to publish new media content, such as videos, images and text assets as portable applications web users can distribute on personalized web sites
- Ability to track audience, interaction, page placement, viral spread and other key metrics
- Extensive analytics to optimize creation, distribution and monetization efforts

- Single point of management to reduce complexity and consistently manage widgets across various channels (blogs, websites, social networks) and content-types

"Sites like NetVibes and MySpace are just the beginning. Widgets will become increasingly important as the web transforms from a publication mechanism into a platform for online services" said Hooman Radfar, co-founder of Clearspring. "With our platform, developers will have the ability to capitalize on the growth of the personalized web with tools to manage and track widgets in an open environment."

"Dennis Digital is continually seeking innovative ways to deliver our branded content," said Russell Kern, Director of Business Development at Dennis Digital, publisher of the leading men's lifestyle website Maxim.com. "Clearspring's widget platform looks to provide a great set of tools for us to reach new audiences on blogs, social networks and other relevant websites."

For more information about Clearspring Technologies please visit www.clearspring.com.

About Clearspring Technologies

Clearspring is the first company to offer hosted widget syndication services with robust built-in tracking and analytics. Clearspring empowers its customers with a full set of tools, services and market intelligence to transform content into widgets, publish them across multiple platforms, and track and analyze the viral spread of widgets, in real-time, across the web. Clearspring is funded by Novak Biddle Venture Partners, Joel Adams, Miles Gilburne, and Bobby Yazdani.

VCMike's Blog

Most Interesting Web 2.0 Company? November 12, 2006

Posted by vcmike in venture capital, startups, widgets, clearspring. trackback

After spending 3 days out at the Web 2.0 Conference I think I probably saw about 50 early stage Web 2.0 companies.

Like most at the conference, I generally was more struck by how many of these startups were really "features" as opposed to real business opportunities.

One company, though, did get me excited—*Clearspring Technologies*. Led on the technology side by one of the WebMethods founders, these guys are a "widgetizer." In other words, they make it very easy for content owners and web developers to create widgets so that others can incorporate this content or application into their own sites, blogs, spaces, etc.

As I've posted before, I think the whole notion of syndicating/distributing web content is one of the more important trends we'll see over the next couple years, and I think there is a great opportunity for someone to make a lot of hay out of being a horizontal value added enabler in this value equation.

Unfortunately for me, VCs were flocking all over these guys at the show. In fact, at one point I was chatting with Clearspring CEO Chris Marentis at the show when Vinod Khosla comes up and, with nary a word to me, drags Chris off into a separate room. Funny, I thought Vinod was out of the web and into energy investing these days?

So what do we make of all this? The Clearspring original concept was developed by Hooman Radfar and Austin Fath, two Carnegie Mellon graduate students. With seed money from tech incubator Idea Foundry, their initial vision was to build a consumer-focused social network that leveraged new Web 2.0 technologies. Over time, the influence of new venture capitalists redirected the company's focus to the provision of hosted services to publishers seeking to deliver their content into social networks via portable software modules, or widgets. Also, the venture capitalists selected Chris Marentis, an AOL alumnus, to be the CEO based on his background and experience. Interestingly, the astute redirected vision focuses on providing the infrastructure to enable the commercialization of widgets to all players involved rather than putting the company in direct competition with the likes of Google, Yahoo!, or Microsoft. It is interesting to note that the Freewebs company mentioned in the *Wall Street Journal* article is a sister company to Clearspring Technologies, related by their common investor, Novak Biddle.

We speculate that as a result of these changed objectives, the endgame shifted from building a substantial social network over time to a strategy of potential acquisition. This endgame closely resembles that of Google's acquisition of YouTube in October 2006. The venture capitalists not only contributed funding to exploit commercialization of the concept but also solidified the vision of the technology and defined a more realistic endgame.

After the present book has been on the market awhile, we will be very interested to see what happens in the life of Clearspring Technologies. Will their endgame strategy change based on their ability to develop better technology and new customers? How will competitors emerge? Will the company be able to manage the expected explosive growth? We will be watching this exciting business closely, and we hope that you will, too, in the context of alternative endgame development.

3.6 MAKING IT WORK

The keys to making the commercialization process work are to be professional and to use sound management principles. Seat of the pants, intuitive, and ad hoc business styles are doomed. Next, we discuss briefly how to make the commercialization process work in overview: that is, strategically. Tactical details are the subject of the following chapters.

3.6.1 Building a Team

When building an innovation team, we choose an organizational structure that promotes teamwork, and work hard to make it successful. In large measure, doing so depends on the backgrounds and personalities of the core team members. Understanding team members' strengths and weaknesses and their motivations is fundamental. We suggest that you review Section 1.2 to establish this frame of reference. For a team to function at its highest level of efficiency, all egos must be left at the door. Remember, this is a business, not a personality or popularity contest.

3.6.2 Establishing Milestones

No boss that we ever had liked surprises, and neither will our colleagues in the commercialization effort. We can avoid surprises by agreeing in advance to what we are going to do and when we are going to do it. In developing our plan, well-defined milestones help to avert confusion and astonishment. If we are tasked to reach one of these milestones, we have to make it happen or explain why not. If we have to explain why not, we had better suggest remedies available to the rest of the team so that we can solve the problem or alleviate the reason for delay.

3.6.3 Evaluating Progress

Good communication among team members is essential to commercialization success. This can be through frequent oral and regular written reports. Voice mail and e-mail are helpful tools, but they are only tools. They are not substitutes for regular personal contacts: telephone conversations and good old-fashioned eyeball-to-eyeball talks. Too many people today believe that electronic devices speed up decision making and eliminate the need for human conversations (a.k.a. interactions). We agree that devices are very helpful in sharing information. But we strongly believe that the best strategies, plans, and decisions are made when we at least hear our colleagues' voice, and better yet, when we look them in the eye. When we want to update somebody on progress, voice mail and e-mail are perfectly acceptable, but if we want consensus and validation, we need to talk with them.

3.6.4   Making Decisions

It is extremely important to decide in advance who will make decisions and how. We all know that committees make rotten managers. For our purposes, the two key decision types are (1) those that involve spending money, and (2) those that assess technological accomplishments. For the first type, the person who provides the money decides *if* it will be spent based on input from others. By providing advice and consent, the others have a considerable say on *what* the money should be spent.

On the other hand, assessing technological accomplishments is a shared function that all participate in, not just the technical folks. Each team member has a distinctive role in this assessment because technological innovations depend on a lot more than just whether or not it works. There are business, legal, financial, marketing, and sales considerations, just to name a few.

3.6.5   Planning the Celebration

One of the biggest mistakes made in the commercialization process is not knowing when we are done: when we have achieved what we have set out to accomplish. Thus, it is absolutely necessary to make sure that everybody understands when we have reached an end point. That can be when we are ready to be acquired, to float an IPO, to be spun-off as a subsidiary, or to sell a patent or license.[12]

A weakness shared by many inventors and technologists is the sin of "excess perfection." 95 percent is often good enough. From a development standpoint, it's more important to get the show on the road and take advantage of timing than it is to be absolutely perfect; besides, striving for perfection causes costs to rise exponentially. This is not to say that flawed technology should be tolerated, but continued development should be for refinement and improvement, not for utopia. Therefore, when we get to where we set out to be, we will have a nice party and move on to the next idea in the portfolio.

---

[12]These are just a few of the possible end points. We think that investment bankers and lawyers will identify a lot more than these.

3.7 KEY POINTS

- To provide focus and discipline to the technology assessment and evaluation process, it's important to have an endgame in mind.
- Growing an idea to maturity is best for great ideas with markets that are large, ripe for development, and projected to last for decades.
- Acquisitions, IPOs, and spin-offs are all popular endgames.
- Development of technology with a view toward selling patents or licenses is also a good alternative endgame.
- Sometimes an acquisition by us can enhance a portfolio of technologies more quickly and economically than could in-house development. In addition, such acquisitions can bring in outstanding technical and managerial talent.
- Undercapitalization and inadequate marketing are major showstoppers in achieving desired endgames.
- Two examples of company endgames are described. In the first, the generalized endgame was realized but not exactly in the way anticipated. In the second example, the innovation is a work in progress. Readers are invited to compare progress over time with the original endgame strategy and any subsequent revisions.
- The key to making the commercialization process work is to be professional and to use sound management principles while building the innovation team: establishing milestones, evaluating progress, and making decisions.
- It is absolutely necessary to make sure that everybody understands when we have reached an endpoint. That can be when we are ready to be acquired, to float an IPO, to be spun-off as a subsidiary, or to sell a patent or license.

4

FINDING IDEAS

In Chapters 1 to 3 we looked at technology commercialization from a strategic viewpoint and attempted to provide insight into the perspectives that various innovation team members bring to the process. Moreover, in Chapter 3 we discussed the importance of formulating an endgame strategy. In the next 12 chapters, including this one, we focus on tactical considerations.[1] We approach these chapters by describing how we would examine individual candidate technologies and how we would approach typical operating situations.

4.1 IF YOU HAVE MONEY, IDEAS FIND YOU

As soon as inventors/innovators discover that they can't fund their concept or idea without help, they look for outside sources of money. We said earlier that borrowing from relatives should be avoided if possible, and banks (including commercial banks) don't want to lend money without expecting the security of more assets than the inventor usually is willing to pledge. So the inventor looks toward venture capital groups or that increasingly popular phenomenon—angel investment groups—for money. Angel

[1]The final two chapters combine both strategy and tactics.

Commercialization of Innovative Technologies: Bringing Good Ideas to the Marketplace,
By C. Joseph Touhill, Gregory J. Touhill, and Thomas A. O'Riordan
Copyright © 2008 John Wiley & Sons, Inc.

investment groups finance small, early-stage companies that need a few thousand to several hundreds of thousands of dollars. John May, founder of several Vienna, Virginia–area angel groups and an author and expert on angel financing, says: "Structured angel groups are the bridge between friends and family and venture capital."[2] He points out that venture capital funds prefer companies further along in the development process and typically measure their investments in the millions of dollars.

Our emphasis for the remainder of the book will be on venture capital investing, because today's innovative technology requires a lot more money to develop than most angel groups are prepared to spend. However, we describe how angel groups work in a bit more detail because they do have a place in some types of technology investing, especially where inventors have done considerable development on their own or where the innovation is simple enough that the sums required to commercialize the concept are relatively small. Today, angel groups typically are comprised of people whose net worth is a least $1 million or who have an annual income of $200,000 or a joint income of at least $300,000.[3]

Some people call these groups "fancy investment clubs." One angel investor characterizes such investing, despite its risks, as more satisfying than playing the stock market and appreciates that it permits angels to participate in concept development and company startup while lending their expertise and mentoring skills. Inventors/innovators submit business plans to the group, usually in a prescribed submission format, and the plan is vetted by a committee that screens down to a selected few. These companies are invited to make a formal presentation at periodic group meetings (normally held about once every six weeks). After the presentation, the angel group determines whether to move ahead, and if so, negotiates the level at which they wish to participate. Angel groups are interesting and useful endeavors, but the types of investing opportunities we are looking at in this book are larger and more technically involved than one that a typical angel group could handle.

Some of the more sophisticated angel investors arrange to piggyback with venture capitalists. In this way, angels can participate in ventures that have greater potential for big payoffs, and the venture capitalists can do some risk spreading. Just as large insurance companies spread and diversify their risk by using reinsurance consortia, venture capitalists mitigate their risk by inviting others to participate in their ventures. Angel investors are one such group. Usually, there is a well-established relationship between the angel investors and the venture capitalists where piggyback arrangements are used.

[2]"An angel on their shoulder," *The Intelligencer*, Feb. 15, 2006, p. C-1.
[3]Ibid.

Risk spreading recently has included faculty from educational institutions and in some cases universities themselves. Both avenues have been helpful in demonstrating local interest and concern relative to promoting innovation. Altruism is a factor, but the reality is that such venture participation has been quite profitable for many leading technological universities.

When inventors/innovators find out that we have money available to commercialize good concepts and ideas, we become very popular. This can be a plague as much as a blessing. To manage the large number of ideas that come to us, we must prepare methods to prevent being inundated by screwy ideas from crackpots. In addition, we must be able to screen out ideas that diverge from where we are headed with our portfolio, as defined by our business plan. In the following sections we discuss how to attract and screen ideas.

4.1.1   Using a Quick-Screening Technique

First, we must articulate a portfolio mission statement so that potential interested inventors/innovators clearly understand the types of concepts and ideas that we are soliciting. Next, we must establish specific criteria that encompass key characteristics of attractive ideas that we would like to explore and then move forward into development and ultimately full commercialization. Then we create a form that spells out our mission statement and evaluation criteria and give it to everybody who wants our money. Done properly and with judgment, the criteria will serve as a first cut to eliminate pests or irrelevant ideas. We intend to be kind and gentle in the process for several reasons: (1) the people coming to us have sunk a good deal of time and effort into their concept or idea, and whether it's good or bad (or really terrible), they deserve the dignity of a polite response; (2) if we are curt, nasty, and arrogant, word will spread and our candidates will dry up; and (3) bear in mind that inventors usually have loads of ideas, so if we turn off somebody because they happened to provide us with a bad idea, another investor could well get their good ones.

A few of the questions that we could ask in a screening form are:

- How does the idea or concept fall within the bounds of our mission statement?
- What is the theoretical basis for the idea?
- Why is the concept novel?
- Do you have unambiguous and exclusive rights to the intellectual property?
- What market is anticipated for the concept?

- How long will it take to develop the concept to make it feasible commercially?
- How much money do you need?
- What rights will you give up and/or share with us in return for our investment?
- Who do you envision are your most serious competitors over the long term?[4]
- What endgame do you visualize?
- Why did you come to us?

This list is not intended to be exhaustive. We encourage those preparing such lists to tailor them to their specific needs and to do so with the idea of controlling the number of responses anticipated.

4.1.2 Doing the Homework

It's very important in the screening process that we understand in considerable detail what's going on in our field of interest. If we are up on what's happening, it also helps in seeking out prospects, which probably is the way we will find the best candidates. Detailed knowledge of the field makes it much easier to reject ideas either because they don't fit the strategic plan or because the prospect doesn't have a full appreciation of the marketplace and/or what's happening in the sphere of new technological developments. Being thoroughly aware of the latest developments will not only be beneficial in screening innovations but will also be invaluable in abbreviating the assessment and evaluation process, thus saving considerable time and money. Ideas about which we know more than the inventor should be quickly discarded.

4.1.3 Having a Network

If we know our business well and keep up with latest developments, chances are that we have an established network of contacts who share our interests. This is the case not only with technologists, but also with most other team members' disciplines.[5] We must keep in touch with those

---

[4]We'll bet you a nickel that their initial answer will be, "We don't have any competitors." After pressing for a more realistic answer, if they continue to give the same response, drop them and move on.

[5]Recall from Chapter 1 that being well-connected is a valued attribute of an investor. By staying well-connected with like-minded investors, the successful investor is more likely able to generate investment capital for winning ideas, reinforcing the adage that "it takes money to make money."

in the network whose judgment we trust, tell them what we are doing, and describe the kinds of ideas and concepts we are looking for. If we do this well, we'll probably identify good ideas through our network before the originators of the good ideas find us. Our networks typically are comprised of friends and relatives, former co-workers, acquaintances in academia, professional colleagues, associates in professional societies, and competitors. In our experience, maintaining cordial relations with competitors has great value. Sometimes we find them to be our most honest (often, brutally so) source of critical information. Clearly, to get this valuable input, we have to return the favor.

To give people in our network an added incentive to be our "concept scouts," we have to let them know that if they come up with promising finds, we'll reward them appropriately. Such rewards could come in the form of cash bonuses or, if it's a particularly good idea, even a small piece of the action. Be cautious however, about tapping into the network. Contacts have to be discerning and careful about what they bring to our attention; otherwise, they could turn out to be time-consuming pests. If they do become pests, let them know gently and drop them from the network.

4.1.4   Having a Referral System and Getting Rewarded for It

Inevitably, some very good ideas will be brought to our attention that have absolutely nothing to do with where we are headed. Even if we could fantasize and rationalize to bring such ideas into the portfolio, we must not succumb to the temptation—there is a better way to handle this situation. Identify other innovation teams with different strategic objectives and approach them with the idea. By including other innovation teams in our network of contacts, we may nourish an important source of new ideas. If other teams in the network don't find a referral appealing, remember that they have their own networks, thus making it easier to find a home for very good ideas.

Don't make referrals for nothing—expect reciprocity. Reciprocity can range from simple trading of ideas from time to time all the way to formal contractual relationships (including specific confidentiality provisions). Although we prefer formal scorekeeping and written contracts, how the process unfurls depends on the type of relationship we have with the group to whom we make a referral, or vice versa. Nevertheless, whether by handshake or by contract, keeping score *in writing* is important so that there are no misunderstandings and so that we don't lose friends and confidants. Recall what we said earlier in relation to borrowing from relatives. The biggest fights come when the spoils of victory are divided, not when we tally up our defeats.

In his book *Open Innovation*, Chesbrough articulates what he calls *open innovation principles*, which relate to the referral system that we describe above:[6]

- Not all the smart people work for us. We need to work with smart people inside and outside the company.
- External R&D can create significant value; internal R&D is needed to claim some portion of that value.
- We don't have to originate the research to profit from it.
- Building a better business model is better than getting to the market first.
- If we make the best use of internal and external ideas, we will win.
- We should profit from others' use of our intellectual property, and we should buy others' intellectual property whenever it advances our own business model.

Understand that he formulated his principles to be aimed at people within larger corporations that were attempting to stimulate innovation from within. Think of those who take Chesbrough's message to heart as potential customers for good ideas that don't fit our model. Furthermore, keep in mind that Xerox missed out on capitalizing on marvelous ideas that came out of their Palo Alto Research Center (PARC) simply because they didn't comprehend the open innovation principles and didn't believe that their intellectual property had value outside Xerox.[7] In fact, some claim that one reason they failed to capitalize was that they didn't want to create competitors. To us, this is silly because they intended to pigeonhole the ideas themselves anyway.

4.2   IDEAS MUST BE CONSISTENT WITH THE OVERALL PLAN

We have talked previously about being careful to pursue ideas that are consistent with our overall plan. It may seem obvious, but the truth is that when we get started we may be overly eager to get moving, and our judgment may be impaired by this eagerness. In addition, when we let people know that we have money available, we will see a steady stream

---

[6]H. Chesbrough, *Open innovation*, Harvard Business School Press, Watertown, MA, 2003, p. xxvi.

[7]An example of technology that PARC did not capitalize on includes the mouse computer pointing system made popular by Steve Jobs and the Apple computer.

of folks who want to tap in. So in the early stages of a venture we may feel like kids in a candy store. Resist the temptation to try everything. Be patient. Be disciplined. If it turns out that we have more ideas than we can handle, we probably need to change the plan and in the interim make more referrals. The following discussion focuses on how to stay consistent with the overall plan and how to maintain proper business control.

4.2.1   Buffets Cause Overeating

The commercialization process is inherently exciting and generates great enthusiasm among participants. What makes it even more exciting is that there are lots of very good ideas that cry out for evaluation. The problem is that we only have so much time and money—*use them both wisely.* To stay on the straight and narrow, we need to designate a member of the innovation team as a *governor*. The governor (a person or group that maintains focus and discipline) is charged with keeping a judicious balance of enthusiasm and control. The role is akin to that of a nutritionist who makes certain that we eat prudently. The governor is usually the investor or their cadre of professionals (e.g., accountants, lawyers).

4.2.2   Making a Quick Estimate of Cost and How Long It Will take

A useful way to stay grounded and not overindulge in good ideas is to make a first-pass estimate, in terms of time and money, of what will be required to achieve success. The best method for making such a rough estimate is to assume that everything will go perfectly. There are three reasons for adopting this approach: (1) It's much easier to do if we don't have to consider all sorts of alternatives and contingencies, and if we accept quick estimates; (2) it shows the size and time frame for investment in relation to other ideas that we are considering; and (3) it gives us an early view of the upside return on investment if everything goes perfectly.

After we have made this quick estimate of budget, schedule, and projected rate of return, it is good thing to begin a spreadsheet that tracks these quick estimates against reality so that we can refine the estimating process based on actual results. If we do this, we may find that our estimating improves over time and that we may actually get pretty good at it.

4.2.3   Remembering to Consult the Budget

Maintaining a fiscal perspective is an especially good way to take advantage of the icy intellects of investors. It is important that the investors counterbalance the technologists when dealing with inventors/innovators.

As we noted earlier, after the introductory period is completed technologists and inventors often become chummy and thoroughly enthralled with the technology, forgetting the finer points about maintaining a budget. Investors must bring them back to earth. This is done through regular project reporting based on a method and format agreed to in advance.

4.3 INVENTORS/INNOVATORS MUST BE PREPARED TO GIVE UP EQUITY

In Chapter 1 we described the personality characteristics of inventors/innovators, especially in terms of their suspicious and paternal nature relative to their concepts. We also pointed out their reluctance often to part with a substantial equity position. If they do not understand that they must share rewards with those who accept the risk with them, we must move on quickly. That doesn't mean that inventors/innovators don't deserve to be allowed some romance regarding their ideas. To the contrary, they are the lifeblood of the commercialization process. It does mean that the amount of equity sharing is negotiable, and they and the innovation team should work quickly and diligently to arrive at a percentage ownership that all parties believe to be fair. If it appears that negotiations will be protracted, or worse yet, stuck, move on to other ideas.

4.3.1 Structuring the Agreement

Stubbornness and lack of imagination are two enemies of arriving at a mutually acceptable contractual arrangement between the inventors/innovators and the innovation team. Stubbornness can kill a deal in either the short or the long term. The problem in the short term is that the parties can become bogged down and simply walk away (usually, in bitterness). The problem in the long term is that when the parties endure painful negotiations and sign an agreement after all, there may be a residual of hard feelings that persists through development and the remainder of the commercialization process. Clearly, this is not good. All parties must work hard to arrive at a win/win resolution. If either party feels used (it usually is the inventor), such a belief will haunt the project forever. We want success in bringing a good idea into practice, and we want this to result in joy, not resentment.

Lack of imagination comes into play when negotiations get bogged down. Negotiations often get stuck because of a failure to visualize all potential alternatives. Clichés can be tiresome, but "there's more than one way to skin a cat" comes to mind here. If an idea is a good one that the innovation team really wants, and the inventor needs the money, there has to be a way to make it work, and all it takes is the imagination to make that happen.[8]

4.3.2   Assuming Success

To be successful in negotiating with inventors, we have to assume that an idea will be a commercial success. Surely that's how the inventor sees the outcome. We have articulated the thought several times before, but we'll do it again for emphasis. Not only will the negotiations improve, but the results will also. Many ideas fail because contingency plans anticipate what can go wrong instead of what to do when we have positive results at key milestones. We should begin by anticipating success and planning for it. If we are mistaken and have not taken potential problems into account, there are have two choices: Either amend the plan or scrap the idea.

4.3.3   Engendering Cooperation

It is important to build team spirit at the outset. This is an essential ingredient of success in the commercialization process. Everybody need not love everybody else, but all must move in the same direction, have the same understanding of the mission at hand, and treat all other team members with respect. It helps a great deal if business is conducted in a thoughtful, professional, and businesslike manner. Given the diverse personalities that comprise an innovation team, this is not always easy but is always vital to success.

4.4   KEY POINTS

- Angel investing groups can be valuable adjuncts to the investing process.
- A screening method is required to manage the large number of ideas that will be offered to the innovation team.
- Detailed knowledge of a field makes it much easier to evaluate ideas.
- It is important to establish a network whose judgment you trust and to encourage them to be your concept scouts.
- The team should have an idea referral system and expect reciprocity.
- There is only so much time and money—*use them both wisely*.

---

[8]We understand that the process may be more complex than this, but as you may have noticed, we are true optimists.

- A useful way to stay grounded and not overindulge in good ideas is to make a first-pass estimate of the time and money that will be required to achieve success.
- Investors must remind other team members of how much money they have to work with.
- Inventors have to understand that they must share rewards with those who accept risk.
- Stubbornness and lack of imagination are two enemies of executing mutually acceptable contracts.
- To be successful in negotiating with inventors, we have to assume that an idea will be a commercial success.
- Building team spirit is an essential ingredient of success in the commercialization process.

5

INVESTING IN IDEAS

There are some important investing rules to keep in mind once ideas have been identified that appear to have strong potential for successful commercialization. The sections that follow elaborate on a few of the more important rules based on our experience. In the last section we pay tribute to Eugene Kleiner, investor *par excellence*, who had a few cogent rules that we would like to share.

5.1 BEWARE OF EYE-POPPING PROJECTIONS

We have never seen an inventor/innovator prospectus or business plan that included a pessimistic projection. That's to be expected because we would be foolish to undertake anything with somebody who believed that they had conceived or invented a dud. Given this propensity toward optimism, the issue becomes how to validate and lend realism to inventor/innovator projections. In general, the need for caution is directly proportional to the size of the projection, so we must act accordingly. We once had a boss who said, "Never trust a forecast that looks like a hockey stick!" We agree. Conversely, just try to imagine if it turned out to be true!

Commercialization of Innovative Technologies: Bringing Good Ideas to the Marketplace,
By C. Joseph Touhill, Gregory J. Touhill, and Thomas A. O'Riordan
Copyright © 2008 John Wiley & Sons, Inc.

All businesses have life cycles that look like the biological curve for organisms: birth, logarithmic growth, lag phase, maturity, and death.[1] Our objective is to find companies that are about to enter the logarithmic growth phase, so steep projections are expected. The innovation team has to test the legitimacy of the projections. One way to do this is to negotiate with the inventor/innovator using a "what if?" scenario. First, we find out what the basic assumptions are that led to the projection. Rather than attack the assumptions as unrealistic, we point out to the inventor that we are thoroughly familiar with the field and wish to test the assumptions by hypothesizing what would happen if conditions changed. By challenging the assumptions (not repudiating them), we can ascertain their validity and get a good idea of whether or not the inventor has a complete understanding of how to deal with changed conditions.

Benefits of the "what if?" scenario are: (1) It provides a good indication of the soundness of an idea; (2) it provides insight into the inventor's understanding of the field; (3) it results in more realistic numbers; (4) it lets the inventor save face in the event that overly exuberant projections were offered initially; and (5) it permits both the inventor and the innovation team to get to know and understand each other better with reduced potential for conflict. If the inventor refuses to defend his or her projections and to share the basis for and debate the underlying assumptions, it's probably a good idea to conclude discussions. A good rule here and in life in general is to avoid wholly unreasonable people.

5.2   REMEMBER THIS IS RISK CAPITAL; ONLY A PERCENTAGE OF IDEAS PAY OFF

Earlier in the book we emphasized that to succeed, we must focus on what goes right, not on what goes wrong. We also urged that we plan for good things happening and make alternative plans for that contingency, not just for failures. We stand by this advice. But the biggest single mistake that investors make is assuming that every idea has to be a home run. This mistake occurs more often to people who don't diversify their portfolio than to those who do. Clearly, a mediocre concept is far more devastating to somebody who has no other opportunity than to people with a well-rounded stable of ideas.

Such a well-rounded array might have one or two barn-burners, several good performers, many mediocre ones, and a couple of real turkeys.

---

[1]Some companies rejuvenate themselves over time, but many others do not. The Old Original AT&T, Bethlehem Steel, and perhaps General Motors are examples of corporate icons that have already seen the best part of the business cycle pass them by.

The range of possible endgames for the barn-burners is limited only by imagination. Good performers can be dealt with in a variety of ways depending on the preferences and experience of the innovation team.[2] Mediocre ideas should be sold off early on, possibly to earn money to fund better concepts or to help in the search for new ideas. Let the turkeys die early.

Expect and plan for various levels of success, and do so unemotionally and in a businesslike manner. Rescue operations divert valuable time from better ideas, so use great care in dispensing cardiac resuscitation to projects that have an uncertain future. Be aware that inventors/innovators rarely are willing to take their beloved ideas off life support, and often they get some degree of support from those technologists who also become emotionally involved with the concept.

On the other hand, what may be mediocre to us may be a treasure for somebody else. When choosing to give up on an idea, it is wise to take time to determine if it can be passed along to a network chum or to an innovation team with whom we have established a reciprocal agreement. It may also be appropriate for an angel group with whom we have an established relationship.

5.3 STRUCTURE THE PAYOFF WHEN THE SHIP DOCKS, NOT WHEN IT SAILS

Perhaps the biggest personal mistake that we made in technology investing was to pay money for an innovation too soon. It was a bitter lesson. We were very eager to get the rights to what we believed was going to be a barn-burner, and we were led to believe that a competitor would beat us to the punch if we didn't act quickly. In retrospect, we wish they had. The idea was a good one and it is being sold commercially today, but it was a slightly above average C+, although initially, we were convinced that it was an A++. So here is a bit of wisdom at the expense of our insouciance. Inventors/innovators invariably want their money (*all of it*) as close to the front as possible. That's understandable, because they sank many hours and dollars into their concept before we even saw it. What they are trying to do is recoup their investment plus interest to make themselves whole again and so that they can have the satisfaction of our approval of this wonderful thing of theirs. In the process they want to shuffle all the risk off to us.

However, even though they are wildly enthusiastic about their inventions, if asked to delay payment until an idea is proven, they may well

---

[2]For more on alternative endgames, see Chapter 3.

become less sanguine about the prospects. In truth, they may be unwilling to accept the risk that they expect us to accept. They must be reminded that if the idea is in fact that great, their reward will also be great *after thoughtful and complete development*. When that time comes, *we absolutely must keep our word*. Honesty and diligence will be rewarded in subsequent interactions with other inventors. When they see how well we treated others when we were successful in commercialization, we will be sought out as much for our sense of fair play as for our technical acumen.

In sum, the inventor should be rewarded after it is clear that we have a winner, not before. We may want to provide some sort of progress payments to keep the person afloat during development activities. For example, we could employ the inventor as a consultant to assist the technologist. But reserve the big payoff until the ship docks.

5.4   BET ON PEOPLE WITH PROVEN TRACK RECORDS

We greatly improve the odds of coming up with a successful concept if it comes from a source that has a proven track record. That doesn't necessarily mean that the person has to have a long list of patents; it does mean that it's unusual for great ideas to emerge unexpectedly. That's why it's important for the innovation team to do their homework, thoroughly understand the field, have a good network, and have insight into who's doing what in the area of interest.

Many of the leading technological institutions of higher learning have in-house organizations that promote innovations for license and sale.[3] These universities actively market their innovation business and sometimes have off-site office and laboratory parks where they help startup companies. This is a good place to look for good ideas in need of development. However, our experience with professors is that they often have grandiose ideas, an inflated sense of their own importance, a negative impression of the intellect of people outside academe, and a desire for lots of upfront money. Unless they lose these afflictions, it's best to let them waste somebody else's time. Usually, professors who have had experience with centers of entrepreneurship at their universities have been inoculated with healthy doses of realism and are far easier to deal with. Finding such people is a great boon, because not only do they bring outstanding ideas

---

[3]Most universities will only license patented technology; they won't sell it. They have in-house legal departments that specialize in such licensing activities. They tend to be tough to deal with because of the academic bent of the inventor and because universities generally don't have a sense of urgency.

into the portfolio, but also a reservoir of talented graduate students who can help either as colleagues of the professor or as our employees.

Others with proven track records are companies that specialize in developing ideas for Small Business Innovative Research (SBIR) and Small Business Technology Transfer (STTR) contracts. Many such companies submit dozens of SBIR and STTR proposals annually. The better ones understand the need to have multiple irons in the fire and frequently come up with a few reasonably good ideas. Their weakness tends to be that they are focused more on writing the next proposal to the government than they are on commercializing their successful innovative research contracts. We believe that an aggressive effort to convince them to take a more proactive role in commercialization can benefit everyone.

5.5   TAKE CARE IN ASSEMBLING THE INVESTMENT GROUP

Sometimes inventors/innovators show up with their own group of early investors. We don't blame such investors for wanting to combine their investment with ours and hit it big. But there are two things we want to avoid. First, we want early investors to understand that we are destined to carry the greatest share of the risk in the multiple facets of downstream commercialization activity, and that they should be rewarded for the magnitude of risk that they accept throughout the entire commercialization process, not just at the beginning. In other words, they should not get special points simply because they saw value at the outset. Second, from the start of our involvement, we drive the bus; they are simply passengers. Not that we don't value their acumen and opinions; to the contrary, we applaud their perspicacity in recognizing the potential of a good idea. However, if we are going to make it work, our team has to be in charge. If early investors can't accept that view, buy them out or discontinue the relationship.

Tribute to a Great Investor:
Eugene Kleiner

A notable giant of venture capitalism is Eugene Kleiner, one of the Traitorous Eight and cofounder of the famous firm of Kleiner, Perkins, Caufield & Byers. We want to call attention to him here because his lifetime achievements show how one person can function in many of the roles of the core innovation team. Probably nobody did it better than Eugene Kleiner. During the course of our research for the book, we came across an obituary for Kleiner in *The Economist*.[4] Their reporter did a great job of capturing the essence of the man. Thus, we quote liberally from that obituary.

> Had you visited the Valley of Heart's Delight, south of San Francisco, in the 1930s, you would have found a pretty place of plum and walnut orchards. Radio hams liked to go there, attracted by the clarity of signals near the ocean. Seventy years later, the valley contained 7,000-odd companies working in electronics, biotech and their offshoots, with 11 more springing up every week. Yet this most recent industrial revolution, like earlier ones, depended on the chance combination of three elements: the scientist with his invention, an entrepreneur to market it, and an investor willing to risk his money.
>
> Eugene Kleiner was each of these, at different times. But he began with no thought of revolution. When he came to California in 1956, a nerdy young engineer in flannel suit and tie, his only desire was to make a perfect transistor. His job was at the Shockley Labs, where he and seven others were employed to turn William Shockley's Nobel-winning invention into what was to become an integrated circuit. The volatile and brilliant Shockley wanted to fit as many transistors as possible on a single wafer of germanium. Mr. Kleiner and his colleagues preferred silicon, which could take heat better; they fell out with the boss, and went off on their own.

As we pointed out in Chapter 1, it was Kleiner's letter to his father's stockbroker that led to the group making contact with the legendary venture capitalist Arthur Rock, and thence the alliance with Sherman Fairchild. At Fairchild Semiconductor, Kleiner discovered that he was a pretty good entrepreneur. He and his colleagues pioneered the relaxed informality that now typifies the Silicon Valley style, and they also used the somewhat revolutionary concept of stock options to entice the brightest and best to come to the valley.

The obituary continues.

> By 1972, Mr Kleiner had plenty of cash. He also wanted to become a venture capitalist himself. The breed was still rare, and even rarer in the guise Mr. Kleiner had in mind: a "technologist" who was involved and got his hands dirty, as well as simply writing cheques. He was never interested in enterprises that did not relish this approach. But in partnership with Thomas Perkins, and later in the firm of Kleiner, Perkins, Caufield & Byers, he gave the starting push to more than 350 companies. Some were duds, of course, like the snowmobile company that ran into the drifts with the 1973

---

[4]"Eugene Kleiner, pioneer of venture capitalism, died on November 20th, aged 80," *The Economist*, Dec. 4, 2003.

666999966669966666999999966666666666666999999999999999966699999999996666

oil embargo; but they also included Compaq, Genentech and Amazon. By 1997, KPCB had backed firms with a combined stock market valuation of more than $100 billion.

...A shy man, he tended to efface himself in teams and collaborations. His letter may have been the spark that brought silicon to Silicon Valley and led, indirectly, to the hundreds of start-ups that established the age of the computer and the semiconductor. Yet his greatest pride was to be not just an enabler, but an inventor. *To the end of his life, he called himself an engineer* [emphasis added].

Kleiner is well remembered because of the "laws" he formulated based on his amazing experiences. We paraphrase them below.

- Make sure that the dog wants to eat the dog food. No matter how groundbreaking a new technology, or how large a potential market, make certain that customers actually want it.
- Build one business at a time. Most business plans are overly ambitious. Concentrate on being successful in one endeavor first.
- The time to take the tarts is when they're being passed. If an environment is right for funding, go for it.
- The problem with most companies is that they don't know what business they're in.
- Even turkeys can fly in a high wind. In times of strong economies, even bad companies can look good.
- It's easier to get a piece of an existing market than to create a new market.
- It's difficult to see the picture when you're inside the frame.
- After learning some of the tricks of the trade, some people think they know the trade.
- Venture capitalists will stop at nothing to copy success.
- Invest in people, not just products.

5.6 KEY POINTS

- Given the propensity of inventors/innovators toward optimism, a key investment question is: How do you validate and lend realism to inventor/innovator projections?
- One way to validate and improve on inventor/innovator projections is to negotiate with them using a "what if?" scenario.

- With capital at risk, only a percentage of ideas pay off.
- Mediocre ideas should not be discarded out of hand; what may be mediocre to us may be a treasure for somebody else.
- The inventor/innovator should only be rewarded after we are certain that we have a winner, not before.
- The odds of coming up with a successful concept improve greatly if the idea comes from a source that has a proven track record.
- It is vital to make certain that academicians understand their role in commercializing concepts that come out of a university setting.
- Companies that specialize in SBIR and STTR contracts can be good partners in commercialization activities.
- Caution is advised in accepting early investors into the innovation team.
- We include a tribute to the great investor Eugene Kleiner, and list his famous laws.

6

ASSESSING IDEAS

Now that we have found good ideas, it's time to figure out if they are as good as the inventors/innovators would have us believe. In this chapter we address questions that must be answered in the assessment process. Then we offer some insights that will be helpful in deciding whether or not, and how, to move ahead with an innovation.

6.1 THE ASSESSMENT PROCESS

When assessing ideas and concepts, to decide whether or not to fund and develop an innovation, an innovation team has to answer many questions. These questions can be divided into three categories: strategic, administrative, and legal issues; technical issues; and marketing and commercialization issues. The three categories can be approached in parallel. In fact, it's probably better that they are, so that the team members can consult during the process. Clearly, answers in one category can have an impact on deliberations in another.

Below we list pertinent questions according to category. After each question we have made brief comments germane to the question. In subsequent sections, certain of the more important issues are discussed in greater detail to lend clarity to items that in our experience, we believe need expansion.

Commercialization of Innovative Technologies: Bringing Good Ideas to the Marketplace,
By C. Joseph Touhill, Gregory J. Touhill, and Thomas A. O'Riordan
Copyright © 2008 John Wiley & Sons, Inc.

6.1.1   Strategic, Administrative, and Legal Issues

- *Does the concept fit within the scope of the strategic plan?* As we have said before, it is unwise to spend time on ideas that do not fit into our strategic plan. Pass on ideas that don't mesh unless they are potential barn-burners, and then find a home for them with other innovation teams and get compensated for the effort.

- *Why do you want and need money from us?* Ask the people who want us to fund their ideas why they came to us. Is it because they ran out of money; can't manage the risk; were refused elsewhere; or heard about us and like our business style and track record? If they have been refused elsewhere, find out why and by whom.

- *Is the business plan or proposal clear, unambiguous, well organized, and well written?* Business plans and proposals tell us a lot about the people who submit them. In our experience, clear, direct, neat, organized, and well-written proposals indicate a thoughtful and disciplined proposer. There usually is a correlation between well-prepared proposals and good ideas. Most often, sloppy proposals are indicative of fuzzy and haphazard thinking. However, take care to discover whether the proposal or business plan was written by a professional proposal preparer. There are many good people out there who make a comfortable living as freelance proposal writers. Work hard to find the real author. Usually, this can be elicited when grilling those proposing an idea at the initial standup presentation.

- *Who really was the inventor, and who did the work that led to the innovation?* It's important to assure that the inventor and the innovator are actually the same person. That's because shrewd innovators often pick up elements of other people's idea and try to sell them as their own. Plagiarism can cause horrendous legal problems.

- *What are the qualifications and track record of the inventor/innovator?* Great concepts seldom come out of the blue. They usually are generated by somebody who has impeccable credentials and a résumé that makes it possible to track the evolution of the idea during the course of the person's career. It helps if the person has been successful with previous commercialization endeavors.

- *Who owns the innovation?* Some people think that it's obvious that the inventor owns the innovation. Not necessarily! If the inventor had to finance early efforts with funds from family, friends, angel groups, or smaller venture capitalists, ownership definition could be a muddy swamp. Find out early who owns what and in what percentage. That way it is much easier to figure out who we are dealing with, and it will make negotiations a lot simpler.

- *Does the owner have unequivocal rights to the innovation?* Whether the inventor owns the innovation outright or a consortium shares ownership, either party has to demonstrate that they have unfettered ownership rights. Make them prove it in writing. We would after all, never buy a house without a clear title[1] (see Section 6.2).

- *Is the legal right fully documented?* This is the proof in writing that we spoke of in the preceding item.

- *Is the legal right exclusive and defensible?* We have lawyers look at the documentation and give us an opinion of how solid it is and an opinion of what happens if it isn't.

- *Is the inventor/innovator willing and able to make full disclosure of all details?* We accept nothing less than *timely* full disclosure. Less than full disclosure and we will walk (actually, run) away. Get evidence of willingness to make full disclosure in advance and in writing.

- *Are any special hazards or environmental problems associated with the innovation?* For an answer to this question, we get our lawyers and technologists together to see if there are any special risk factors that would cause us to pass on the concept. If there are any areas of which we are unsure, we don't hesitate to bring in outside expertise.

- *Should we move ahead with the idea?* We convene the entire innovation team to make this decision after all other questions in all other categories are answered.

6.1.2   Technical Issues

- *Is the concept original?* As we have said before, if we have kept up with the state of the art for our area of interest, this probably will be an easy question to answer. However, it is possible that it will not be completely obvious. In such a case, we have to require the inventor to give us proof that it is original.

- *Is the concept sound scientifically and theoretically?*[2] I am reminded of a technology evaluation I made many years ago. An inventor claimed that he had a technology comprised of a combined magnetic and radio-wave device that prevented the buildup of scale in boiler pipes. Neither my fellow engineering colleague nor I wanted to travel to the demonstration site, but the big boss wanted us to go. We told him beforehand that what was described to us was not sound

---

[1]We've never heard of such a thing as "invention title" insurance, but it might not be a bad idea.

[2]In the comment on this question, the senior author is speaking in the first person.

scientifically *or* theoretically, but he had a buddy he owed a favor.[3] My fellow engineer and I traveled on a local flight that stopped four times on the way out and five times on the way back (as I remember, it was an old DC-6). All I have to show for the trip is the biggest (and prettiest) chunk of crystals and boiler scale you ever saw. I keep it in my den to remind myself of the fact that turning lead into gold is scientifically impracticable.[4] In subsequent years, the lesson never failed me.

- *How does it work?* We ask the inventor why it works, and then we figure it out ourselves. If the two answers aren't the same and the inventor can't explain why, we had best move on to more promising pursuits.

- *How well does it work?* Remember, we are looking for earth-shaking and revolutionary technology, not small incremental improvements (see Section 6.4).

- *Can we make it work better?* It is entirely possible that we can see a unique facet of the innovation that the inventor has missed, and we sometimes do—much to our delight and usually that of the inventor.

- *Is the process reproducible?* If Cold Fusion was reproducible, the economy of Saudi Arabia would be a lot different than it is today. Unfortunately, it wasn't. Many people declared Cold Fusion to be a boon to humankind before definitive testing failed to confirm reproducibility. Conduct whatever tests are necessary to demonstrate that others can do what the inventor has done, and do it several times for good measure. In fact, for the innovation to be commercializable, it has to be reproducible reliably at all times.

- *What technical work has been performed to prove the idea?* Have the inventor show in great detail how the experiments were conducted that proved to the inventer that the concept worked. We usually ask to see a demonstration.

- *How well is the idea documented?* Have them show us their laboratory notes and all data notebooks. Do not believe loose-leaf notebooks. To have legal standing, data must be recorded in ink in bound notebooks, and key pages must be witnessed, signed, and dated, also

---

[3]Oddly, I ran across an advertisement for a very similar device just the other day. The vendor was kind enough to disclose that their technology was "controversial." I should say so!

[4]The Nobel prize–winning physicist Glenn Seaborg actually did turn minute amounts of lead into gold in 1980, but he had access to particle accelerators that regular folks like us may never even see, much less have access to.

in ink. Good inventors/innovators are abundantly familiar with this scientific and legal protocol.

- *What does the inventor believe remains to be done?* Generally, inventors are pretty good about knowing what needs to be done to make a product a commercial success. Quiz them and then confirm it ourselves.

- *What do we believe remains to be done to solidify the concept?* See the comment in the preceding item.

- *Will it work better, cost less, and function more reliably than existing technology?* All of these are crucial questions. We have to work hard and do considerable research to answer them. Make a detailed plan of how to attack each element of the question, and for outstanding ideas, expect that the answer to each will be a resounding "yes!".

- *Can we lower costs?* In most cases we are able to find ways that inventor costs can be reduced: generally through improved design, simplified operation, and better materials.

- *How long is it going to take to reach a first significant milestone?* If it's going to be a long time, it better be worth it.

- *How much will it cost to develop, design, build, and fully commercialize the innovation?* The technologist's ability to make quick and accurate cost estimates is a crucial skill.[5] Two things that drive the development phase are costs and schedule. If either is exorbitant, the innovation team will probably abandon the concept.

- *Can the innovation be developed, designed, and manufactured (built) safely, reliably, and cost-effectively?* Based on detailed evaluation, the technologist must answer these questions affirmatively.

- *How much will it cost to prove the concept and develop design criteria?* This is a subset of the question above.

- *How reliable is the concept?* The development phase should be designed so that this question can be answered based on the data. A preliminary estimate will have to be based on prior related experience.

- *Can we make it more reliable?* The answer depends on a well-designed feasibility study.

- *Will it be easy to build and fix?* We must make it so.

- *Do we need outside help to decide whether the idea is a good one and to develop it?* It depends on the idea.

- *Does the inventor/innovator have laboratory and test facilities with appropriate analytical tools?* It certainly would be helpful if they did.

---

[5]Some people think that *quick* and *accurate* are mutually exclusive. They are not. Competent technologists do it all the time, and they are very good at it.

Otherwise, we will have to find someplace that we can contract/rent or build the required facility ourselves.

6.1.3 Marketing and Commercialization Issues

- *Is the innovation unique, ingenious, and a significant (earthshaking) leap forward?* The answer to this question is the product of the best thinking of the entire innovation team because many factors have to be considered. Moreover, such considerations cannot be made in a vacuum. It must be hashed out thoroughly before moving ahead.
- *Who needs the innovation, and does it meet well-defined customer needs?* The entrepreneur and his or her staff must validate the inventor's target market and generate their own targets through research and their knowledge and experience of the field (see Section 6.3).
- *How many potential customers are there?* This is a subset of the preceeding question.
- *Does the inventor/innovator have a track record of successful innovation and commercialization?* If the inventor/innovator does have a successful track record, his or her projections and estimates can be viewed with a great deal more credibility. Lack of suspicion makes everybody's job easier.
- *Is the innovation suited for the application envisioned?* Sometimes the marketing staff can come up with a better application for the innovation than that put forward by the inventor. That's why marketing staffs are picked for their creativity. But they better come up with such new applications early before too much money is spent on what will turn out to be a secondary or tangential application.
- *How long will it take to develop, design, demonstrate, and commercialize the innovation?* The technologists are asking essentially the same question. Coordinate answers with them.
- *Who are potential competitors?* In Chapter 4 we bet you a nickel that the inventor's initial answer would be, "We don't have any competitors." After pressing the inventors/innovators for a more realistic answer, if they continue to give the same response, drop them and move on. On the other hand, maybe we know the answer better than they do, and realistically we should. So be careful of being too hasty.

When we have answered all of the foregoing questions, we will be in a position to make a decision on whether or not to move ahead. If the answer is "go," we are ready to begin the development phase (see Chapter 8).

6.2   THE NEED FOR EXCLUSIVE RIGHTS

You are saying to yourself, "Didn't they talk about this before?" The answer is that we did; however, in this section we take a little different tack as to why exclusive rights are important. It's an expensive proposition to perform effective due diligence on an innovation, as the reader can see from the extensive list of questions above. Unless we get exclusive rights, we risk having our hard work clear the path for somebody else to reap the benefits of our considerable investment. Suppose that we decide to pass on the innovation. If we have exclusive rights, at least we can recoup some of the investment by selling these rights to somebody else. It's also important to demand rigorous confidentiality as part of the due diligence operation, in case we decide to back off. That's because the work that we did could be invaluable in giving the successor a running start in development of the concept. This is often referred to as the second-mover advantage.[6]

We must be careful in what we discard. Hard-won information, especially in the technology business, has value. So it is not wise to get frustrated and junk records and reports if the innovation doesn't fit our plan or if we are disappointed that the concept didn't meet expectations. Remember Pontin's *first rule of innovation*: "The first attempt to commercialize an invention almost never succeeds."[7] We don't want to be in a position of having paved the way for somebody else without being compensated properly.

Another important reason to get exclusive rights is to keep the inventor/innovator from shopping the idea around while we are making our assessment (due diligence). Even though due diligence and technology assessments are not identical, sometimes innovation teams mix the terminology and imply that they are one and the same. Strictly, due diligence is validation through a discovery process that the claims[8] embodied in the prospectus, proposal, or business plan of the inventor/innovator are correct. A technology assessment is the process that determines if the invention/innovation/concept has merit from the viewpoint of the innovation team and will work.

---

[6]Jason Pontin, "From the Editor: The rules of innovation," *Technology Review*, May 2005, p. 12.
[7]Ibid.
[8]These claims can encompass financial and marketing considerations as well as technical claims.

6.3   TECHNOLOGICAL ASSESSMENTS ARE EASY; MARKETING AND BUSINESS ASSESSMENTS ARE DIFFICULT

This may seem simplistic, but if costs and pricing are not factors in technological assessments, either the technology works or it doesn't. Hence, theoretically, the outcome of the assessment is easy to measure. Surely there are degrees of effectiveness in accomplishing the technical intent of a concept, but determining if people will buy an innovation even if it works wonderfully is another matter. We don't mean to minimize the work of the technologist in evaluating the invention. To the contrary, if the technologist doesn't bless the innovation in glowing terms, the rest of the discussion in this section is academic. The fact of the matter is that technologists operate in a mainly objective area. They test hypotheses and decide whether the model that they have constructed matches experimental results. Again, there may be some variation in results, but in general, from an objective viewpoint, it either works or it doesn't, and it is a factual finding, not an opinion.

Does a market exist for the product? Will anybody buy it? How much can we charge for it? What kind of profit margin can we expect? How long will the market last? Is there an international market? Where do we manufacture or produce the product? These and many other pertinent marketing and business questions lead to far more subjective answers than technical questions. What is not easily understood is: "How do we make money from the invention?" Or as Pontin says, "The business model is imperfectly understood."[9] Somebody on the team has to come up with that well-understood business model. This is why the roles of the investor and the entrepreneur on the innovation team are crucial. They guide the team in arriving at a realistic and workable business model that converts great technology into something that people are eager to buy and that we can make money in the process (see Chapter 14).

How do they create that business model? The investor and entrepreneur work in parallel with the inventor and technologist. They conduct the marketing and commercialization assessment, while the others (the inventor and technologist) do the technological testing. The tasks don't have to be done sequentially. In fact, when both jobs are finished, the team can move directly to the decision as to whether or not to continue with the innovation. Input for decision making is equally important from both the

---

[9]Pontin, op. cit.

technological and business processes; it's just that there is more subjectivity and uncertainty on the business side.

6.4   IDEAS THAT ARE 10 PERCENT BETTER AREN'T GOOD ENOUGH

To justify a decision to move ahead with development, both the technological and business assessments must show that the innovation is dramatically better than the present state of the art. Innovations that are a little bit better just can't make it, for several reasons. First, price margins have to take into account all commercialization costs, including assessment, evaluation, and development, and generate an attractive rate of return that justifies the risk of investing. Investors will not take risks based on thin margins, nor should they be expected to.

Second, new ideas sell well only when they are recognized as being revolutionary and represent a quantum jump in technology at a greatly reduced cost. Let's face it, government and corporate purchasing agents are not willing to risk their careers by taking a chance on a new, and as far as they are concerned, unproven concept. Unless we blow their socks off with astounding performance and lower costs, they will stonewall us even if their bosses urge them to try out the new technology.

Third, best-selling new ideas are those that have no *apparent* competitors at the time of their introduction. Although there may be no direct competitors who sell the same or related technology, customers probably can accomplish what we are selling using other means.[10] What we have to show is that our new method is capable of doing the job better, faster, and cheaper than the method currently in use.

Another idea-killer uncovered in conducting the marketing and commercialization assessment is finding out that there is an extremely limited market for the innovation. The following is an anecdote that we believe is apocryphal; nevertheless, it illustrates an important point. In their assessment of an impressive idea, technologists determined that an innovation was truly revolutionary and from a technical viewpoint would be remarkably successful. Unfortunately, those performing the marketing and commercialization assessment determined that there was only one customer in the entire world who could use it, and that customer needed only one copy. Thus, if we want to move ahead with innovation development, the idea must be a lot better than what is out there now, and it must appeal to a large market.

---

[10]So in a sense there really may be competitors after all.

6.5   NOT SKIMPING ON TIME OR MONEY WHEN A GREAT IDEA SHOWS UP

As George Orwell said in his book *Animal Farm*, "All animals are equal, but some animals are more equal than others."[11] If we believe that we have a barn-burner based on results of preliminary evaluations, we must make certain that we conduct a thorough assessment of that concept early and not be penurious in doing so. We want to define the idea in sufficient detail so that we can move ahead quickly. Additionally, if results continue to be very promising, we may want to start development efforts (and perhaps even generate a prototype) while negotiating with the inventor. It helps our claim to ownership if we accept more risk early. Obviously, doing so will solidify our claim on rewards, but the risk and reward must be balanced appropriately.

This is not to imply that we should be lackadaisical with "ordinary" ideas. To the contrary, unless the ideas that we evaluate have merit, we shouldn't consider them. But let's face it, as evaluations proceed, some are imbued with magic, and we know it early; so be prepared to comprehend when that moment comes and devote time and money to make certain that the idea is assessed fully.

If that moment comes and we spend money to confirm our intuition and positive experimental and developmental results, we must make absolutely certain that the intellectual rights to the work that we sponsored are protected. A problem to be avoided: An inventor believes that they have invented the greatest thing since sliced bread, and our work not only confirms their expectation but also shows promise beyond even their wildest hopes. So what do they do? The inventor starts to believe that they have sold the idea too cheaply and they begin to try to wiggle out of the deal. Don't let them do it. We must document in excruciating detail the special time, effort, and funding that we have devoted to bringing the concept to barn-burner status. What the inventor has to understand is that if we were smart enough to be able to identify the huge potential that the concept has, we are the ideal partner to exploit it.

6.6   TAPPING THE FULL RESOURCES OF THE TEAM BEFORE MOVING AHEAD

As we pointed out earlier, just because a concept works technically doesn't mean that we can make money at it. Thus, all innovation team members

---

[11]George Orwell, *Animal Farm*, Harcourt, Brace, New York, 1946.

have to be involved in the final decision to move forward. We must be able to identify clearly a well-defined market for our product and be able to determine that the market can generate attractive rates of return on our investment.

Another area of concern that is often overlooked is related to legal considerations. Some very good ideas may be less appealing because they invite legal challenges because of potential patent infringement. Often the U.S. Patent Office lets a patent sneak through that is overly broad, and virtually any concept presumably will infringe on that patent, including our idea. If the concept we have is a great one, it may be worth the fight, but we won't know just by bearing in mind the technologist's opinion. We have to account for the views of the investor, entrepreneur, and the expert professional advisors we have retained, and together we make a reasoned decision as to whether or not we want to endure the potential challenge.

Recall that we have identified the entrepreneur as the quarterback who chairs the process of deciding whether or not to move ahead. The key is the involvement of all team members. As we said before, we want unanimous approval to move to the next stage. Nobody should ever be in the position of saying "We told you so!" in the event of failure.

6.7 MOVING AHEAD WITH DEVELOPMENT, THEN REVISING THE PLAN

When we have reached the stage where we are ready to move to the next level (i.e., the development stage), the innovation team amends the plan to accommodate the new status of the concept if the original plan is found wanting. Get it in writing and make sure that the innovation team is in agreement before proceeding. Logically, our view of the concept may be different than the one we had initially after thorough testing of the idea in all its aspects. Moreover, that view could be more positive than at first. Hence, we may choose to revisit our thoughts, plans, and expectations prior to moving into the development phase. Our plans could be much more focused than initial ones and could be more specific in terms of budgets and schedules for accomplishment. There shouldn't be big surprises or departures from the original plan because we were optimistic from the outset. On the other hand, now we should be much more specific about what we are going to do and when we are going to get it done.

6.8   KEY POINTS

- During the process of assessing concepts and ideas, the innovation team has to answer many questions for it to decide whether or not to fund and develop the innovation. These questions can be divided into three categories: strategic, administrative, and legal issues; technical issues; and marketing and commercialization issues.
- A list of pertinent assessment process questions is provided.
- Exclusive rights to good ideas should be obtained; otherwise, we risk having our hard work clear the path for somebody else to reap the benefits of our considerable investment.
- In deciding what concepts to discard, it pays to be careful. Hard-won information, especially in the technology business, has value.
- An important reason to get exclusive rights is to keep the inventor/innovator from shopping the idea around while the team is making its assessment (performing due diligence).
- Technological assessments are objective and easier to understand than marketing and commercialization assessments, which are far more subjective.
- To justify a decision to move ahead with development, both technological and marketing assessments must show that the innovation is *dramatically* better than the present state of the art, and it must appeal to a big market.
- When the great idea shows up, it is wise not to skimp on time or money.
- All innovation team members have to be involved in the final decision to move forward with development.
- When the team is ready to move to the next level, they may need to amend the plan to accommodate the new status of the concept.

7

PAYING FOR AND CONTROLLING IDEAS

When it comes to defining equity, ownership, and control, core members of the innovation team and their advisors can agree only generally as to what these terms mean. Even then they have their own perspectives. The inventors/innovators want to maintain creative control; they really don't want anybody messing with their babies. To the investor, control means financial control through majority ownership. The technologist sees control in terms of managing how the technology is developed, applied, and improved, whereas the entrepreneur means managerial control over the entire enterprise. So how do these varied perspectives relate to how we pay for and control innovative ideas?

There are a number of concepts that we have to bear in mind when answering this question. First, an innovative idea is intellectual property. Second, intellectual property is a valuable asset. Third, equity is the money value of an asset. Thus, to own and control an innovative idea, one has to pay to establish equity. So the fact is that the investor and the entrepreneur have got it right from a legal and practical standpoint. Thus, if we acquire a majority position in the ownership of intellectual property or a company's stock (either privately held or publicly traded), we have acquired both equity and control. Hence, this chapter is written primarily from the

Commercialization of Innovative Technologies: Bringing Good Ideas to the Marketplace,
By C. Joseph Touhill, Gregory J. Touhill, and Thomas A. O'Riordan
Copyright © 2008 John Wiley & Sons, Inc.

investor and entrepreneur viewpoint of what we buy and how we pay for it in order to establish control.[1]

7.1   BUYER AND SELLER WISH LISTS

If we try to guess how people want to be paid for good ideas they have generated, the payment modes would depend on the wants and desires of each person or group. Frankly, what motivates people is different from person to person. But to suggest an infinite variety of ways to be paid isn't going to help much in this chapter, so what we have chosen to do is to construct what we believe is a consensus "wish list" of what ideal payment looks like from the perspectives of both the buyer and the seller. It is not meant to be definitive, but it does form the basis for further discussion in subsequent sections of this chapter. And frankly, the wish lists, although speculative, probably aren't too far from the typical case.

The wish lists were constructed not from the perspective of getting everything either party wants, but rather, getting everything that is fair and reasonable. It represents positions whereby the buyers and sellers could expect minimal negotiations to reach a win/win final agreement. In other words, the lists resemble more what we could live with as opposed to asking for the moon and arguing down from there.

In later sections we address strategies that are important in making payments to establish equity. For precise methodologies on investment banking and legal aspects pertaining thereto, we encourage readers to consult information sources that offer expertise in those areas.[2]

7.1.1   Buyer Wish List

- We don't want to pay for the idea upfront until we have a chance to conduct, at the very least, thorough due diligence in the assessment phase.
- We are willing to pay a modest upfront bonus to the inventor/innovator to obtain exclusive rights to evaluate the concept, thus preventing the inventor/innovator from shopping the idea to others simultaneously.
- We are willing to pay the inventor/innovator a reasonable consulting fee during the period when we are conducting discovery and interrogatories.

---

[1]We have attempted, where appropriate, to present the inventor/innovator view as well.
[2]We repeat what we said earlier. We are not investment bankers or lawyers, and we promised these two honorable professions that we wouldn't pretend to be them if they wouldn't pretend to be technologists.

- We are willing to pay a "walk-away" fee in an amount agreed to at the outset of discussions, and we permit the inventor/innovator to keep the upfront bonus, which granted us exclusive evaluation rights, if we terminate our investigation.
- In the event that we choose not to pursue the idea further, we want to be compensated for any improvements to the concept and any data generated during the due diligence effort. Such compensation can be in the form of cash or can be a percentage ownership of the revised (by us) intellectual property.
- We are willing to acknowledge and pay for the value of investments made prior to our involvement, but only under the following conditions:
  - √ Total equity will be calculated as follows: It will be the sum of the value of what we agreed to pay for the idea to begin with and the amount that we subsequently invested in the commercialization process (e.g., all technical, marketing, research, legal, consulting, and other fees, plus administrative costs). Thus, it includes all of our investment in the innovation. Excluded from the amount we agreed to pay at the outset are any performance-based incentives subsequent to marketing and selling the product.
  - √ Payment will be in stock. The percentage ownership given to prior investors will be calculated as the initial value we pay for the idea divided by the total equity as described above. We agree that we may choose to buy out the prior ownership for an amount to be negotiated at the time of the buyout offer.
  - √ If the prior investors wish to negotiate a share of the profits over the life of the innovation, we will agree to do so only at the time of initial agreement. We will not negotiate sharing profits after due diligence, the development phase, product design and manufacturing, and marketing and selling. We believe that stock ownership in the company will result in sufficient rewards.
- As the majority owners, we are the sole arbiters of how the company is to be operated, managed (including accounting), and sold, if that is the endgame selected.
- We want the inventor to sign a noncompetition contract for a five-year period.
- We are willing to hire the inventor/innovator and selected key staff as employees after acquiring all rights to the innovation, but that is a preference, not a requirement. If we do offer the inventor employment, we want it to be a five-year commitment.

- If the inventor develops other ideas while in our employ, such ideas will become our property. However, we are willing to share ownership with the inventor in a meaningful way. Such an arrangement is to be negotiated as a condition of employment.
- We want strict confidentiality agreements to be in place at the beginning and throughout our association.
- We require the highest measure of cooperation. Recalcitrance and insubordination will not be tolerated.

7.1.2   Seller Wish List

- We are willing to accept a stock arrangement for our concept, but we want some cash upfront.
- We want to share in the profits as the product is sold.
- We want to be well compensated if the prospective buyer decides not to move forward with us. If termination is not done in good faith, we want the compensation to be punitive.
- If the prospective buyer terminates the commercialization process with us, we want all rights to the idea to be conveyed back to us.
- We will not stop shopping our idea during conversations with the prospective buyer until we have a formal agreement in hand, together with a cash consideration.
- We want a consulting fee while the buyer is performing due diligence.
- If we have entered into an employment contract with the buyer and the contract requires a definitive length of service, we want to have a formal severance agreement for termination, for any reason, thereafter.
- We want the ability to buy out our employment agreement for a reasonable price after one year of service. We want the buyout price to be established when the employment agreement is executed.
- If we come up with other patentable or proprietary ideas during employment with the buyer, we want a mechanism in place that will grant us a substantial share of ownership in that idea.
- If bonuses are granted to the management of the firm that employs the inventor, the inventor wants an equitable bonus that reflects their contribution to the company's success, similar to management's bonus.
- We hope that we and all of our associates are treated with courtesy and respect at all times.[3]

---

[3]We know that this wish cannot be mandated. It is a function of company culture and leadership and can be neither measured nor enforced; however, we believe that the seller should receive this courtesy and respect.

7.2   USING WISH LISTS TO REACH AGREEMENT

Several aspects of the buyer and seller wish lists are incompatible and require thoughtful negotiations to reach agreement on the terms of payment. For us, the buyers, the optimal strategy for acquiring innovative technology is to get our feet wet gradually, with the objective of achieving majority ownership if the idea proves to be a great one. Conversely, if the idea turns out to be a dud, we want to be able to walk away without any strings attached or residual liability. This choice is akin to having our cake and eating it, too. Although this may sound unfair, remember that we have the money to make commercialization happen, and the original owner (the inventor/innovator) needs our investment.

The flip side is that no inventor/innovator we want to deal with will want to part with majority ownership. If the person did, he or she is showing grave doubts about the concept and we should run briskly to the nearest exit. But the inventor/innovator must understand that once we invest our money, we assume the risk of development and commercialization and we should be accommodated accordingly. On the other hand, if we behave poorly, he or she knows that we are not the only fish in the ocean, and if we demand too much, he or she can choose to move on to other potential investors.

Thus, it is prudent for both sides to come to an agreement in a way that is mutually acceptable, and to do so expeditiously. So how do we go about deciding where the two sides meet to agree? This is a delicate negotiation that depends on how good the idea really is. Because it takes several steps to get that information, both sides will have to make assumptions about the projected performance of the concept. From the outset, the inventor assumes the best: "It will be a fantastic success." To expedite negotiations and to arrive at a reasonable and equitable agreement, the investor and entrepreneur should assume the same thing. Thus, the parties ultimately have to decide how much equity they want to wind up with, and how much money they want to accept (or give) to get there.

Each negotiation is different, so we won't recommend any percentages or numbers except to say that the people with the money should wind up in substantial control, and the inventor should enjoy long-term residuals if the idea is a barn-burner in the marketplace.

7.3   IS BUYING THE COMPANY A GOOD THING?

Try to remember that the goal of the richest technology company in an ideal world is to own *all* ideas and to license them to others for implementation, and then sit at home and cash the license-fee checks. Even in the case where the endgame is growth to maturity, there comes a point where the innovation team can liquidate its position. Bearing that in mind, the goal of our portfolio is to own ideas, not necessarily to own companies.[4]

So why would we not want to own a lot of companies? To us, owning a bunch of startup operating companies is to technology commercialization as real estate owned (REO) is to a bank—it's a pain in the neck. Our energies are diverted from the primary mission of uncovering great innovative technology into what sometimes turns out to be a baby-sitting operation. Little drives a well-oiled innovation team wild more than seeing a company that they own being managed poorly. The temptation for intervention simply becomes too intense.

If we don't own the company and our coaching, financing, and mentoring don't work, we can walk away. If we own the company and all the help is to no avail, we are stuck with a turkey. Either we have to spend the time, money, and energy to fix it or we lose everything. Thus, when we are approached by an inventor who wants us to buy the company, not just his or her innovation, we try to come up with an alternative that satisfies what the person is trying to accomplish without buying the company.

7.4   INTELLECTUAL PROPERTY: THE MOST VALUABLE ASSET

The model we have chosen for our perspective in the commercialization enterprise presumes that we will always have exclusive rights to the intellectual property we own. The principal reason for this strong belief is that the true value of our portfolio assets are measured in terms of the intellectual property over which we have complete control. In other words, this is our ultimate store of treasure.

Ideally, intellectual property in the portfolio will be closely interrelated if we have chosen our area of interest carefully. Hence, we have assembled a group of ideas that complement each other and add strength to the entire portfolio. If we dilute that strength by permitting ideas over which we do not have complete control to be part of our stable of intellectual property, we weaken the overall strategy. In other words, it's usually a terrible move to accept a nonexclusive asset.

7.5   PAYING WITH FUTURE PROFITS WHENEVER POSSIBLE

A truly successful concept can be determined only after it happens. Moreover, to be a true success, we have to be profitable. So ideally, we should

---

[4]We anticipate that during the commercialization process we will have to own companies for a while, *but the ultimate objective is to own ideas*.

not pay for the idea until after commercialization is complete—but life doesn't work that way. Often, at some point inventors are at the end of their rope financially and desperate for funds not only to continue to develop their concepts, but also to feed their families. Clearly, in buying their intellectual property we have to recognize the fundamental needs of the inventor. Additionally, the innovation team should understand that the longer we make inventors wait for their money, the larger the share they will want. Really, that's fair, because in making them wait, you have forced them to partake in a far greater level of risk than if they were paid immediately. Therefore, we must reach an agreement someplace in between. That point most often is decided very unscientifically and depends almost entirely on human psychology.

As we mentioned elsewhere, one way to deal with this issue is to provide an inventor with a decent consulting fee during the assessment, evaluation, and development phases of commercialization, and generously share the profits of success with him or her. But based on experience, sometimes even this doesn't work.

7.6   KEY POINTS

- Buyer and seller wish lists are offered that suggest items that each party would like to have in exchange for the inventor's intellectual property. The lists are positions that could result in win/win agreements reached with minimal negotiating.
- Optimal strategy for acquiring innovative technology is getting one's feet wet gradually, with the objective of achieving majority ownership if an idea proves to be a great one.
- Inventors and investors have to decide how much equity they want to wind up with, and how much money they want to accept or to give to get there.
- The goal of our portfolio is to own ideas, not necessarily companies.
- Our most valuable asset is intellectual property.
- The model we have chosen for our perspective in the commercialization enterprise presumes that we will always have exclusive rights to intellectual property.
- Ideally, we should not pay for an idea until after the commercialization process is complete.

8

DEVELOPING IDEAS

We have reached the point in the commercialization process where the innovation team decides that technology assessment has demonstrated that the idea is meritorious and can be commercialized successfully and profitably. So now the concept is ready for the development phase. Although the entrepreneur is active in the development phase, it's really the technologist who leads the way.

Concepts that are acquired by the innovation team come in various stages of maturity. Some are still budding nascent ideas, whereas others, especially those that have been kicking around for a while, are very near adulthood. Hence, the development phase can entail considerable effort or hardly any at all. Finding out where we are in the concept life cycle is an important task of the technology assessment. It is crucial in deciding how much money should be budgeted for development activities.

The primary task of the development phase is to obtain sufficient information so that results of the development effort can be used to design and build a product ready for placement into customers' hands. Usually, this involves building and testing a prototype, or in the case of software, a beta test version. A good analogy is construction of a "concept car." The car is unique at first, but it serves as the model of all the copies that follow. The concept car is tested thoroughly and is modified many times before mass production begins.

Commercialization of Innovative Technologies: Bringing Good Ideas to the Marketplace,
By C. Joseph Touhill, Gregory J. Touhill, and Thomas A. O'Riordan
Copyright © 2008 John Wiley & Sons, Inc.

The goal of the development phase is a *basis of design* for the new product. The basis of design is also referred to as *design criteria*. Design criteria are used to produce the detailed product design.

8.1 REMEMBER: THIS IS BUSINESS, NOT RESEARCH

The greatest joy of some inventors/innovators is fiddling around with their projects. We don't know who said it, but the following quote comes to mind: "The journey is more satisfying than the destination." Many inventors dread success psychologically because it seems to put them out of work. This is especially true if they have only one good idea. Additionally, some of them resemble overly protective mothers, who hate to see their children grow up. So they pretend to be looking for perfection, but in reality they are delaying the moment that they believe will render them unnecessary.

A common tactic used by inventors is to insist that more research has to be done to overcome the "slight" weaknesses of the conversion of the idea into a workable product. Notice that inventors don't fault the idea, because it was solely theirs. It's the reduction to practice that is flawed, and that is the responsibility of the innovation team: the technologist, in particular. This common ploy occurs despite the inventor's apparent eagerness to proceed briskly toward commercialization.

So how does the team convince the inventor to be a genuine helper in development rather than a stumbling block? The team has to convince the inventor that research and exploration are indeed joyful pursuits, but if they earn money (the sooner, the better) they can use it to generate more new and hopefully even better ideas. Many companies use a process referred to as *preplanned product improvement* to articulate a strategy which acknowledges that the initial version of the product may not be optimized but needs to hit the marketplace to establish market share. Subsequent "new and improved" versions can then be produced to capitalize on the initial market presence. Using this type of strategy, the innovation team can work with the inventor to "get the product out the door," with the intent to make it better when conditions permit.

Development progress can be speeded up measurably by a fully engaged inventor because most good ideas have an element of art associated with them. If technologists are left to their own devices, the pace of progress could be painful as many little wheels are reinvented. Inventors probably learned tricks and shortcuts during their efforts to perfect their inventions that can help to avert false starts.

Invite the inventor to attend all regular progress meetings so that they can see the pressure that technologists have to endure when grilled by the full team regarding schedule and budget issues. It's very important that the role of the inventor be spelled out clearly before he or she shows up at meetings. In general, the inventor should be called on to provide details of the idea as it relates to development. Moreover, it would be a good idea if the inventor explained how he or she is supporting the efforts of the technologist.

8.2   MAINTAINING CONTROL OF DEVELOPMENT EFFORTS

This section is a variation and an extension on the theme of Section 8.1. In the research, evaluation, and assessment phase of examining the concept, the role of the inventor is very important. The objective of the team is to gain a thorough understanding of what the idea is all about and to have the inventor convey the idea clearly to the technologist and other team members. Hence, the inventor is pivotal to those activities and knows how important they are. This importance wanes as others learn as much about the invention as the inventor knows, so as the research phase ends and development activities begin, control shifts to the technologist.

The human interaction and communication skills of the technologist will be tested because they have to exert control of development efforts while keeping the inventor involved in the work, albeit in a subordinate role. Remember that the inventor feels deeply connected to the idea, and rightfully so, but it is imperative that the technologist keeps things moving ahead. Once hurdles have been surmounted, avoid revisiting questions that have already been answered.

A productive device for helping to focus the inventor forward rather than backward is to point out the need to address many important challenges that remain ahead: for example, how do we design, demonstrate, standardize, package, sell, monitor, fix, and improve the technology? Our ability to tackle these issues successfully could well make the inventor a very wealthy person.

8.3   THE GOAL OF DEVELOPMENT IS THE BASIS
OF DESIGN

When we are finished with the development phase, we should be in a position to design the product we intend to commercialize. Process engineers, computer programmers, and other technologists absolutely love the

FIGURE 8.1 Physical–chemical treatment pilot plant.

development phase. It gives them the opportunity to test various product configurations under a range of conditions. Moreover, development activities permit the technologists to build the best pilot plant or prototype possible, stress it to the breaking point, reconstruct it, and then rebuild it. The reasons for doing so are fairly obvious. We want to assure that the product will operate reliably in the complete range of real-world conditions encountered by the customer.

Figure 8.1 shows a pilot plant we helped to design that was used to develop design criteria for an innovative physical–chemical wastewater treatment facility. To test a prototype thoroughly, the technologist will operate the product to the limits of failure. These limits are not chosen arbitrarily but are based on careful planning prior to the outset of development testing. Remember to plan and perform pilot runs carefully. Some of the pilot runs cannot be duplicated because of time and budget constraints. However, process results should be perfectly reproducible; otherwise, something is terribly wrong.

Planning helps to reduce data acquisition costs, detailed design costs, operation and maintenance costs, and capital investment in physical facilities. In addition, it helps to assure application of appropriate technology during the design phase. (see Chapter 9). Planning focuses mainly on establishing design criteria. Design criteria (the most important element of the development phase) are derived from study and investigation data generated in this stage of activities. The following steps define the design process and provide insight into how design criteria fit sequentially into a generalized design program.[1]

The Design Process

- **Problem identification**
- **Problem characterization and quantification**
- **Problem assessment and definition**
- **Delineation of alternative solutions**
- **Feasibility studies**
  - √ **Bench, pilot-scale, and semiworks**
  - √ **Simulations**
  - √ **Effectiveness/efficiency**
  - √ **Economic evaluation**
  - √ **Reliability**
  - √ **Manufacturability/constructability**
  - √ **Safety**
  - √ **Maintenance and operation**
- **Design basis development**
- **Alternative selection**
  - √ **Process simulations**
  - √ **Risk evaluation**
  - √ **Heat and material balances**
  - √ **Cost estimates**
  - √ **Regulatory compliance**
- **Design criteria development**
- **Detailed engineering design**
- **Procurement**
- **Manufacturing/construction**

---

[1]C. J. Touhill, "Process engineering: the bridge between concept and design," Kappe Lecture, American Academy of Environmental Engineers, Annapolis, MD, 1992.

- **Startup and trial runs**
- **Operation**

Effective design criteria serve as the formal basis of design. When the technologist turns this documentation over to a competent designer, the final detailed design of the product should be straightforward. Correspondingly, when the designer is finished, manufacturing and/or construction should proceed with few hitches. This is not to imply that the entire design process is easy. To the contrary, it is very complex and requires great patience, discipline, and diligence.

8.4 THE IMPORTANCE OF FEASIBILITY STUDIES

Development activities are different in the case of innovative technologies than for established technology. For example, if we are building a chemical or pharmaceutical processing plant for a product currently on the market, we approach development and subsequent design much differently than if the product is new. The main difference is that many of the questions and conditions that need to be defined for the final design have already been done for the established product. For the innovative product, we need to perform feasibility studies that are intended to build a prototype that embodies the following desirable characteristics of the finished manufactured product:

- It should be safe to manufacture and use.
- It must accomplish its designated function efficiently and economically.
- It should be able to be manufactured or constructed using simple, well-established techniques or methods which themselves are easy to develop and use.
- Its materials of construction should be safe and last a long time.
- It must be reliable.
- It must be manufactured at the least possible cost consistent with high quality.
- It must be easy to operate.
- It must be easy to fix if it breaks.
- It must not waste materials or energy.
- It must comply with applicable regulatory requirements.

Therefore, we have to experiment with physical dimensions, materials of construction, rates of flow (or similar measures of throughput), process efficiency, reproducibility, effects of environmental conditions (e.g., temperature, humidity, ultraviolet radiation, dust), and any other variables that are determined to be critical to product function. Basically, we build the prototype up, stress it to its limits, vary testing conditions, tear it down, and do it again until we are satisfied that we have an optimized model. Then we document the range of operating conditions that describe the optimized model so that somebody can build it. The result is what we call the design criteria—the objective of development activities.

When we produce design criteria using the results of our feasibility study (a pilot plant, a beta test, a process simulation), we sit down with the design engineer and flesh out the criteria so that two very important things are accomplished:

1. All of the designer's questions regarding the feasibility study are answered, and the designer understands fully what was done in the study.
2. The designer has a set of design criteria from which they agree that they can build the product. The designer is then ready to prepare detailed plans and specifications for manufacturing or building the product.

Be certain that all data are archived and that all design criteria and detailed plans and specifications are documented fully. These documents should permit any competent professional to reproduce experiments, pilot-plant runs, and product manufacture using only the documents as a guide.

8.5   THE VALUE AND MEANING OF ESTIMATES

When we are given a cost estimate, it's very important that we know how to evaluate it. Is it precise or simply a wild guess? There are accepted conventions that define the accuracy of capital cost estimates. One of the better ones is that proposed by the American Association of Cost Engineers and articulated by Peters and Timmerhaus.[2] The list below defines and explains the basis for levels of estimation for capital investments.

[2]M. S. Peters and K. D. Timmerhaus, *Plant Design and Economics for Chemical Engineers*, 3rd ed., McGraw-Hill, New York, 1980, p. 157.

1. *Order-of-magnitude estimate:* ±30 percent probable accuracy of estimate. Based on similar previous cost data. Also known as a *ratio estimate*.

2. *Study estimate:* ±30 percent probable accuracy of estimate. Based on knowledge of major items of equipment. Also known as a *factored estimate*.

3. *Preliminary estimate:* ±20 percent probable accuracy of estimate. Based on sufficient data to permit the estimate to be budgeted. Also known as a *budget authorization estimate* or *scope estimate*.

4. *Definitive estimate:* ±10 percent probable accuracy of estimate. Based on almost complete data, but before completion of drawings (plans) and specifications. Also known as a *project control estimate*.[3]

5. *Detailed estimate:* ±5 percent probable accuracy of estimate. Based on complete engineering drawings, specifications, and site surveys. Also known as a *contractor's estimate*.[4]

Obviously, the estimates get better as we proceed through the design process. That's one important reason why we pay close attention to developing thorough design criteria.

8.6 KNOWING WHEN TO CELEBRATE AND WHEN TO CRY

The development phase is probably the most crucial point in the commercialization process—where we are able to recognize victory or defeat. Intuitively, we would think it would be during assessment activities, but it's not. In the assessment we are looking to see if the concept has merit. In development we are trying to see if we can build the product economically, safely, and reliably. For a host of reasons, a great concept may not be able to be reduced to practice. It requires talent and experience to be able to distinguish between victory and defeat. Clearly, the farther down the line in the commercialization process, the greater the costs that are incurred. Thus, we have to know when to commit more significant funding to the idea and when to quit. To make this determination, it is very helpful to set down criteria in the strategic plan to help decide on the status of the development *objectively*. Such criteria could include: establishing an estimated rate of return on investment, determining an acceptable level

---

[3]The estimate that emanates from the completed feasibility study (i.e., the basis of design or the design criteria) should enable preparation of a definitive estimate.

[4]When the designer turns plans and specifications over to the builder or manufacturer, they should include a detailed project estimate.

of risk (legal, financial, operational, and strategic), and setting a tolerable budget and schedule, for example.[5]

Earlier we talked about ideas that come to our attention that don't fit a strategic plan (see Section 4.1.4). We recommended that there be a system for referring such ideas to others. The same thing can happen in development activities. Certain ideas might not capture our fancy but may be attractive to somebody else. Try to find a home for these ideas and be compensated for that effort. We advise never giving away or burying an idea without looking for a place where it might be appreciated, except in the case of an outright dud. Ration this effort to finding a place to sell the idea based on how much we have invested in it and how much we believe that we can recover. Experience in doing this will help to determine how hard we have to work to place the idea.

Through experience we find that innovation teams tend to celebrate too early and cry too late, and larger and more cynical investors tend to give up too soon. One way to keep inpatient investors honest is to have intellectual property rights revert to the original owner in their entirety if the innovation team gives up. Another way is to have that subset of the innovation team that is more patient and believing get first crack at buying the intellectual property—at a bargain price. Obviously, all of these contingencies have to be agreed upon in advance and incorporated into specific contracts.

8.7 KEY POINTS

- The primary task of the development phase is to obtain sufficient information so that results of the development effort can be used to design and build a product ready for placement into the customer's hands
- Many inventors dread success psychologically because it seems to put them out of work. Remind them that this is business, not research.
- A productive device for helping to engage an inventor throughout the development process is to point out the need to address many important challenges that remain ahead.
- Elements of the design process are enumerated.
- Effective design criteria serve as the formal basis of design.
- Feasibility studies are intended to build a prototype that embodies desirable characteristics of the finished manufactured product.

---

[5]Clearly, other criteria could be added depending on the preferences of the innovation team.

- It is very important to have a clear idea of the level of accuracy of capital investment cost estimates.
- The development phase probably is the most crucial point in the commercialization process where we are able to recognize victory or defeat.
- Innovation teams tend to celebrate too early and cry too late, and larger and more cynical investors tend to give up too soon.
- Try to find a home for ideas that might not capture our fancy and be compensated for our efforts.

9

DESIGNING AND BUILDING TECHNOLOGY

Now that we have the basis of design as developed in Chapter 8, we are ready to design and build the product for commercialization. For purposes of this book, the term *building,* can be taken to mean creating, making, fabricating, manufacturing, constructing, or producing. In essence, the end result of the building process is the product that we are trying to commercialize and sell. Our emphasis on design presumes that actual manufacture of the product usually will be taken into consideration during the design process. Moreover, we assume that the mechanical and computational processes[1] that enable manufacturing are either state of the art or are designed in conjunction with the product. Perhaps it is our bias as technologists, but we figure that if you can design it, you can build it. That obviously is easier said than done with those few products or processes that require wholly new methods; nevertheless, such instances are not the norm. Hence, we focus mainly on product design in this chapter, incorporating product building into what we refer to as the overall design process.

---

[1]We recognize that some innovations will involve biological, chemical, and biochemical processes as well.

Commercialization of Innovative Technologies: Bringing Good Ideas to the Marketplace, By C. Joseph Touhill, Gregory J. Touhill, and Thomas A. O'Riordan Copyright © 2008 John Wiley & Sons, Inc.

9.1   THIS IS WHERE THE SPENDING OF REAL MONEY BEGINS

Aside from the initial investment of the inventor/innovator, which can be considerable, this is the point where money begins to be spent seriously.[2] What went before design (i.e., research, evaluations, negotiations, and even development) can't match the magnitude of the budget that will be devoted to designing and building the product. As a rough rule of thumb, design engineers estimate that for purposes of planning a capital improvement project, approximately 10 to 15 percent of the total project costs will be for the design phase, and the remainder for construction. For our purposes in this book, we assume that *designing* the system that manufactures the product costs roughly one-tenth as much as physical system *building* costs. In addition, of course, we have the actual *operating* costs.

A grave mistake made by many manufacturing entities in their capital cost projections is that they focus so much on major costs of building a manufacturing system that they fail to consider design budgets properly. So when technologists/designers ask for a design budget that is 10 to 20 percent of the total system capital cost estimate (which is entirely reasonable), those responsible for building the system immediately begin to look for ways to reduce design costs. Implementation of innovative technology isn't as easy as building a manufacturing system for a mature commodity product that lends itself to "cookie cutter" or "off-the-shelf" designs. But somehow this mentality (skimping on design budget) is not uncommon. We strongly urge that technology designers be provided with an adequate budget to complete a design that anticipates encountering unforeseen challenges in the design process. Experience tells us that a thoughtful design budget that is the product of solid planning results in a building budget that is easier to track and control. Similarly, the budget for building the manufacturing system should provide contingencies for adjusting the manufacturing process to correct inefficiencies and to enhance process performance.

Design plans and specifications should be prepared in such a way that any qualified and competent contractor could work from these documents and reproduce the system perfectly. Not only is this good engineering practice, but also it represents sound business practice. For example, this documentation is essential in the event that the alternative endgame is to sell the company at the conclusion of the design and building phase.[3]

---

[2]By *seriously*, we mean in larger amounts. We don't suggest or mean to imply that previous efforts were not undertaken in earnest and with great diligence.

[3]Inventors/innovators generally are deficient in documenting their early efforts, so using their initial information in design preparation is risky. Spend the time to verify their data.

A place that innovation teams can get into trouble is in building prototypes. Frequently, prototypes are used during the development phase to run experiments and conduct pilot runs with an eye toward utilizing them as the design model. Thus, in addition to using prototypes to generate data to develop design criteria for full-scale implementation, sometimes they become the design itself. As a result, if inefficiencies are built into the prototypes, they get multiplied many times if they are the design model. There are two ways that inappropriate prototypes get built. First, the person who designs the prototype in the development phase is focused on the experimental aspects and most often isn't qualified to design a model suitable for full-scale implementation. Second, some of the best pilot-plant technologists who can test new ideas with great facility are what we call "junkyard" engineers. Although often absolutely brilliant in putting together a pilot plant from spare parts and extracting gobs of excellent useful data with them, they have little appreciation for the sophistication required in the finished design model. Thus, unless there was a planned and conscious effort to use the prototypes as the first copy of the manufacturing system, don't use it as your design model.[4]

It's a rare bird who is able to be a good process engineer extremely capable at generating design criteria in the development phase and at the same time has the capability to be a great detailed designer of the manufacturing system. Therefore, technologists must be able to know when they have to bring in experienced designers from the outside. Obviously, confidentiality must be maintained, but if our innovation team has a reliable detailed designer that we can call upon routinely, it would be wise to use them rather than stress our process engineers by pushing them into unfamiliar territory.

9.2 SIMPLE DESIGNS ARE THE MOST ELEGANT

The reason people laugh at Rube Goldberg contraptions is because they represent a complicated way of performing a simple operation. Moreover, the materials that such contraptions are made of often include a lot of "spit and glue." There are two points here: (1) simple designs are best, and (2) use of appropriate materials to build manufacturing systems is essential.

When designing the model product (the original), the designer must concentrate on incorporating in it as many features as we intend to

---

[4]From this point forward, to distinguish between the devices that are used for testing in the development phase and the actual product that we are manufacturing, we refer to the former as the prototype and the latter as the design model.

incorporate into each copy of the final product. The innovation team cannot lose sight of the need to make each one exactly the same. The temptation is strong to make the original the perfect model: in truth, they all have to be perfect.

The design model should be easy to build, easy to use, easy to service, and easy to fix. Therefore, considerable thought must be given to model design to achieve all of these characteristics, yet be simple. A danger with simple designs is that they are easy to reverse-engineer. That's why it's important to have strong patent protection. On the positive side, simple designs can give us very rapid market entry and thus establish a commanding lead over the competition. If we are able to ramp up quickly and get momentum, we can point to a large and recognized market in the event of patent infringement.

For over a century German engineering has been envied all over the world. Their products tend to be expensive in the short term, but they are competitive because they leave the impression of lasting forever. Thus, life-cycle costs compete favorably in the long run. We asked a good German friend of ours who we work with regularly to explain this phenomenon. He said, "It's very simple, really. We approach designing and building manufacturing systems much as the Swiss approach watchmaking. We spend a lot of time making a superior design and we use the best materials of construction available to build the system and its product."

We believe that our German friend is on the money with his analysis. Quality materials of construction are an essential element in assuring product quality and longevity. His comments are even more relevant for innovative products. Frankly, it's hard enough to get people to buy what we have to offer without their having the impression that our product looks cheap. We all have the mind-set that says, "If it looks and feels cheap, it's no good!" In addition to the feeling of quality that first-class materials of construction convey, they do last longer. That is precisely the notion that we want our customers to have of our product.

9.3   THE DESIGN TECHNOLOGY SHOULD BE AS GOOD AS THE TECHNOLOGY DESIGNED

This may seem obvious, but we can't do twenty-first-century designs using nineteenth-century design tools. Hence, we have to use state-of-the-art design technology. Unfortunately, many people chintz on design technology, believing that they can save money by using inferior design tools. It just doesn't work that way, for a very important reason. We must do the design right the first time so that somebody doesn't roll over us using better and more modern design tools. The key is not to permit competitors to have the advantage; we have to be able to generate a design that is flexible, adaptable, and easy to improve. Besides, if modern design technology is state of the art, by definition it must represent the best, fastest, and cheapest way to do the job.[5]

Therefore, time must be spent investigating the best tools for designing the product and the system to build it. Responsibility for this investigation resides with the technologist with help from the inventor/innovator. Where appropriate, outside consultants should be used in the design process.

Contrary to the opinions of many young whippersnappers, engineering design using electronic methods and means has evolved quickly for many years. We can remember some of the computers of the 1960s, which facilitated design using innovations such as the light pen, still regarded as a neat and helpful development. The development of electronic design tools over recent years has made it possible to have a Reading, England design completed at the end of a business day and sent electronically to Clinton, New Jersey for review and then shipped off to Thailand to be committed to final plans and specifications which are on the desk of the Reading engineers when they show up for work the next morning. Moreover, these global designs are made possible by commonly used engineering software and hardware that are thoroughly compatible worldwide.[6]

9.4 THE MANUFACTURING SYSTEM SHOULD BE BUILT TO BE FLEXIBLE

Because we are building or manufacturing a product that probably has not been created or built before, the manufacturing system may also never have been developed before either. No matter how careful we are in developing design criteria and in planning the detailed design of the system, experience will teach us ways (often subtle) to improve the manufacturing process. In addition, the product itself probably will change when we get customer feedback. These factors mandate that the manufacturing system be built flexibly so that enhancements can be incorporated into the system easily. One way to do this is to compartmentalize various unit operations. By doing so, the changes do not perturb the entire system, only those segments that are affected by the needed change or improvement.

One of the reasons that the manufacturing system may need to be changed is because a cheaper and more efficient way to make the product has been discovered. Another reason might be that after continued

---

[5]This supposition is correct most of the time.
[6]For example, who in the engineering profession has not heard of AutoCAD?

customer use, a modification is found that will improve the quality and/or longevity of the product. That's why we need to maintain close and friendly relationships with our customers. Sometimes customers come up with the best ideas for system improvement. Thus, we do not want to lock ourselves into an inflexible manufacturing system without having extensive product manufacturing experience. Designing flexibility into the system will help us as we get feedback from early operating histories.

A Good Example of Bringing It All Together: Orville and Wilbur Wright

Perhaps one of the most revolutionary leaps for technology in the twentieth century was the first powered flight by Orville and Wilbur Wright on December 17, 1903. Raised in a household of purpose, boundaries, and mechanical acumen, the two brothers provide an example of an effective innovation team. Wilbur was the technologist as well as the articulate champion of constant improvement and intellectual teamwork. Singleminded and composed, he provided the steady hand during their remarkable collaboration and was their public spokesman. Orville was

FIGURE 9.1   Wilbur and Orville Wright.

the inventor. Quieter than Wilbur, he was creative, curious, and impulsive. Like many other great inventors, he never earned a degree, yet followed a self-study routine that built a solid engineering foundation. His mind was agile and his ideas flowed quickly and naturally from the stimulation of their experiments.

Their remarkable partnership began in the printing business and blossomed into bicycle manufacturing and repair. Overlooking the emerging assembly line revolution of that time, the Wright Brothers bicycles were handmade, of high quality, and durable. They passed these characteristics along to the conception and manufacture of their aircraft. The bicycle business proved to be a fertile proving ground for aerodynamics. Similar to the challenge with aircraft design, bicycle mechanics included sensitive stability margins that required static and dynamic engineering solutions. There was additional similarity in the requirement for light structures, an understanding of fluid dynamics, and power transmission.

The Wright brothers departed from their contemporaries, who concentrated on empirical field testing as the basis for aeronautical insight by capitalizing methodically on the previous experiments of Lillienthal and Chanute. In doing so, they developed basic theory and then proved that theory through testing. This sound scientific approach contrasts sharply with present-day belief that innovators of that era "flew by the seat of their pants"[7] or by Edisonian trial and error. In the broadest sense, it was a four-step process:

1. Develop the theoretical concept.
2. Test the concept through controlled experimentation.
3. Derive lessons learned.
4. Refine the theory, and repeat the process.

As we said earlier, good science helps to focus on problem solving in a realistic way and minimizes wasting time and energy on false starts that might not be readily apparent if fundamental theory is not employed. Concentrating on first principles, the Wright Brothers kept it simple by starting their work in 1900 with gliders. With two years' foundation in unpowered aerodynamics, they employed a structured development plan that favored scientific research over trial by error. This led to breakthrough insights on the coefficient of lift through exquisite wind tunnel instrumentation, as well as fresh theory in the fluid dynamics of a propeller. Their focus on developing individual components before integrating those elements into the total system was an early example of compartmentalization. It

---

[7]Sorry, but we simply could not resist the pun.

also is indicative of the principles of good engineering design. Watching actual films of Wright Brothers' flights helps us understand the blend of simplicity and elegance.

While there was genius in their vehicle integration, the individual component design was both simple and elegant. When they faced roll reversal in the 1901 glider, they deftly introduced a vertical stabilizer for yaw stability, a movable rudder for consistent control, and then coupled the rudder with wing warping for synchronized flight! To decrease weight for the engine as well as the overall vehicle, their team cast the crankcase from aluminum, a first use of this material for aircraft. Each of these problems could have doomed their effort, but instead produced clarity, innovation, and results that surpassed their expectations.

Even before their record flight in 1903, Orville and Wilbur Wright attempted to protect their technology through a comprehensive patent filed in March 1903. The technology offered a unique solution in three-axis stability and control, as well as "structure combining lightness, strength, and convenience of construction."[8] Although competition in the United States and reverse engineering in Europe frustrated an uncontested financial return, their patent was the cornerstone of a favorable court decision for Orville after Wilbur's death. Even at that time, the value of intellectual property was appreciated. Subsequently, better methods were devised to safeguard good ideas.

9.5 KEY POINTS

- In this chapter we presume that product manufacturing is taken into consideration during the design process and that mechanical and computational processes that enable manufacturing either are state of the art or are designed in conjunction with the product.
- As a rough rule of thumb, design engineers estimate that for purposes of planning a capital improvement project, approximately 10 to 15 percent of the total project costs will be for the design phase and the remainder for construction.
- Technology designers and builders should be provided with an adequate budget to complete a design and implement a system that anticipates encountering unforeseen challenges, correcting inefficiencies, and enhancing process performance.

[8]U.S. patent 821,393, May 22, 1906.

- Design plans and specifications should be prepared in such a way that any qualified and competent contractor could work from these documents and reproduce the system perfectly.
- Process engineers are key actors in the development phase, and detailed designers are major contributors during the design phase. It is rare that a single person can manage both roles well.
- Readers are advised to beware of "junkyard" engineers.
- Simple designs are the most elegant.
- Good-quality materials of construction are an essential element in assuring product quality and longevity.
- State-of-the-art design tools should always be used.
- Electronic software and hardware continue to revolutionize how and where engineering design takes place.
- Designing flexibility into the manufacturing system helps to make adjustments based on feedback from early operating histories.
- Several of the central themes of this chapter are brought together in a brief vignette relating to innovations of Orville and Wilbur Wright.

10

DEMONSTRATING TECHNOLOGY

Now our product is built and ready to go. The next task is to demonstrate that this great innovation works better and more cheaply than any rival technology. We are convinced, but we need customers to be as persuaded as we are. Based on what we have seen to this point, we surely believe that once we tell the world about our innovation, the product will sell itself. This is a good time to return to a quote from Chapter 1 to reinforce a painful reality. "Unfortunately, the old truism, 'build a better mousetrap and they will beat a path to your door', doesn't always work. In fact, our experience shows that unless you know how to commercialize good technological ideas, people won't take your mousetrap even if you gave it away for nothing."

So how do we go about converting doubters? We have to demonstrate in unequivocal terms that the innovation is spectacular. This isn't easy for many reasons; some of which we discuss in this chapter.

10.1 NOBODY WANTS TO BE THE FIRST TO USE A NEW TECHNOLOGY

It's very difficult to get people to take a chance on anything, much less something new and innovative. Presumably if we give away early copies

Commercialization of Innovative Technologies: Bringing Good Ideas to the Marketplace,
By C. Joseph Touhill, Gregory J. Touhill, and Thomas A. O'Riordan
Copyright © 2008 John Wiley & Sons, Inc.

of a product, we may capture the hearts of some customers. For example, if we convince people to try the product at our cost, then if it fails they can tell their boss that it was a freebie, so nothing is lost. But if it costs something, even if the number is ridiculously small by our reckoning, and it fails, our customer figures that his head will roll when the boss finds out. In fact, experience shows that some potential customers want us to pay them to be the "guinea pigs" and to indemnify them for any losses of any sort for anything during the demonstration. It isn't easy to sell a free demonstration, but we have to do it because this is an activity that can make or break the product.

We just have to accept that nobody wants to be the first to take a chance. Even if we can demonstrate that a product works based on extended, large-scale tests, people may still be reluctant to try it. In view of this, how do we approach the critical demonstration step? The fact is that we must make some strategic concessions. Here are several that have been tried by us and others.[1]

1. If the innovation works as claimed over a specified period, the customer will attest to and agree that we can advertise the success at their location in return for specific incentives. These incentives may include some or all of the following: We pay for installation and dismantling costs, we reimburse them for any losses or damages that may occur during and because of the demonstration, and we give them free use of the system for the remainder of the product's useful life or some mutually agreed upon time period (i.e., a limited or restricted exclusive license).

2. In addition to some or all of the above, the customer (particularly if it's a big customer) may ask for a piece of the action in terms of equity ownership. We resist doing this unless there is a very compelling reason. So far, we haven't found one for any of our demonstration partners.

3. A third incentive that we have encountered, especially solicited by larger companies, is one where the company agrees to the demonstration but attempts get an exclusive license to the product that effectively prevents their competitors from using it if the demonstration is successful. They have to be very careful about that strategy because it smacks of unreasonable restraint of trade, and for obvious

---

[1]The examples given are subject to considerable negotiation and ultimately may include more concessions than those cited.

reasons we have to exercise care in accepting such a condition. Frankly, we have never done this and probably never will.

4. Software and, less frequently, computer hardware companies use beta testing not only to demonstrate their technology but also to get customer feedback on their innovations. Microsoft permitted users of their Windows software to download free copies of Windows Defender, software designed to protect user computers against malicious and unwanted software. Most people are unaware or unconcerned that downloading and using Windows Defender allows Microsoft to gather information about "spyware" and its impact and occurrence.

We don't especially like it when potential customers try to stick it to us with the concessions itemized above (although we routinely accept beta testing without much complaint). We prefer to identify companies with an acute need for our product and negotiate a demonstration agreement with them. While the technologists are doing their thing in the assessment, evaluation, development, and design phases, the entrepreneurs are finding and lining up these needy souls. Candidates tend to be companies that are over the barrel either economically or from a regulatory standpoint and may even be in shaky financial condition. If we are willing to perform the demonstration at our cost, and give them the incentive of favorable pricing on the purchase if the demonstration is successful, they often behave like the plain Jane who is grateful to have somebody ask them to the prom. If we can help them avert disaster, they will become our best customers and give us embarrassingly good testimonials. On the fantasy upside, if the turnaround is particularly dramatic, we may trade the product for a piece of their equity. On the other hand, if the demonstration is successful and the distressed company still struggles or fails, we can still point to our success when marketing to others.

In reality, demonstration agreements wind up somewhere between the onerous conditions favored by the customer and the ideal position of finding a company that we can rescue from the jaws of a dragon. But like it or not, it is absolutely essential that demonstration agreements be executed and implemented to show subsequent customers that they are not the first to use the product.

As we said above, a very good example of demonstrating new technology is beta testing of computer software. We recommend that beta-test terms and conditions from software vendors be read carefully to learn how they have structured legal agreements to protect themselves from liability.

10.2   EVERYBODY WANTS ALL THE DETAILS ON HOW OUR SYSTEM WORKS (FREE OF CHARGE)

It's not unusual for a company to demand product details, including confidential ones, prior to agreeing to host a demonstration. Our response is that unless the company first signs up for a demonstration, the answer is an unequivocal "no!". A similar problem that pops up in technology demonstrations is that the company hosting the demonstration may want insight into the inner workings of the product. Believe it or not, this curiosity is evident even among technically unsophisticated users. Sometimes it's for legitimate purposes, but often it's because they are nosey or because they think that they can duplicate results without us. Remember that strange things can happen at companies that are under stress, and one of them is believing that if they can pick our brains they can implement the concept without us. Do not share such information with the demonstration host without strict confidentiality agreements and suitable incentives. One such incentive is a firm contractual commitment to a significant sale. Another is exclusive rights to sell similar products at all other host company locations.

We must strive to retain rights to all operating data from the demonstration. Host companies balk at this because they need to have specific information on how the product performs for their application. Moreover, they are concerned about the sensitivity and confidentiality of their operating data. This is understandable, but if we obtain generalized information that is not pertinent to the host's particular application, we expect to have exclusive and confidential rights to that data. We promise to share with the host all data that is vital to the conduct of the host's in-house operations, and we agree to preserve the confidentiality of that data.

Remember that information is intellectual property and is the life blood of the innovation team. Don't give it away for nothing!

10.3   A DEMONSTRATION DESERVES SOMETHING IN RETURN

In this section we reemphasize points made in Sections 10.1 and 10.2 but in a slightly different way. We know that we have to demonstrate that the product will perform well and in accordance with our claims; otherwise, people just won't buy it. We also understand that continuing to demonstrate to more people that the product works will enhance its reputation. Further, we appreciate that companies don't like to try new ideas and require incentives before doing so. Finally, we recognize that it's going to cost money to do demonstrations—but, we want something in return, ideally the following:

1. An unrestrained opportunity to test the product at the host company's location for the company's particular application
2. A reasonable opportunity to try alternative operating modes, at our expense, if those alternatives do not have an adverse influence on host company operations[2]
3. A commitment to significant sales to the host company if the demonstration is a success[3]
4. Retention of the rights to all data that are not used by, or critical to, host in-house operations
5. An agreement to advertise demonstration success and to receive host company endorsements
6. Access for prospective customers to view the demonstration in operation, provided that visitors adhere to host company security procedures

We are willing to negotiate the terms and conditions of these items, but do not believe that any of them are unreasonable.

10.4   WHEN A SHOWCASE DEMONSTRATION WORKS, INVITE EVERYBODY IN THE WORLD TO COME AND SEE IT (AND NOT BEFORE)

If we have a great product, we must not be afraid to have everybody come and see it work. That's why it is so important to have the host of a demonstration agree in advance to permit prospective customers to visit the demonstration site and see it for themselves. The team should work very hard at structuring an access agreement that preserves the confidentiality and security required by the host company. We are reminded of a visit to a German automaker's plant where we were checking out a new process. We were allowed to view the demonstration, but the innovation team with whom we were dealing had to pay for the extensive draping of new car models so that we would not see the host company's most highly guarded secret at that time—new model paint colors!

---

[2]For example, we would like to test during off-shift periods or downtime when the host is not operating.
[3]Make certain that we define (in writing) the parameters of success in advance of the demonstration so that the host cannot renege.

Understand that many host companies are also eager to show off successful demonstrations. They are proud to be recognized as innovators and as offering their customers the latest state-of-the-art technology. The team should help them to convey that impression and be aware that sometimes the success of the two parties is intertwined. Our team entrepreneur should work closely with the host company public relations staff to generate publicity and to facilitate public access to see the demonstration in progress.

We continue to be amazed at the attention that press releases about new technology receive. Most serious, intense, and beneficial attention comes not from popular sources such as network television or mass-market newspapers, but from technical journals and trade magazines. In fact, in our experience, articles in the popular press often generate weird responses from strange people who believe that we are stealing an invention that they have been working on for the past 30 years. Only rarely in our careers have meaningful contacts been made from publicity in the popular media. Technically tuned-in readers of technical journals and trade magazines, on the other hand, want to learn all they can about innovations that can be helpful to them or that can pose a challenge to their own version of the technology.

Be prepared to react to significant inquiries about a demonstration. Have a well-coordinated plan as to how to respond to every query, and if the demonstration is truly revolutionary, the number of potential contacts can be daunting. There are ways to deal with large numbers of contacts: remote videoconferencing, regional presentations, Web videocasts, and DVD mailings, for example. We rely on our retained public relations consultants to devise the most appropriate manner of communicating. Failure to respond to inquiries can be the kiss of death.

Be aware that our competitors want to find out all they can about what we are doing and how we are doing it. That's understandable. We would do the same thing. Hence, the publicity has to be structured such that we can stimulate prospective customers without giving away family secrets in the process.

A big mistake that some people make with demonstrations is that they get caught up in the excitement of the moment and invite prospective customers to come to see it prematurely. Not only do demonstration runs have to be reproducible several times, they also have to be consistently reproducible at all times. When we invite people to see our demonstration, we have to be absolutely certain that it will work. Even accomplished and experienced technology companies goof. During April 1998 at the Comdex Spring Convention, amidst much hoop-la, Bill Gates tried to demonstrate the newest version of Microsoft's operating system, Windows

1998, when it crashed and burned before his and millions of others' eyes.[4] "I guess we still have some bugs to work out," he said good-naturedly. "That must be why we're not shipping Windows 98 yet." Unfortunately, the gaffe fueled the perception of Microsoft-haters that the company was issuing bug-infested software, and later than promised as well.

Bill Gates has been embarrassed several other times despite yeoman efforts by his staff to protect him from failed demonstrations. In January 2005 at the CES gathering in Las Vegas, while giving the opening keynote address, Gates attempted to give a demonstration of the unreleased Xbox game, *Forza Motor Sport*. He was chagrined when the program crashed and showed the infamous "blue screen of death."[5] If that wasn't enough, at Microsoft's 2006 annual financial analyst meeting, the Windows Vista product manager attempted to show how easy to use the speech recognition technology built into Vista would be.[6] The product manager spoke the following into the computer: "Dear Mom." The result was a disaster. The gentle salutation was read by the Microsoft software as "Dear Aunt, let's set so double the killer delete select all." As the reporter who wrote about the failure noted: "Attempts to correct or undo or delete the error only deepened the mess."[7] The failed speech recognition product demonstration debacle was blamed on echoes in the convention hall, but unfortunately, the damage has been done.

So we see that even when they are supersensitive, the big boys have problems. Let this be a lesson. When we wheel out a demonstration, *it has to work right the first time and every time*. It's hard enough to get people to remember successes. Don't let them remember failures—they'll remember them forever![8]

10.5 HOW MANY DEMONSTRATIONS ARE ENOUGH?

How many demonstrations are enough is a crucial question. It costs a lot of money to consummate and execute a demonstration. This is a decision that is best addressed by the entire innovation team. Obviously, investors want as few demonstrations as possible because of the cost. Technologists, supported by the inventor/innovator, want to be absolutely certain that the

[4]R. Lockridge, "Windows 98 crashes during Gates' Comdex demo," *CNN Interactive, Computing*, Apr. 20, 1998.
[5]T. Sanders, "Philips turns knife over Gates' failed CES demos," Forbes.com, Jan. 10, 2005.
[6]E. Auchard, ""When good demos go (very, very) bad," Reuters, July 28, 2006.
[7]Ibid.
[8]Readers can still see a QuickTime movie of the Windows 98 crash on the Internet.

product works, so they may tend to want more demonstrations rather than less. But it's likely that the entrepreneur has the best handle on when we are done. One answer is that we are done when customers believe that the idea has merit, that it works, and that they should try it.

Knowledge of the target market is essential in deciding what's enough. Despite successful demonstrations for application in one industry, we might have to test the technology in each industry that we have targeted. Surely we will try to point out how our technology interrelates between industries, but if the decision makers are purchasing agents, getting them to think broadly isn't the easiest chore in the world. So we must decide which industries offer us the greatest potential market and use demonstrations to target these markets. We remind you that these strategic decisions have to be made early and have to be matched by thorough and judicious planning.

Beta testing of computer software is a different breed of demonstration than a pharmaceutical production process, for example. With a pharmaceutical plant, one demonstration clearly could be enough but that won't work for computer software. For example, Microsoft offered their Anti-Spyware Beta1 (the precursor to Windows Defender) to anybody who wanted to download the program. Before doing so, they had a specific plan in mind for how they would assess the success of the software, how they would gather information on performance, and how big the potential market would be. Thus, they had a careful plan in place to determine when enough is enough. Other computer software companies that sell applications to branches of the federal government offer special incentives to the agencies to get them to participate in beta tests. Their beta tests are designed at the outset with an end point that is well defined.

10.6   KEY POINTS

- It's very difficult to get people to take a chance on new and innovative technology. They want somebody else to be first.
- It isn't easy to sell a free demonstration, but it has to be done because it is an essential step in commercializing new technology.
- A vital step is the identification of companies with an acute need for our innovative technology, then negotiating a demonstration agreement with them.
- It is absolutely essential that demonstration agreements be executed and implemented to show subsequent customers that they are not the first to use the product.

- Demonstration data must not be shared with anybody without having strict confidentiality agreements and suitable incentives in place.
- Remember that information is intellectual property and is the life blood of the innovation team. Don't give it away for nothing!
- When we make a demonstration, we do so having specific objectives of what we want in return.
- When we invite people to see our demonstration, we have to be absolutely certain that it will work.
- When we do a demonstration, *it has to work right the first time and every time*.
- We are done with demonstrations when customers believe that an idea has merit, that it works, and that they should try it.
- Knowledge of the target market and thoughtful planning are essential in deciding how many demonstrations are enough.

11

STANDARDIZING TECHNOLOGY

In response to the question of what colors would be available for his Model T automobiles, Henry Ford said, "Any customer can have a car painted any color that he wants so long as it is black." Despite his penchant for pithy quips and aphorisms,[1] Ford was deadly serious about the car color issue. He wanted to make cars inexpensive enough that most families could afford them, and he believed that mass production was the way to do it. Moreover, he believed that standardization was the essential element in bringing his vision of car building to fruition.

Somehow there is a tendency for those involved in the early stages of innovative technology to lift their noses at the thoughts of assembly lines and mass production. They feel that producing a gazillion copies of their "baby" demeans the original brilliant concept; each application should be designed to fulfill the specific need at hand. Not so! The whole point of bringing good ideas to the marketplace is to optimize commercialization. Thus, product standardization is crucial to success. In this chapter we focus on how and why standardization contributes to such success.

---

[1]It is alleged that Ford hired professional writers to produce many of the aphorisms attributed to him.

Commercialization of Innovative Technologies: Bringing Good Ideas to the Marketplace,
By C. Joseph Touhill, Gregory J. Touhill, and Thomas A. O'Riordan
Copyright © 2008 John Wiley & Sons, Inc.

11.1 CUSTOM SUITS TAKE LONGER TO MAKE AND ARE MORE EXPENSIVE

Successful commercialization implies broad, beneficial application of the inventor/innovator's concept and idea. The product should fill an important need, do so at an affordable price, and hopefully, make the backers of the process, device, or system (i.e., the innovation team) a decent profit. Remember that an important objective of the production process is to be able to use economies of scale effectively. Standardization helps to achieve this objective.

By nature, inventors and technologists thrive on problem solving. This attitude causes them to focus on problems one at a time. Typically, they diagnose the problem, formulate a solution, execute the solution, and then move on to the next problem. Left to their own devices they would generate many solutions, but it would take a long time to make a dent in filling the needs of those who require answers now. By the time they got around to us, we probably would have chosen a competing technology to meet our immediate pressing need. That's why investors and entrepreneurs must channel this creative energy into a production process that can *promptly* fill the needs of a host of customers. Simply put, the innovation team must focus its energies on mass-producing the product rather than creating it one application at a time.

That doesn't mean that if the product doesn't work exactly right when it's tried for the first time, the customer will move on. To the contrary, often, simple alterations and adjustments can make it acceptable. The process of making alterations and adjustments is discussed in detail in Chapter 13. In the present chapter the focus is on how we get to the point where we have lots of affordable and excellent product models that can be altered to begin with. Look at the automobile industry today. Many people pick out a car on the lot based on price and availability. But most customers have particular preferences that they want, and they are willing to pay (sometimes handsomely) to have these options included in the vehicle they ultimately drive away. With linked dealership computers, it's very easy for a car salesman to identify a car that contains all of the options desired, and get it to the customer virtually overnight. Everybody understands the concept of adapting their needs to the standard or basic model. With today's online computer ordering, the proletarian consumer *thinks* they are designing and building their own automobiles to their own specifications and preferences. Folks want the feeling of power that this ruse gives them, but in reality they are buying standardized vehicles. Actually, they should be glad they are, because if they were getting truly custom cars, they'd be paying Rolls-Royce prices.

Ideally, the first order of business in standardization is to design the prototype in such a way that it will be the model and basis for the manufactured product. It may take a little longer and cost a bit more to do that, but in the long run, production costs will be far less. (See Chapter 9 for a discussion of the differences between prototypes and design models.) Realistically, we can't always anticipate exactly what the design model will look like until we have a prototype, and eventually the prototype may have to be modified based on the results of experimentation.[2] Nevertheless, if possible, we should try to build the prototype with standard features that can be applied in manufacturing.

The second and more important step is to make sure that we are not creating an oddball. Recall the big battle between Betamax and VHS video recording machines? We now have a new battle between Blu-Ray and HD DVD that is far from resolution. We don't want to come down on the side of technological approaches that become dinosaurs. Thus, we must pay close attention to established and evolving industry technical standards. There are many excellent professional organizations that establish and monitor technical standards. ASTM International (originally known as the American Society for Testing and Materials), the International Organization for Standardization (ISO), the American Society of Mechanical Engineers (ASME), the American Society of Heating, Refrigerating and Air-Conditioning Engineers (ASHRAE), the IEEE Standards Association (Institute of Electrical and Electronics Engineers, Inc.), and the American Water Works Association (AWWA) are just a few of the leading organizations that develop and promulgate industry standards. The team should learn what standards apply to any concept, because customers are unlikely to buy a nonconforming product (see section 10.1).

The suit analogy cited in the section heading is a good one, because it reveals the kind of thought process that is necessary to satisfy customer needs. Have you ever inquired about the cost of having a suit custom-made? A custom suit costs about three to ten times as much to buy as does one off the rack, assuming similar-quality materials. In addition, the suit is not immediately available; it generally takes a few weeks for a custom suit to be finished.

---

[2]Customer preferences as measured by the marketing department are also important in this process.

But people come in a wide variety of shapes and sizes, so it is unreasonable to assume that a single model could fit everybody. Hence, what manufacturers have done is to standardize suits in accordance with certain body dimensions (e.g., waist size, inseam, sleeve length) and manufacture them in a standard range of sizes (sometimes further categorized as short, regular, and tall). We choose a suit that comes as close as we can get to fitting comfortably and then have minor alterations made so that it will fit "properly." For the purpose of selling our product, we need to do research that defines the scope, size, and number of models appropriate for our market.

For example, if our innovation is computer software, we may have only two versions: one for home use and one for businesses. If we have a process that treats water, flow rates become an important design factor. If we have a device used in homes to reduce allergens for especially sensitive people, we have to decide how big the device should be and where it will fit into the central heating, cooling, and ventilation system. What dictates the number of standard models of a product is satisfaction of customer needs within the fewest possible models. One excellent way of optimizing use of the fewest models is to employ a modular approach, and we describe that briefly in Section 11.3.

How do we know whether our standard design is going to meet the needs of the marketplace? Many successful vendors use beta testing with valued and trusted clients to test preproduction models to assess whether the intended product resonates well with the client's needs and expectations. Software designers such as Microsoft have a well-developed network of beta testers who test and assess early designs of products, giving the company valuable feedback to be incorporated into the final standard design. Another example of soliciting customer feedback is illustrated by car shows where new designs are unveiled. Concept cars not only tickle the fancy of the automotive enthusiast but also serve as a fertile feedback mechanism for manufacturers. Additionally, displaying concepts in a show forum gives quick feedback on how an idea stacks up against competitors' ideas.

In sum, we have to conduct research to determine and understand thoroughly the needs and situations of our customers before we cast the standard design in concrete and establish the number of design models. Learning about the success of competing products can be very helpful because system operators don't change their habits easily and are reluctant to implement "new" methods. Additionally, the product must conform to industry standards. If the innovation is truly unique, we have to recognize that we may be establishing a trail that others may have to follow relative to standards: It's best to be the leader—and way ahead. We want our product to become the established standard.

11.2   STANDARD DESIGNS ARE CHEAPER AND EASIER TO OPERATE (AND FIX)

As Davidow said in his excellent book: ***"A product that never fails is the ultimate way to deliver good service."***[3] With standard models, customers can buy a dependable product from available inventory and often get a significant break on price. In addition, they can get delivery almost immediately. Hence, standard designs are both economical and convenient for customers.

An important rule in standardizing design is to keep the product simple. For example, BMW is a popular and very well built automobile, but many people find their new I-Drive system to be overly complicated and frustrating. People hate products that are complicated and difficult to operate. They lose patience with them much more quickly than they do with systems that are easy to operate. In addition, experience shows that products that are easy to operate are also easy to fix. So customers tend to fix products themselves if the design has been kept simple. Perhaps that's why there are so many automobile hobbyists who focus on older cars that are easy to work on. Not many people today can afford the expensive diagnostic machines necessary to service and maintain "computer chip" cars.

We don't want customers to lose patience because they have to send a product back to be fixed. If the product works well, they don't need us to fix it. Too many things can go wrong when they send it back: We can take too long, charge too much, or not fix it exactly the way the customer wants. And if we are not careful to design the product to be simple, we might not enjoy fixing it ourselves.

One way to supplement simple designs is to write great instruction manuals. Do you recall those cryptic instruction manuals that used to come with Asian products a few years back? We don't know what language they were written in, but many people couldn't understand them, which made them very angry. Sometimes the fractured English was so bad that the manuals were actually funny. Don't do the same thing to our customers. In Chapter 13 we talk about technical support. Technical support staffs are difficult to assemble, train, and keep focused, so if we can avoid having customers contact the technical support team, we will stay ahead of the game. One way to do this is to spend time and effort to come up with very good instruction manuals. A criticism of instruction manuals for innovative products is that it may convey critical insights to our competitors. That's rubbish! A crummy instruction manual is more

---

[3]William H. Davidow, *Marketing High Technology*, Free Press, New York, 1986, p. 57.

likely to lose customers than an outstanding instruction manual is likely to serve as a road map for competitors.

There's a great quote: "When all else fails, read the manual!" It's funny, but true. The best products are those that are intuitive. It's wonderful when we open a box, plug in the device, and away we go. The obverse is the dreaded message on the box that says "some assembly required." Hence, in the process of designing and standardizing, special emphasis must be given to making a productive as "intuitive" as possible. In addition, make absolutely certain that the product comes assembled or that we do the assembly at the customer's desired location.

11.3   MODULARIZE WHERE POSSIBLE

Merriam-Webster's Online Dictionary defines *modularity* as "constructed with standardized units or dimensions for flexibility and variety in use." Modules are especially valuable when a product is for use in a rapidly expanding application. For example, suppose that a customer is manufacturing an electronic product that requires ultraclean water. Further assume that they are hoping for lots of production increases quickly but don't have the financial wherewithal to fund too much ahead of time. So they want us to provide them with modules that they can string together just before their expanded need. We have water treatment units that will process 10,000 gallons per day. The customer's optimistic strategic plan calls for annual growth that would require fivefold production output and hence a fivefold larger treatment facility. The best solution to meeting their need probably is to add 10,000-gallon per day modules as the need develops. In this modularization approach, we win and the customer wins.

There are many benefits to be derived from modularization of products:[4]

- We can cover a much broader range of customer needs by stringing modules together.
- Modularization results in fewer models being required in the manufacturing process.
- Modularization reduces costs for both the manufacturer and the customer. Some modules can be reused in other products, speeding development schedules while reducing development costs.
- Ease of construction and operations generally are enhanced when modules are employed.

---

[4]In the business of writing software code, a frequently used phrase when reusing code is "you get bonus points for copying."

- Repairs are easier. Sometimes it's as simple as popping out a defective module and putting in a new one. With most electronic devices and household appliances, that approach is a great deal cheaper, due to the fact that labor costs often are much higher than the cost of the part itself.
- When there are fewer standard modules, the skill level of the manufacturing staff can be reduced without impairment of product quality. This in turn reduces costs and increases production volume.

Modularity can come in several forms. One is shown in the example above of the water treatment modules, where same-sized units can be strung together to meet a growing need. Another form is "bolt-on" functional improvements to a basic core capability such as a personal computer (e.g., external hard drives, scanners, printers, speakers, perhaps even joysticks). A third form involves changes in scale. For instance, we want to buy a Shop-Vac. All the models have the same basic design, but we can get it in a 2.5- or a 5-gallon size. We refer to this form as *modularity of design*.

Interchangeability of parts (including spare parts) is an important adjunct to modularization. Not only is manufacturing more effective when parts are readily interchangeable, but also repairs are done faster and easier. Remember to consider the dimensions and units of measurement when building a production model and buying materials for assembly. Increasingly, metric units are the standard because of the expanding global marketplace. However, English units are still preferred in many industries in the United States. Therefore, consider the target market carefully when deciding what unit of measure to use.

11.4   COOPERATE WITH SUPPLIERS AND PARTNERS

Life can be made much simpler if people with whom we interface use the same standards, dimensions, materials, and even colors that we do. When we order parts or systems from suppliers, they have to know in great detail everything that we expect from them. The relationship between us and our supplier should be considered as a covenant between our companies. But don't be lazy: Write detailed specifications when ordering anything from anybody and make sure that all parties are in mutual agreement before the deal is consummated.

Companies renowned for their expertise in supply chain management, such as the Dell Corporation, stress the importance of the relationship between a manufacturer and its suppliers. Dell emphasizes the criticality of the supplier providing the highest quality delivered at the right time to the Dell manufacturing facility. In return, Dell regularly forecasts on a two-week cycle what they need from a supplier. The results are no surprises for either the manufacturer or the supplier. A visit to the Dell manufacturing plant in Round Rock, Texas highlights the impact of this covenant on manufacturing. The "just-in-time" supply relationship enables Dell to custom-build machines using a module construction technique within a day of placement of the order. Working with transportation suppliers, Dell is then able to ship the machine to the consumer within hours. Dell cites the superior relationship with their suppliers as one of keys to their success and holds their suppliers accountable for the quality and timeliness of their components.

Remember, when we incorporate a supplier's part in a product and the part goes bad, at worst the liability is ours and at best it is shared. Pass on to suppliers and partners all of the discipline and all the requirements that we demand of our own employees.

11.5   KEY POINTS

- Product standardization is crucial to successful commercialization of an inventor/innovator's concept and idea.
- Standardization helps to achieve the important objective of using economies of scale effectively.
- The innovation team must focus its energies on mass-producing a product rather than creating it one application at a time.
- Simple alterations and adjustments will generally make a standardized product acceptable to customers.
- Close attention must be paid to established and evolving industry technical standards. The product must conform to applicable industry standards. Deviation from industry standards may well create a freak.
- Conducting research to determine and understand thoroughly the needs and situation of customers is essential when defining the scope, size, and number of models appropriate for the target market.
- Standard designs are both economical and convenient for customers.
- An important rule in standardizing design is to keep the product simple.
- One way to supplement simple designs is to write great instruction manuals.
- When product use is intuitive, there is less need for instruction manuals.

- Modularization reduces costs for both the manufacturer and the customer and makes manufacturing, construction, operation, and repair easier.
- Interchangeability of parts (including spare parts) is an important adjunct to modularization.
- Carefully consider the target market, either United States or global, to decide what units of measure to use in building a product.
- Detailed specifications must be prepared when ordering anything from anybody. Pass on all of the discipline and all the requirements that we establish for our own employees.
- Companies renowned for their expertise in supply chain management, such as the Dell Corporation, stress the critical importance of relationships between manufacturers and their suppliers.

12

PACKAGING TECHNOLOGY

At this stage of commercialization, the product is in the process of being manufactured as standardized models. The next step is to sell it, but before that can be done effectively, there remain a few very important items before selling begins in earnest.[1] For the purposes of this chapter, *packaging* is defined as the culmination of strong market research, advertising, image building, and proprietary rights protection. When we hit the streets to sell a marvelous idea, we must be fully prepared. In this chapter we focus on some of the most important issues in this preparation and give a classic example of how one company carried it off.

12.1 OVERCOME THE STIGMA OF BEING FIRST

In Section 10.1 we said that nobody wants to be the first to use our technology. In our experience there is no greater challenge in selling new technology than this customer attitude. But how do we package technology to address this crucial issue? There are several ways to do so. The first

[1]We approach essential elements of commercialization in this book as though each is undertaken sequentially, when in actuality many of these elements are conducted in parallel.

Commercialization of Innovative Technologies: Bringing Good Ideas to the Marketplace,
By C. Joseph Touhill, Gregory J. Touhill, and Thomas A. O'Riordan
Copyright © 2008 John Wiley & Sons, Inc.

and best way is to appeal to customers who are known to want to be on the cutting edge of technological innovation. Many such customers have well-recognized records for making innovations work. The reason is because they have cast their corporate image as being a leader in the use of the latest and greatest technology.[2] Hence, they have a major incentive to pick innovations wisely, and when they do, to make them work efficiently and economically. These companies should be at the top of our prime target list.

A second approach is to offer incentives to customers who are afraid to be first but would be industry leaders and trend-setters if we could land them. Companies that fit this mold may be afraid but not petrified. In other words, they are simply cautious and need a boost to get them to take a chance. Otherwise, they are knowledgeable, economically sound, and willing to be innovative, albeit a little conservative in so doing. Moreover, they are approachable.[3] Incentives may include:

- Exclusive rights to our technology within their industry
- Substantial financial incentives (e.g., discounts) for a fixed period of time
- Extensive hold-harmless clauses related to product use
- A share of the profits for a fixed period of time
- An equity position in our company
- Information updates based on data generated at other locations[4]

Obviously, we want to give them as few incentives as we can (preferably none), so there is a lot of negotiating involved in getting companies to try a product.

A third type of company that might be approached is one that desperately needs our product and is eager to use it but doesn't at present have the money to buy it. This is where the investors and entrepreneurs can strut their stuff. They can make a thorough business assessment to see if use of the product will enhance the condition of the buying company sufficiently so that its strapped financial status will be improved dramatically. In return for taking a chance on them, they will have to offer us incentives. Such incentives might include partial ownership of the company, for example.

---

[2]Some individuals do the same thing.

[3]Don't waste time with companies that are arrogant or ignorant or those that regard us as door-to-door salesmen.

[4]Be careful with this incentive so that confidentiality obligations for other customers are not violated.

Finally, there is the broad universe of companies that can benefit from the use of our product. These companies were identified in our market research as having a need but no special or unique characteristics like those mentioned above. Good old-fashioned marketing and selling (pavement pounding and cold calling) are used to get them to buy. For this last category, we must be careful not to linger too long with lukewarm companies that want us to give away the store. Let them know that the technology has been demonstrated and that we are not going to spend a lot of time romancing them, and then if they don't buy in a reasonable time frame, move on.

Governmental entities are often easier to sell in the early stages because their needs can be unique and because sometimes they are encouraged to favor innovation through enabling legislation. However, government (especially the federal branch) frequently wants unique concessions such as royalty-free rights to employ a particular the technology with any agency, anywhere, at any time. In addition, confidentiality protection can sometimes be problematic because of public disclosure regulations. On the other hand, selling to the government can result in large sales and tremendous publicity in a relatively short period of time. We must be careful that governmental sales dovetail with where we are headed and that such a direction conforms to our strategic plan.

Typically, early adapters of any of the types mentioned above want tight and generous guarantees and warranties. That's not wholly unexpected and may not be unreasonable, but we have to be very careful about how far to go in accepting risk, especially for third-party liability. We rely heavily on good legal advice in terms of how far an early adapter can push us, particularly because of the precedents that upfront concessions can set.

In return for our incentives and concessions granted, we want something for our benefit. We strive to get glowing testimonials from our early customers. Obviously, we have to turn in a performance that warrants such praise, but the testimonials should be given freely and enthusiastically. In addition, the customer must be aware that we intend to use the testimonials liberally in our advertising. Remember to let the customer know when and where we will be advertising and get their permission in advance. It's also a good idea to send them copies of what goes to the media so they won't be surprised.

The biggest thing to remember is that after the first sale and the first successful operation we can say to subsequent customers, "You're not the first to use our product. XYZ Corporation continues to use it successfully, and here are rave testimonials regarding what we've done for them!"

12.2   DETERMINE WHAT NEEDS TO BE DONE TO MAKE TECHNOLOGY APPEALING

This section is closely related to many of the issues discussed in Chapter 11, where we were concerned about conformance to industry standards; the scope, size, and number of product models; and in general, the technical characteristics of the product. Here we are focused on market needs and potential applications. Notwithstanding our desire to sell modular off-the-shelf products, we have to do our homework and learn what wrinkles and options we can generate in order to make the product more attractive for targeted customers. That doesn't mean that we are straying too far from the standard model approach, nor does it mean that we won't charge extra for options, alterations, or adaptations. What it does mean is that we must recognize what customers need and then focus on their applications. The degree to which we give attention to options, alterations, and adaptations is related directly to market size and potential profit margins. In fact, if the market is big enough with very good profit potential, we may even consider a quasi–custom suit approach, albeit reluctantly.

As a rule, we want product packaging to convey the perception that we have adapted the product for application in a specialized industry. That can be accomplished by advertising in technical journals and trade magazines, exhibiting at trade shows, and through selected mass-media and mailing campaigns. A well-designed Web site can be especially helpful. The impression we want the customers to have is that we understand the industry completely because we are part of it. Testimonials can be especially helpful when they come from leaders in the targeted industry.

Deciding where to locate distribution centers is important if the target industry has centers of concentration: pharmaceuticals in the Middle Atlantic states, particularly New Jersey; chemicals in West Virginia, the Ohio River Valley, and on the Gulf coast; and computer software in the Bay area of California. Not only can we get a product to the customer quickly, but also we establish linkages as a neighbor dedicated to serving that industry if we locate distribution centers properly and with forethought. This is part of image building associated with packaging.

After the product has been embedded in the target industries, packaging needs will mature and will need to be revised. For instance, once we have an established track record, we may shy away from options, alterations, and adaptations and let customers handle this aspect themselves with some advice from us, when appropriate. Such a change should be taken with great care and should be the product of close customer contact and thoughtful market research.

12.3   THE ART OF BEING COOL

Throughout the book we've concentrated on innovation that featured exceptional engineering creativity. One of the best examples of twenty-first-century technology packaging certainly embodies that characteristic but adds a right-brained perspective that has captured the imagination of modern culture. The iPod, along with Apple Inc.'s associated product lines, is not only sophisticated technology, it is *cool*.

There is no hesitation here on being the first to deploy a consumer idea. Apple is on the leading edge of technology. Their culture seems to push them to the limit and to be the "first with the most" in innovation. With the iPod, Apple jumped into the breach with a very compelling package that included a reliable machine, a flexible and intuitive software interface, and a virtual store that reaches out to the customer.

Apple doesn't evaluate the market, it shapes the market. Although their business model allegedly is detached from customer concerns, they are reinventing the electronic life of consumers. Even though many might say that there is no requirement for 60 gigabytes of music, photos, and video in one's shirt pocket, thousands can't live without it once they've been exposed to the iPod experience.

Apple's advertising is steamrolling the competition. They communicate a startling vision of life style and implied values. The commercials are bright, swirling, and exuberant. The immediate message is unconstrained freedom. The iPod becomes a universal symbol for that life style, an emblem of being synchronized with boundless electronic access.

On the computer side, their long-term campaign caricaturing PC and MacIntosh users not only reinforces the thought that Apple products are hip, but also brands the rest of the PC world as mechanical, inhuman, and a bit dense. The only advertising response from the competition appears to be mimicry.

Accordingly, they've established a counterculture *image* that is seductive to mainstream America. Even the physical packaging is an extension of the central theme and won them an award for packaging excellence. When these aspects are combined, the iPod and the many other Apple integrated products are more than a technology project. They become a contemporary artform that transcends the consumer world. They are *cool*.

Apple fortifies the image through their successful retail stores that are spreading across the United States. The stores are the perfect backdrops for celebrating each product. Eschewing the Best Buy warehouse effect, Apple takes each iPod product and displays it in a clear singular space, brightly lit, with the gravity of a priceless museum artifact.

Despite these strengths, Apple has not forgotten the importance of *protecting its proprietary rights*. The first line of defense here is that the iPod is a closed system. Although this deters third-party development, it indemnifies software standards and configuration control. In terms of branding, Cisco is suing Apple on the use of the iPhone trademark.[5] In an interesting twist, the suit suggests that Apple may be infringing on Cisco's proprietary rights. In any case, this is enduring evidence that proprietary rights are crucial in technology development.

Apple has packaged their iPod technology with skill and *elan*; it appears that the iPhone will follow suit. There are some caution signs along their path to financial growth. Their closed systems may complicate the work of enterprise customers. Additionally, their meteoric success and intellectual fireworks might lead to an increase in arrogance and market blindness in the future. Nevertheless, we might not find a better example of packaging technology than Apple Inc.

12.4   PROTECT OUR PROPRIETARY RIGHTS AGGRESSIVELY

The message here is simple: Don't be nice when somebody tries to steal an idea. Thump them quick and hard. Eddie Mayehoff, playing the father (Jarring Jack Jackson) in the film *That's My Boy*, told his son (Jerry Lewis), "Hit 'em low, hit 'em hard, and if they get up, hit 'em again!"[6]—and he was right. In today's marketplace, we must establish conclusive ownership of ideas and engage decisively any interlopers who attempt to steal them. Moreover, if the idea is as good as the innovation team believes, we must have accomplished legal advisors set to go early in the commercialization process. Reverse engineering is inevitable, so we have to anticipate our response in advance. Choose legal advisors who are familiar with our innovation and its associated industry and who have a proven track record of protecting proprietary rights. We instruct our lawyers to act vigorously in early cases because those cases set the tone for latter challenges, and if we are very aggressive, the plagiarizers will back off and try to steal another idea from somebody else.

We intend to get patent coverage consistent with our dream marketplace[7] and in accord with our strategic plan. In other words, because

---

[5]At the time of this writing, it appears that the dispute is nearing resolution.
[6]In this 1951 classic movie, the greatest player in Ridgefield College history (Mayehoff) uses his influence and reputation to get his only son, a sickly, uncoordinated nerd (Lewis), on the college football team—with comic results.
[7]Places that we have targeted in both the short and long term in our strategic plan.

most of our early target customers may be in North America, we might only apply for patents in the United States, Canada, and Mexico. This could be a grave mistake because if the product has potential for global use, it should be protected globally. Thus, we recommend strongly that if there is not a compelling reason to do otherwise, patents should be applied for in all countries that offer patent protection.[8]

We don't expect that we will receive letters or telephone calls informing us that another company is infringing on our patents. We must be vigilant in finding such infringements on our own. It really isn't as difficult as it seems. If we know the customers and the target market well enough, we should be able to tell when somebody is messing with our ideas. The trick is to be able to investigate and confirm suspicions early and then turn the lawyers loose on the offenders.

Before we set the dogs on infringers, one strategy is to see if we can't turn them into allies. If they see the benefits of our innovation, perhaps we can give them an incentive to be our agents rather than our enemy. Hence, we might consider having them work on commission or grant them a license to sell on our behalf. The reason that this tactic doesn't work as often as we would like is because if the infringement is done consciously, the infringers probably aren't the most trustworthy people in the world. On the other hand, if the infringers are honest people who truly may have a technology that is very close to ours, reaching an accommodation with them could be worthwhile. But if we reach an accord with somebody, make absolutely certain that the integrity and quality of the product does not suffer. The cost of litigation is exorbitant, so we have to look for ways to absorb competitors if we can. If not, we have to go get them.

We can't confuse competition with infringement. There are lots of people in the business who are as smart or smarter than we are. Therefore, we shouldn't waste time suing somebody who really is a legitimate competitor. The way to deal with them is to outsell them.

12.5   KEY POINTS

- Product "packaging" is the culmination of strong market research, advertising, image building, and proprietary rights protection.

---

[8]Some countries have no meaningful patent protection, and some that do, have no enforcement to speak of. We are vulnerable in such countries. Generally, countries where infringement is a problem aren't good markets to begin with, so the problem of infringement there can be ignored without too much harm. On the other hand, if the product is shipped to a patent-protected country, we should be diligent in pursuit of the offender.

- The best way to overcome the stigma of being first is to appeal to customers who are known to want to be on the cutting edge of technological innovation.
- A second approach to overcoming the stigma of being first is to offer incentives to customers who could be industry leaders and trend setters if we could land them.
- A third type of company that might be approached is one that desperately needs our product and is eager to use it, but doesn't have the money to buy it at present. If it makes economic sense to work with them, seek incentives to do so.
- Under the right conditions, government can be a good early adapter/customer.
- Get glowing testimonials from early customers.
- We want product packaging to convey the perception that we have adapted a product for application in a specialized industry.
- Deciding where to locate distribution centers is important if the target industry has centers of concentration.
- The Apple iPod and its other branded products, including the iPhone, are outstanding examples of how to use total packaging to capture and embrace a unique spot in today's electronic culture.
- Proprietary rights must be protected aggressively, but seek ways to avoid litigation first.
- Competition should not be confused with infringement.

13

APPLYING TECHNOLOGY

In Chapter 11 we emphasized the formulation, design, and manufacture of standard and basic product models. In this chapter we focus on altering these models and applying them to satisfy specific customer needs. In addition, we comment on the need for exemplary technical support and customer service.

13.1 OFF-THE-RACK SUITS REQUIRE ALTERATIONS

When we were talking about the establishment of standard models in Chapter 11, we used the analogy of custom suits versus those off the rack. The analogy is a good one in this instance, too. Very rarely do ready-made suits fit exactly right off the rack. In fact, most suit trousers do not come hemmed or cuffed at the bottom to begin with; thus, alterations are virtually guaranteed. Consider the range of sizes available for ready-made suits. If this broad range of choices can't meet the exact specifications of customers (and it usually doesn't), try to imagine the likelihood that our product will be a perfect fit off the shelf. Clearly, we have to be prepared to adapt the product in some manner to meet customer requirements.

We want the alterations to be as minor and as easy as possible. This goal can be accomplished by anticipating in advance what the type and

Commercialization of Innovative Technologies: Bringing Good Ideas to the Marketplace,
By C. Joseph Touhill, Gregory J. Touhill, and Thomas A. O'Riordan
Copyright © 2008 John Wiley & Sons, Inc.

range of alterations will probably be. This is done by performing thorough market research and incorporating results of this research into product design, which must reflect the potential scope and sort of alterations that are likely to be required by our customers based on our knowledge and understanding of industry needs. Obviously, the closer that customer needs are to the industry norm, the more minor the alterations should be. The innovation team should decide on an allowance for alterations as part of the base purchase price. If all we are doing is tweaking a little here and there, customers expect that the cost should be included in the price of the product—and they are right. The last impression that we want to convey is that we are nickel and diming them.

Determining the point where we start charging customers for alterations is very important not only from the standpoint of profit margins but also from the viewpoint of customer satisfaction. Do it carefully, rationally, and with the business strategy clearly in mind.

13.2 ALTERATIONS AND OPTIONS ALWAYS COST MONEY

Because alterations and options always cost money, we must decide which costs we will eat and which we will pass on. As a rule of thumb, we should charge the customer for all options and adaptations and for those alterations that we did not identify and allow for in developing our pricing strategy model. The biggest mistake (made most often by inventors and technologists) in dealing with a customer's desire to make major alterations is to get angry. Somehow certain members of the innovation team take it as a personal affront when a customer representative wants to change the product. This attitude is absolutely wrong. It really is an opportunity to get better profit margins than we could get on the base model. Therefore, we should bend over backward to satisfy customer preferences, provided of course that the customer is prepared to pay for the changes.

Indeed, we view this customer weakness (i.e., wanting to tinker with the basic design) as a golden opportunity to sell those features that can improve performance. Technologists and those involved in the marketing and selling of a product should be trained to make the customer aware of how to get such enhanced performance—all at an appropriate price, of course. Certainly, improved performance has to be demonstrable, and evidence should be prepared in advance to show the cost-effectiveness and positive return on investment of the change. The reasons for doing this are to show that there are tangible benefits to the purchase of extras, and to avoid any hint of gouging. We urge that the sale of features that are still in development, untested, and that may not be feasible be avoided. Don't oversell, and certainly don't promise what isn't available.

13.3   MAKE TECHNICAL SUPPORT EASY AND ACCESSIBLE

Even though our innovation meets all the customer's expectations, the customer will continue to be nervous because it is new. Nervous people yell for help at the first sign of something going wrong, and they want *immediate* attention. They don't want to have to wade through a path of number pushing on the telephone while being told (by a mellifluous prerecorded voice) that despite the wait, "your business is important to us." "If it's so darned important, how come I can't talk with somebody *now*?" Then when they finally get to a human being, the person (in heavily accented English) slogs through a bunch of administrative questions before revealing that they have no idea how to solve their problem or address their needs. We want to do the exact opposite; we want to make the process of interacting with customers easy and pleasurable.

When the product becomes used widely as a commodity, the people to whom we will sell the company may adopt the approach described in the preceding paragraph, but we'll be gone by then. However, as long as the company is ours, we'll emphasize exemplary customer service and endeavor to avoid the traps cited above.

First, when the sale is made, the buyer will be given the name and contact information for a specific person who will be responsible for servicing the product. Moreover, if that person is unavailable for any reason the customer will have a backup person identified. There should also be an emergency telephone number. This protocol will eliminate the number-pushing path. Instead, our customers will hear a real live voice or at the very least, get the voice mail of somebody they know.

Second, we will not wait for the customer to get antsy. Our person designated to service the customer will check in regularly to see how things are going. In the early stages, when the customer list is modest, check-in will be frequent because we are as eager as they are to learn about product performance (more about this later). As sales increase, we make certain that we have sufficient knowledgeable staff so that contact can be made at least monthly, preferably face to face.

Third, we will assure that the service representatives are trained technically to be able to address most routine problems encountered. In addition, these service representatives will understand procedures on how to engage the company's best applications specialists and engineers in the event of complicated problems. We cannot afford to have customers suffer undue downtime because our product doesn't work right (even if it's their fault because of improper operating methods). Hence, we will attack their problems quickly and effectively no matter whose fault it is, and sort out the causes later.[1]

Fourth, we want our service representatives to be close to the customers culturally and geographically. If our marketplace is global, this may be a problem initially and could involve a lot of travel for our best applications specialists and engineers. But as sales increase, we expect to be able to locate trained representatives close to our customers. Ideally, these representatives will be part of the local or regional community and share its cultural identity. We also aim to have our local representatives speak the native language of the customer fluently.

Fifth, to the extent possible, written communications (e.g., correspondence, technical reports, brochures, and operating instructions) will be in the native language of the customer unless they agree otherwise. Exceptions may be for those troubleshooting documents that deal with complicated matters that aren't encountered very often.

Finally, share the company organization chart with the customer and include the president's telephone number. We want customers to have a route to the boss if things go really bad. Experience tells us that it's far better to have an irate customer fume all over the boss than to have them engage a lawyer to sue us.

If we have worked hard to get this far and diligently followed the steps outlined in previous chapters, we don't expect that we will have any tough problems. But we do believe that if we implement the approach described in this section, potentially difficult situations will be kept under good control. In the event that bad things do happen, remember the magic words of technical support: "We're sorry. We'll fix it!" And if it's real bad, we might have to do it at our cost.

13.4   GOOD SERVICE GENERATES MORE BUSINESS

Here's something that all good salespeople know: Satisfied and content customers rarely bid out their jobs.[2] They find ways to keep coming back

---

[1]If the customer is the cause and we can prove it, we may want to back-charge them for the costs and efforts, especially if the costs are significant. The trick is to go about recovering the money with considerable diplomacy. We may even want to let it go if we can arrange to get major new orders.

[2]The exception is government. The requirement to bid government work can be difficult, but with a unique product and solid proven relationships with the governmental entity, that positive experience can be of immeasurable help in landing follow-on work.

to known suppliers because it makes their job easy. They want a product that performs nearly flawlessly; quick and efficient service when there's trouble; and reliability, dependability, good communications, and a warm relationship with the people who represent that product. Things that can sour a solid relationship is if customers feel that they are being taken for granted, ignored, or overcharged. Face it, they are just like us. They want good products that work right forever at a decent price. Additionally, they are willing to pay a little more if they get great service with a smile.

Not only will satisfied users be good repeat customers, they can also be among your best sales helpers. Testimonials, referrals, and references are worth a great deal. We encourage our people to ask for these perquisites of good service. Most industries have technical and professional organizations where people gather to share experiences. Gently urge customers to use such interactions to tell their friends and colleagues how well we performed for them.

One of the best things that a particularly satisfied customer can do is to show other prospective clients how a product works at their location. It's difficult to expect that a customer will permit a potential competitor to visit their facility, but if they like what we've done for them, they will be good hosts for us and our visitors. There may be restrictions in terms of where the visitors can go and what they can see, but that's not unreasonable. Moreover, the customer may charge us for the time and effort that their personnel spend in getting ready for and conducting the visit. Be prepared to be generous in covering these costs. Our experience shows that the willingness of a satisfied customer to allow an outsider into their facility is far more impressive in convincing prospective clients than their actually seeing the innovation in operation.

13.5 KEY POINTS

- Because of the diversity of customer requirements, we have to be prepared to adapt our product in some manner to meet these needs.
- Alterations should be made as minor and as easy as possible by anticipating in advance what the type and range of alterations probably will be.
- The point where charges for alterations begin must be determined carefully, bearing in mind the issues of profit margins and customer satisfaction.

- A customer's desire to make major alterations should not be met with anger. It may be an opportunity to get better profit margins than could be obtained on the base model.
- Interacting with customers must be easy and pleasurable.
- A trained and culturally attuned service representative should be located near the customer, and that person should check in with the customer on a regular basis.
- Satisfied clients make good repeat customers who are willing to help us get more work through testimonials, referrals, references, recommendations, and allowing outsiders to visit their site to see our product in action.

14

MARKETING AND SELLING TECHNOLOGY

We begin with a quote from Davidow: *"... Technological superiority alone no longer guarantees success or even a position in the race. Good devices will not sell themselves. ... Increasingly, marketing will determine the fate of companies."*[1] We are not so presumptuous that we believe that we can tell people how to market and sell innovative technology. There are many other books that do an excellent job of explaining the strategy and tactics of landing new customers. For example, the quote above is taken from a book that we recommend for all those seriously interested in commercializing innovative technology: *Marketing High Technology* by W. H. Davidow.[2] Nevertheless, we would like to share a few observations and experiences that may be helpful in the marketing and sales process.

14.1 THE DIFFERENCE BETWEEN MARKETING AND SELLING

Everybody in marketing and sales seems to have their own favorite definition of what they do, confusing many who operate outside that sphere.

---

[1] W. H. Davidow, *Marketing High Technology*, Free Press, New York, 1986, p. xviii.
[2] Davidow's book was quite popular when it was published 20 years ago, but today it tends to be dated because technology has moved well beyond the concepts of the time. Despite its dated references, Davidow's book still has value in terms of the fundamental lessons it teaches relative to marketing high technology.

Commercialization of Innovative Technologies: Bringing Good Ideas to the Marketplace, By C. Joseph Touhill, Gregory J. Touhill, and Thomas A. O'Riordan
Copyright © 2008 John Wiley & Sons, Inc.

Hence, for the purposes of this book we will hazard our own definition, not to settle the differences of others, but to permit the reader to understand our perspective.

- *Marketing:* We identify the target customer(s) and ask: "What do you need?"
- *Selling:* We have a valuable product that will fill the customer's need, so we ask: "Do you want to buy it?"

In marketing and selling, the trick to being successful is to know the difference between a neat innovation and a great product. Too often we get all misty-eyed about an innovation that we believe will change the world. In fact, it may well be a terrific concept and conjure up all sorts of amazing benefits for our target customers. But we need marketing to turn the service or device into a product having a personality that shouts "buy me!" Salespeople understand that transition from device to product. They need solid marketing to identify the target customers. They need advertising to ease their way into customers' offices. They need clear focus on what the product can do and how it can fill the customer's need, and they need the sales materials (brochures, manuals, samples, demos, and supporting literature) necessary to close the sale.

We believe that marketing and selling are two very distinct activities that are inextricably linked, with selling generally being acknowledged as a subset of the overall process of marketing.

14.2   SELLING VALUE, NOT COST

If our product truly is innovative, most of our targeted customers will not have seen or used this type of technology before. Hence, techniques employed in selling commodity items are completely useless to us. The best approach is to emphasize that we can do something for customers that can't be done any other way and/or that we will save them money (hopefully, lots of it) in the long run. We must emphasize value and not cost. Buying on the basis of cost is usually associated with products that have many competitors, are readily available, address routine needs, have consistent quality among a variety of competitors, and are not unique in their application. They are like supermarket items. Ask our wives which commodity items they buy in supermarkets or discount store and they all give the same answer, "We buy the one that's on sale!"

In truth, it's a very rare innovation that resolves a problem that can't be solved using another approach, even if the technology is very different from ours. For example, water softeners using ion-exchange materials were state of the art for many years. Then reverse osmosis technology advanced to the point where it became cost-effective for household use. In many areas of the country, drinking water quality characteristics were highly favorable for reverse osmosis application compared with ion exchange. So there was a shift toward this new technology. Initially, reverse osmosis for household use was sold as a breakthrough water treatment method. Over time it has captured a significant share of the household water treatment market, yet ion exchange continues to be a viable alternative. How did reverse osmosis compete after the initial novelty wore off? The next stage of selling focused on ease of operation, the reduced need to dispose of spent brine, less corrosion of materials, ease of membrane replacement, and longer life of the units. All of these factors had a positive impact on costs. Household water treatment salespersons emphasized complete life-cycle costs and benefits and sold the reverse osmosis units on that basis. It also helped that very quickly companies that sold ion-exchange units started to offer reverse osmosis units, too. Health consciousness became a selling factor when it was pointed out that sodium concentrations in water treated by reverse osmosis were much lower than those treated by ion exchange.[3]

So what are the lessons of this example? Here are a few:

- The *novelty* of innovative technology was a distinct advantage at first; particularly after it was demonstrated that the new method was superior for certain water conditions.
- Longer term benefits due to more attractive *life-cycle costs* were emphasized in the second phase of selling.
- The third phase of selling offered a choice of technologies, where the one selected was chosen based on the characteristics of the water source in addition to other *performance characteristics*.
- Reverse osmosis sales improved considerably when *positive health benefits* were cited compared with the principal competing technology (ion exchange). In other words, the other technology just couldn't deliver this benefit.
- In summary, for the example cited, cost was a consideration, but value made the sale.

When we get to the point that we are selling on the basis of cost alone, it's probably time to move on to the next phase of the plan.

---

[3] Sodium in water creates potential problems for people with high blood pressure and heart disease.

All that's great, but how do we establish a sale price for our product? It's really very simple: Charge what the market will bear. If the product accomplishes what a competitive product can accomplish, but faster and better, we can establish a price higher than the competitor's. How much higher? Elementary economics tells us that the optimal price is where we maximize profits: the point beyond which customer reluctance to buy because of price causes drop off in profitability (a classical example of *elasticity*). Generally, it's a mistake to settle on a product price by summing up all the development and manufacturing costs and then adding a generous markup. Certainly that's one way to do it, but if the idea is truly innovative, we might be leaving money on the table using that approach, regardless of how rational the method may seem.

14.3   DON'T WASTE TIME WITH PEOPLE WHO AREN'T SERIOUS

There are a lot of people who express curiosity about new ideas. They do so for a variety of reasons. Some are eager to assess and keep up with the state of the art. Some have an academic curiosity and want to learn how and why a product works. Some want to show us how smart they are. Some want to see if they can plagiarize the idea by copying directly or by using patent-skirting techniques. There are lots of other reasons for curiosity, but the conclusion relative to those who simply are curious is always the same: They make lousy customers. They pump us for information, yet share little themselves, and they never seem to reach a conclusion. Thank them for their interest and move on—quickly. Eagerly share information with buyers, not with snoops. They waste our time.

Another category of person who wastes our time is the "fraidy cat." Working with them is maddening because they give every indication of being buyers. They tell us how much they love the product and, in fact, the entire concept. They even provide details as to how they intend to put the product into use. But they have trouble with decision making, leading us to the edge and then backing off time after time. Again, when it becomes apparent that we are dealing with a fraidy cat, tell the person that we'd love their business: "Call us when you are ready to buy." Keep in touch with them through written notices and occasional phone calls and e-mails.

There is a third and more malevolent type of "potential" buyer. It's sad but true that some people waste others' time on purpose. They have agendas that are very different than ours and tend to be conspiratorial in ways that we don't understand. That's the bad news. The good news is they tend to be that way with everybody, so they acquire bad reputations in the industry. Hence, if we have done our research and know the industry well, we know who they are and can avoid them altogether.

Clearly, not everyone is simply curious, afraid, or malevolent. The problem is that we generally don't have a good idea of who these folks are until we meet them and confirm our marketing research or their industry reputations. A simple remedy is to decide early, before we make customer contacts, how much time we are willing to devote to each and establish when we will move on if we don't see action. In our experience the prospective customers who are hardest to dump are the ones we personally like the most.

14.4   THE IMPORTANCE OF MARKET SHARE

Davidow is a firm believer in the crucial importance of market share. He says: "Marketing must invent complete products and drive them to commanding positions in defensible market segments."[4] He goes on to cite the conclusion of a General Electric study which showed that companies with greater than a 30 percent market share almost always were profitable, and conversely, those with less than a 15 percent share almost always lost money. Later in his book he uses the General Electric study conclusions to recommend a strategy for his readers. *"A company must make it a goal to capture at least 25 percent of a market segment. It should never enter a market unless it is almost certain it can capture at least 15 percent."*[5] We don't believe that the rule is inviolable, but we agree that if our market share doesn't fall into the greater than 15 percent level, there had better be a very, very good reason to pursue that market.

14.5   MARKETING TOOLS

Salespeople have many techniques to keep in front of a customer. We will talk about a few, recognizing that our list is far from complete. If we are trying to sell technology and don't have a Web site, we will probably be judged to be absolutely antediluvian. We do not see how anyone can take a technology company seriously nowadays if they can't access a Web site quickly and get the information they are after. It's marketing's job to anticipate the questions that customers might have. People want a clear

[4]Davidow, op. cit., p. 13.
[5]Ibid., p. 140.

explanation of what we do, who we are (our staff and their backgrounds and qualifications), where we are, what we sell, how much it costs, and how to get in touch with us. Rather than providing a lesson in Web design, we encourage readers to browse the Web to see how other high-technology companies have designed their sites. Try to choose sites that are related to what you are trying to accomplish, and hire a professional Web designer to make the site attractive and interesting.

Customers of high technology are not dopes. Generally, they do a lot of homework before they even contemplate buying innovative products. The homework includes researching technical journals, attending trade shows, and listening to technical presentations at seminars and professional society meetings. Their technologists actively keep up with the state of the art, so we have our technologists write journal articles, attend and make presentations at professional society meetings with the aim of convincing them that we know what we are doing and that we have a high degree of credibility. Inevitably their bosses are going to ask them, "Are these guys for real?" You want customer technologists to answer, "Absolutely!"

Well-written press releases are worth their weight in gold. When one of the authors was working at Battelle as a young engineer, he was astounded by the volume of responses that one of his successful projects generated following a widely distributed press release. Inquiries came in from all over the world. Many were from the curious, but the number of substantive contacts was a big surprise. Fortunately, Battelle had mature pros who anticipated the type of response that good news on an important project would bring and who were prepared to field all the questions professionally and promptly, even in those cases where crackpots wrote or called to tell us that we were infringing upon their patents (clearly we weren't). So our advice is to use press releases strategically and be prepared to field responses quickly and precisely or lose both credibility and potential excellent clients.

14.6   MEASURING PERFORMANCE

How do we know if a marketing plan is successful? Davidow has devised a list of 16 questions, or as he calls them, factors, that if dealt with effectively will permit companies to market productively.[6]

1. *Do programs comply with the "strategic principle"?* Most companies fail because they never clearly identify the markets they are pursuing.

[6]Ibid., pp. 160–168.

2. *Does marketing understand why customers will buy the product?* Marketing people can't sell customers on a product's benefits if the marketers don't know them.

3. *Does a crusade mentality exist?* If the product is an important one, the company had better be on a crusade.

4. *Is customer satisfaction guaranteed?* To satisfy a customer, a product must be backed by the services that the customer requires.

5. *Does the product match the sales and distribution channels?* A product may be good in every respect, but there may be no good way to get it to the customer.

6. *Will the promotion program work?* A product's positioning should be the cornerstone of every piece of sales literature, advertising, and promotion.

7. *Is the product different?* Products succeed and become profitable when they are dramatically different in significant ways.

8. *Does a marketing plan exist?* Usually, an unwritten plan is indicative of no plan at all.

9. *Is pricing fair?* Marketing personnel should be able to explain to management why the price established is fair to both the customer and the company.

10. *Are the marketing programs integrated?* Companies have true marketing programs only when all the pieces fit together.

11. *Is marketing in touch with the customer base?* The only way to find out what is going on in the marketplace is to be there.

12. *Does marketing respect sales, and vice versa?* Where there is real teamwork between sales and marketing, great products become more successful, and even the weaker areas can be made to succeed.

13. *Does marketing drive the organization?* Marketing is the organization that must make development groups aware of customers' needs and must make the manufacturing organization knowledgeable about capacity and cost issues.

14. *Are products managed throughout their life cycles?* Good marketing departments are constantly aware of the status of the entire product line and manage both new and old products throughout their life cycles.

15. *Is a forecasting system in place?* Unless a good forecasting system is in place, problems are bound to be caused by changes in demand.

16. *Does marketing have quality control?* Service to customers is measurable.

We are not necessarily recommending that Davidow's factors be used, but we do urge that a system be devised that permits measurement of marketing performance and effectiveness. Certainly, using Davidow's factors would be a good starting point in coming up with such a system. Regular reports to go along with bookings, billings, and profit and loss statements will be valuable performance measurement tools for innovation team management.

14.7 TECHNOLOGY QUOTAS AND RETENTION REQUIREMENTS ARE A *MUST*!

If the principal revenue stream derived from an innovation is through licensing, a dullard customer can kill us because of inactivity and incompetence. Contract agreements with a licensee must be very specific about the performance expected. We try to make this the central issue when attempting to find a suitable licensee and negotiating a license agreement. They have to move ahead quickly and diligently to meet our expectations relative to sales, because their sales determine our license fees. Performance arrangements include quotas in accordance with well-defined schedules over the life of the agreement, and they also contain retention requirements. Retention requirements necessitate that explicit goals be met at predetermined times for the agreement to remain in force. In other words, if the licensee does not meet sales goals, the licensee is not retained and the license agreement is terminated. So in choosing a potential licensee, choose wisely.

The reason that quotas and retention requirements receive considerable attention is because there were some notorious abuses in the past. With the rise of a titan economy in Japan in the 1970s and 1980s, many entrepreneurs were stumbling all over themselves to cut deals with this new global economic giant. Inexperienced "deal makers" looked to Asia for financing if they didn't get money soon enough from their home country venture capitalists. Some of the innovations offered to Japanese companies conflicted directly with strategic plans that these companies had for closely related products. So the approach of Japanese industrialists was to sign a license agreement with the innovators and then sit on the license and do nothing. Letting the licensed innovation fester effectively removed a competitor from the marketplace. There are many innovation teams that are older and wiser because of that experience.

Sometimes licensees run into bad luck or bad timing despite their great energy to sell the licensed innovation. In such an event, be kind and thoughtful before the trigger is pulled on the hapless licensee. Presumably considerable time has been spent in romancing, negotiating, and training them on how to exploit the product. That investment could possibly be saved if nonperformance is the result of bad luck and not lack of effort. We try to work with licensees to get them back on track by lending our technical, financial, and marketing skills. We have to decide how much help we want to give so that we don't jump into a bottomless pit with a licensee who just doesn't have it. We plan our rescue efforts carefully.

Always deal with licensees in a professional and helpful manner. Micromanagement of licenses and constant berating regarding missed targets are not conducive to establishing the kind of smooth, friendly relationships that characterize the most successful license arrangements. Moreover, word of brutal treatment of licensees gets around quickly and broadly, so we can understand why others might not want to work with us if we behave poorly.

14.8 KEY POINTS

- In our definition of marketing, we identify customers and ask them what they need. In selling, we ask them if they want to buy our great product.
- In marketing and selling, the trick to being successful is to know the difference between a neat innovation and a great product.
- The best approach to selling value and not cost is to emphasize that we can do something for customers that they can't do any other way, and that we will save them lots of money in the long run.
- When selling product value, novelty, favorable life-cycle costs, desir able performance characteristics, and special considerations (such as positive health benefits) should be emphasized.
- When we get to the point that we are selling on the basis of cost alone, it's probably time to move on to the next phase of the plan.
- The best approach to pricing is to charge what the market will bear.
- Those who are curious and not really serious about our technology make lousy customers. They fall into three categories: simply curious, afraid, or malevolent.
- Deciding how much time we are willing to devote to each customer contact and establishing when we will move on if we don't see action must be established early.
- "A company must make it a goal to capture at least 25 percent of a market segment. It should never enter a market unless it is almost certain it can capture at least 15 percent" (Davidow).

- It is essential to have a well-designed Web site.
- To build credibility with customer technologists, it is important to write technical journal articles, participate in trade shows, and attend and make presentations at professional society meetings.
- Strategically placed press releases and a well-conceived method for addressing responses to the releases should be used liberally.
- Davidow has devised a list of 16 marketing factors that if dealt with effectively will permit companies to market productively. We have listed the factors in Section 14.6.
- Technology quotas and retention requirements provide for explicit goals to be met at predetermined times for license agreements to remain in force. If the licensee does not meet sales goals, they are not retained and the license agreement is terminated.
- In the event that a licensee runs into bad luck or bad timing, efforts should be made to work with them to get things back on track by lending our technical, financial, and marketing skills.
- All team members must behave professionally. Word of brutal treatment of licensees gets around.

15

TRACKING TECHNOLOGY

The commercialization process is not over when an innovative product is sold. To the contrary, if we make a sale and then walk away, our days as entrepreneurs are numbered. In this chapter and those that follow, we deal with tasks that are very important to the long-term success of good innovation teams after the sale is made.

15.1 MAKE CERTAIN THE BUYER IS APPLYING THE TECHNOLOGY CORRECTLY

Uncle Gene is a very intelligent man with great energy, an inquiring mind, and a depth of common-sense that's so awesome, it's scary. He decided to buy his first personal computer when he was 77 years old. He had never used a PC before. Purchased when he called a telephone number he saw in a newspaper advertisement, the PC arrived with only rudimentary instructions, and all in-depth user manuals were on disks and the hard drive. In his opinion, after trying to use the computer for a couple of years, the company that sold him the computer[1] should be subjected to high-level carpet bombing along with their foreign-based technical support staff. He

---

[1] It is a well-known and highly respected company.

Commercialization of Innovative Technologies: Bringing Good Ideas to the Marketplace,
By C. Joseph Touhill, Gregory J. Touhill, and Thomas A. O'Riordan
Copyright © 2008 John Wiley & Sons, Inc.

is able to use e-mail, search the Internet in a sort of rudimentary way, write an occasional note, and play the simpler games that came with the computer. He regrets the purchase and believes that he was hoodwinked, notwithstanding the fact that his 11-year-old great-grandson loves it. What went wrong?

First, Uncle Gene had a poorly conceived notion of what a computer can do, but his friends convinced him that they were terrific for many chores. Second, he had no prior acquaintance with computers, so he was not familiar with how to use one. Even manipulating a mouse was a novelty to him. Third, when the computer wouldn't work because of his inexperience or when it locked up through no fault of his own, his calls to technical support personnel were an exercise in frustration both because of his difficulty in understanding the foreigners[2] who were trying to assist him, and because he had trouble telling them what the problem was. Frankly, he didn't even know how to describe the problem. So this man, who is widely known and respected throughout the county in which he lives and is frequently consulted by many people for his wisdom and judgment, is a walking advertisement for competitors of the company that sold him the computer. Actually, he is a walking advertisement for how frustrating and useless computers can be.

There are many lessons in this story from which we can learn:

- *Make certain that the customer needs the innovation.* Some of the angriest customers we have ever seen are those who believe that they were sold a device, process, system, or software that they really didn't need. A short-term sale isn't worth the long-term grief and the damaged reputation that comes with it. Stick with a highly focused marketing plan that carefully targets appropriate prospects.

- *Don't leave customers alone until it is clear that they can function independently.* There is a very good chance that if our idea is truly novel, most people won't know how to use it or to apply it to their need. If that's the case, we have to walk the customer through the application process and convince ourselves that they understand and can use the technology with proficiency without our continuous presence.[3] This pertains not simply to teaching them the mechanics of turning it on and off and manipulating it as intended. It also pertains to instructing them on how they can extract maximum usefulness and value from the innovation.

---

[2]To compound the problem, Uncle Gene's hearing isn't all that good.
[3]It's very important to assure them after we leave that we will be available if they have any difficulties or if they can't recall everything we taught them.

- *Provide good written instructions.* After we teach people how to apply the innovation to address their requirements, sometimes all they need is good documentation to remind them what we taught them. Hence, good instruction manuals can help customers to save face and help us to avoid repeating things endlessly. Customers really don't want their hands held forever; they want to use the innovation themselves without our help. Frankly, if they wanted hand-holding *in perpetuity* they probably would have paid us as an outsourced contractor who furnishes and uses our own equipment.[4] There are other ways to provide written instructions besides just giving the customer a printed book. There are some wonderful online methods for instructions and training that are superior to written manuals and instructions. Simple use of a telephone conversation and a shared electronic presentation are extremely powerful and don't cost a dime. Access to that information becomes the focus rather than simply the book or manual.

- *Give customers exemplary technical support.* The best technical (and most expensive) support is delivered face to face. We must plan for such exemplary support and budget to provide it. To the extent possible (especially immediately after the sale), have a person identified who is readily available to go to the client's location to address the problem and fix it. Remember that our technology is new and different and must be learned over time. Don't be arrogant or unclear when providing technical support. If users believe that we regard them as "too dumb to understand this great technology," in addition to never selling them anything again, we'll find that we have enemies who will spread the word like wildfire.

- *Bend over backward to keep a customer satisfied.* Remember that most of the initial customers were targeted because they are industry leaders. The last thing we need is for such leaders to be advocating vehemently that we be wiped off the face of the earth. Stop them before they embark on that path. The corollary is even more important: If we treat them right, we've got customers forever (or at least until we fail to give them the attention and service they believe they deserve).

- *Arrange for a regular inspection program to assure that customers continue to use the technology correctly.* Uncle Gene is irate because he believes to this day that the computer manufacturer doesn't give a hoot about his problems. Recently, he said: "The only time I hear from those bums[5] is when they want to sell me an upgrade or printer

---

[4]In Section 15.2 we suggest that there may be a market for such "hand holding" (i.e., we operate the systems).
[5]The word Uncle Gene used wasn't "bums".

cartridges!" Surely Uncle Gene's situation is different than that of our technology customers. But think about it. If our customers have things well in hand, our effort in the inspection program will be minimal. But if they need help, we will be able to nip problems in the bud and keep them from getting bigger. In either case, the customers will be appreciative of our assistance and hopefully, spread word of our diligence.

Another way that we can keep our customers happy is to include regular training for users and operators for purposes of keeping them sharp and to incorporate the latest upgrades. But never forget: Initial training is the key element in assuring a smooth transition to the new technology. Whereas regular training is a great idea, initial training is *mandatory*. We may consider performing the training at little or no cost if we can sell a lot of upgrades that way. However, we believe that Uncle Gene would be very angry if he believed that he had to pay twice for what he thought was included in the price to begin with.

15.2   HOW ABOUT IT IF WE OPERATE YOUR SYSTEM FOR YOU?

Several times in our careers it would have been much simpler if we operated a product for a customer. In a few cases we actually did just that with glowing success. A company we worked for had an exclusive license for a technology that pulverized coal and mixed it with an industrial by-product that had a high energy value. When the two streams were blended in the correct proportions, they served as an excellent fuel for a customer process that had a high energy demand. For several reasons, the customer was concerned about buying the energy system and operating it themselves. First, the technology was relatively new and untested in the United States. Second, failure to operate the system properly had the potential of creating significant environmental problems, including particulate release and discharge of partially combusted waste products. Third, the customer did not have staff on board in whom they had confidence to operate such a complex system. Fourth, they were reluctant to commit to a major capital project at a time when there were substantial other demands for funding. Fifth, they were very uncomfortable about liability issues in general. Therefore, we agreed to operate the coal blending and feed facility on a tolling basis with a "take-or-pay" agreement.

First, we need to provide a few definitions. A *tolling contract* is an agreement to put a specified amount of raw material per period through a particular processing facility. For example, an agreement to process a specified amount of alumina into aluminum at a particular aluminum plant would represent such an arrangement. A *take-or-pay contract* is an agreement between a buyer and seller in which the buyer will still pay some amount even if the product or service is not provided. This was the type of operating contract into which we entered with our customer. We did so because we knew that we would have a better qualified operating staff than the customer would and we were reasonably certain that it would work like a charm for us and that we could do so at a nice profit. We weren't so sure about the customer's operating people. If they messed up, it could be a black eye from which we might never recover. Thus, we were very enthusiastic about the operating contract. To make a long story short, it worked without a hitch, and both parties believed they had gotten a bargain.

On one occasion we entered into an operating contract in self-defense. An innovative process that we developed to clean up a utility's ground-water contamination problem was not operating properly despite our best efforts to work with the customer. As a result, they refused to pay us. We said that we had designed a process that would meet all regulatory requirements if it were operated as we had instructed. They disagreed; in fact, they disagreed with just about everything we said. Our solution was as follows. We said that we would operate the process with our own personnel for a period of six months; meet all regulatory requirements; and have on-stream performance at least 95 percent of the time. Moreover, if we were successful, they would promptly pay all outstanding invoices and pay all our operating costs for that six-month period. If we failed, they owed us nothing. In their arrogance, they believed that we were absolutely foolish. There was no way that we could make the process work after all the trouble they had, they thought. They were wrong! Not only did we meet all of the contract requirements, we did so with an on-stream performance approaching 99 percent.

There are many other instances where operating a system for a customer is the best course of action, but these two examples encapsulate many of the major lessons to be learned from operating a system ourselves.

- Make certain that the customer has the staff and capability to operate the system. Otherwise, we should do it ourselves.
- If the customer is willing to permit us to operate the system and we can make money at it, consider that option seriously.
- If we operate the system for the customer and they convert a capital expense to an operating expense, make certain that we get a proper return on investment for the use of our money.

- Don't let an incompetent customer blame us for their inadequacies. Be prepared to take over operations as soon as we see that they can't handle it. Otherwise, we could lose our reputation and a lot of money besides. Provide for such an eventuality in the system sales agreement.
- Don't let the situation deteriorate into rock throwing.[6]
- Only do business with honorable people.[7]

Obviously, there are many types of technology that don't lend themselves to operation by us. But when there is a possibility, think about it. It might just lead to another innovative business.

15.3 PUBLICIZE SUCCESS

We discussed the importance of favorable publicity when demonstrating technology, but it's absolutely crucial after a commercial sales success. Thus, when we are convinced that our technology is performing wonderfully on a consistent basis, we must aggressively use all avenues of publicity (e.g., technical and popular media, press releases, trade shows) to showcase our winner.

Get professional help for getting the message out. Too often we think of ourselves as being tuned into all avenues available to reach potential customers. In our experience, professionals in the public relations business see the world much more clearly than we can because of our tendency toward tunnel vision and overexposure to our own technology (a form of myopia). We continue to be amazed at how smart public relations people are despite our strong and continuing belief that they are "technically challenged."[8] We are thrilled that we have finally come to our senses and now use their great skills to spread our vision and message. Add this capability to the list of other professional helpers: lawyers, bankers, accountants, investment counselors, and other specialists.

We encourage satisfied customers to speak out in behalf of our mutual success. After all, weren't they intelligent for choosing to use our terrific technology? So when our public relations consultants are putting together campaigns, we urge them to include as many of our customers in their

---

[6]There is an old adage: "Never wrestle with a pig. People a distance away won't be able to tell you apart." We believe that public rock throwing sullies the reputation of both parties.

[7]Occasionally, it is not apparent if the customer is honorable or appears that way only at first. Be an optimist; take a chance.

[8]In turn, we hate it when they stereotype technologists.

campaigns as possible.[9] Let the customers share in the glow of being initiators of success. Moreover, try to identify by name specific people who have participated in the successful application of technology. If they enjoy the glow of publicity, they will appreciate it forever and recommend us to everybody they know because now our success reflects positively on them and they appear to be the geniuses who made the idea work.

15.4 KNOW WHEN TO MOVE ON

If we have gotten this far into the commercialization process for this particular technology, it's probably time to consider where we are in our strategic plan and how current status relates to the endgame we had in mind originally. In other words, *it's time to execute the endgame*. If our plan called for selling a license, selling the entire company, having an IPO, creating a subsidiary, or some other type of transaction (see Section 3.1), this is the point at which we decide that it's time to move on to the next great innovation.

Sometimes we have to force ourselves to behave in a completely rational manner, because it's tough to send "the kids" off on their own regardless of their degree of maturity. So we tend to procrastinate and linger, particularly when we're still having fun and making a product we love at a profit. One of the hardest jobs is to know when it's time to go. If we want to linger, we should figure out how to do so without getting in the way of those who now or soon will have ultimate responsibility for future success or failure.

15.5 KEY POINTS

- Many important tasks remain after initial sales are made.
- We gave an example of what happens when technology is not applied correctly. Lessons learned from this example are:
  - √ Make certain that the customer needs the innovation.
  - √ Don't leave customers alone until it is clear that they can function independently.
  - √ Give customers good written instructions.
  - √ Give customers exemplary technical support.

[9]Try very hard to keep customers from different entities separated in these campaigns because bunching tends to dilute their individual importance and may even put competitors at odds.

√ Bend over backward to keep customers on our side.

√ Arrange for a regular inspection program to assure that the customers continue to use the technology correctly.

- Another way to keep customers happy is to conduct regular training for users and operators for purposes of keeping them sharp and to incorporate the latest upgrades.

- Sometimes systems work best and customers are happiest if we operate the system we sell.

- Professional help should be used when publicizing success.

- This is the point where we decide it's time to move on to the next great innovation. Know when to make it happen.

16

MONITORING TECHNOLOGY

The main focus of this chapter is on innovative technology that has been licensed, leased, or otherwise conveyed to another party (even if it is a subsidiary or an affiliated company) and where compensation for the contractual arrangement is measured in numbers of transactions, sales, or profits or any combination thereof. The goal is to collect all revenues that are due. In addition to monitoring the basis for compensation, later in the chapter we discuss the need to have sales prospects see the innovation in action, and we talk about our need to examine operating data from the viewpoint of both revenue collection and process improvement.

16.1   MAKE SURE WE ARE COLLECTING ALL REVENUE THAT IS DUE TO US, AND DEVISE A SYSTEM TO MAKE IT HAPPEN

We need to have a fair and foolproof system to determine how much money we have made from sales of a product or process by those who are our representatives through licenses, leases, or other contractual agreements. The system has to be agreed upon in advance, and ideally should *not* be dependent on subjective or qualitative judgments. The closer we

Commercialization of Innovative Technologies: Bringing Good Ideas to the Marketplace,
By C. Joseph Touhill, Gregory J. Touhill, and Thomas A. O'Riordan
Copyright © 2008 John Wiley & Sons, Inc.

come to this ideal, the less chance for misunderstandings and disagreements. Such a system must be constructed to minimize the temptation to cheat. In fact, intercompany relations improve dramatically if everybody is convinced that it's impossible to cheat the system. A good system that gives the appearance of being automatic is a real timesaver and focuses attention on increasing sales rather than divvying up the profits. The system should be open, easily understood, and clearly encourage marketing and selling rather than bean counting.

The system devised must be able to be audited without difficulty and must be supervised by an independent third party mutually agreed upon in advance. It is good practice to have the system auditors be separate and distinct from the accounting firms that normally service the contractual parties. If the product or process is used or applied in a highly technical and complicated way, the auditors must be able to understand how the technology works and the basis for its performance. If performance is measured over a range of effectiveness and the revenue derived is based on the degree of effectiveness, this complicates the system and mandates and accentuates the need for technical skill and proficiency in the auditing procedure.

We have to avoid situations where it takes a long time to determine the split of fees and/or profits. In fact, the system must give results as close to real time as possible. That doesn't mean that we have to wait until audits are complete to know what revenue to expect. To the contrary, distributions should be made as soon as feasible, with adjustments made after audits, if required. Waiting for results causes lots of problems. We want to be able to base our profit and loss statements and balance sheets on hard data as much as practicable and use estimates only when absolutely necessary. Real-time results substantially reduce apprehension between us and our contracted representatives.

In our experience, perhaps the stickiest of all business problems occurs when earnings have to be restated. The road to the CEO graveyard is strewn with the bodies of executives who have had to go back to their boards and shareholders and tell them that their prior numbers were wrong.[1] Thus, we have to devise a system for measuring revenue and profitability that is easily understood, timely, and very accurate. It is not only important to the entity that is receiving payments as the licensor or leaser but is also essential to the generator of revenue. Whereas restatements are difficult to the former, they are fatal to the latter.[2]

---

[1] Boards really raise Cain when prior-year performance, now revealed to be inflated, resulted in very healthy bonuses for management.

[2] A fatality may mean that bogus bonuses are gone forever.

16.2   ARRANGE FOR VISITORS TO HAVE FREE ACCESS TO CUSTOMER SITES

It is a distinct advantage when selling to new customers to have them observe successful projects in actual working situations. Visitations lend credibility to claims and eliminate or reduce the possibility that the prospective clients would believe that we are exaggerating performance. Clearly, the objective is to have the prospects reach their own conclusions based on direct observation. We can help them to judge project performance more favorably by involving enthusiastic customers from the facility visited. In fact, the prospects are more likely to be impressed by customer praise as opposed to ours.

Access is a sensitive issue. It must be arranged well in advance. Actually, arrangements should be provided for in the original contract with the customer whose facility we intend to visit. Early users or adapters must be made aware at the beginning of our negotiations with them of our desire to have access later. Experience shows that if they are reluctant to allow others to enter their plant, the issue must not be pushed too hard. Some customers are very shy about permitting visitors, especially potential competitors, onto their plant sites. Therefore, we must be acutely aware of this sensitivity and provide for it through the access contract and confidentiality agreements required from visitors. In addition, when we take a prospect to a customer's site, we must have them see only what they need to. Don't tempt them to be too nosy.

We can help to soothe the sensitivities of customers whose facilities we are visiting if we prepare a document in advance that:

- Describes the locations in the system that we would like to show off
- Identifies the type and range of operating parameters that we would like to demonstrate
- Defines the degree of involvement of facility personnel

Moreover, we should prepare an agenda that indicates when we will show up, how many people will be attending, who they are, what positions they hold, how long they will be there, and what time we will leave. We should offer to have a debriefing with the facility owner after the visit, if appropriate.

We should be highly selective in who we invite to visit a customer's facility because it is usually regarded by plant management as an imposition, not only due to the confidentiality concerns, but also because visits are disruptive. They take time away from routine operations, and normal plant procedures may have to be altered substantially to protect trade and proprietary secrets. In short, it is a pain in the neck, so make certain that the prospects we choose are worth it.

We can help to get permission if we offer incentives to do so. One way that is used in a wide variety of businesses is to pay an incentive bonus if the visiting prospect buys after seeing the innovation in operation. In addition, we should be willing to pay incentive bonuses to all users if one of their referrals (without visiting the plant) results in a sale. The bonus for allowing plant access should be larger than for a referral. We don't have to be as generous with visitation or access incentives as we did when we were demonstrating our technology (see Section 10.1). Whereas successful demonstrations often are close to "life or death" situations, visitations are easier to get simply because we have more opportunities and more customers. Hence, we don't have to make the incentives are large as we did for the demonstrations.

When we do make a visit, it should be a big event and a big deal. The romance should focus not only on the prospect but also on the customer who is permitting access. Treat the occasion as though it is a major awards ceremony. The reason for doing so is because we want the prospective buyer to remember the affair for a long time and to leave the site convinced that they will buy, or better yet, to sign on the bottom line while they are there. It's extremely important to keep the customer being visited happy enough to permit more visits. Work closely with our own public relations consultant and that of the facility owner to get the most mileage and publicity out of the visit, provided, of course, that security is not a problem.

16.3   OBTAIN ACCESS TO OPERATING DATA

Although arranging to have sales prospects visit customer sites to observe operations in person is best, sometimes it's easier and more appropriate to share selected operating data with them. This means that they don't have to travel, that access agreements are not required, and that the site customer is more comfortable. Confidentiality could remain a problem, but there are ways to mitigate such concerns. Probably the best way is to consolidate data from several customers without identification of which site generated the data. A problem with this approach is that sales prospects may believe that we are displaying only the best data, to optimize performance figures. In fact, that is probably what will happen, so we must be open and share our assumptions, operating conditions, and degree of data selectivity. Then the prospect can be on guard and is obliged to assign their own extent of credibility conveyed by the data. If there are areas of particular concern or if the prospect needs details not revealed in the data selected, it is possible that some type of accommodation can be made to obtain the required information. One way is to identify somebody at the facility whose data were selected to be available to answer questions in writing, by telephone, or by e-mail. It would not be a bad idea to compensate the facility contact or the customer company in some way. For example, we could provide them with cash bonuses, free updates, or extended technical support agreements in return for their cooperation.

We would also like the customer to share their data with us on a regular basis, at least at first. Later, after it's clear that what the performance data show over time is quite predictable, we may want only periodic data summaries. The site customer is more likely to be amenable to share data if they receive a clear benefit from this sharing. Some possible benefits are:

- Identifying operating problems earlier and fixing them before they become significant.
- Determining where and when to apply system improvements designed to patch deficiencies or to improve efficiency and output.
- Improving customer sales by demonstrating product quality and performance.
- Discovering places where operating procedures can be improved and costs reduced.
- Publicizing data jointly in technical journals so that we can share with customers favorable publicity about exemplary product quality and performance.

We must demonstrate clearly that the data we obtain from the customer are needed and that our use of it will be beneficial to them. Moreover, we have to show them that the data will be used wisely and for good purposes. After we analyze the data, it is absolutely necessary to share the analysis with the people who supplied the data and to help them apply it constructively.

There are many people from all over the world who are eager to learn about new technology. It is crucially important to protect the data from those who would use it for unsavory purposes such as corporate spying and espionage. We must also be aware that many countries do not afford patent protection. There are people in such countries who are not the least bit embarrassed to copy a product and sell it without any thought regarding compensation for us; just ask Rolex or Omega or even Microsoft.

Data sharing over the Internet between firms and their customers is a rapidly evolving methodology. Hence, if data sharing is agreed upon, the data can be obtained in real time and conveyed through secure Web sites. Once the security issues (e.g., clearances, passwords, encryption) are taken care of, transmittal of data is inexpensive and easy.

16.4 KEY POINTS

- We need a fair and foolproof system that determines how much money we make from sales of our product or process by people who are our representatives through licenses, leases, or related contractual agreements.
- The system must be agreed upon in advance; it must *not* be dependent on subjective or qualitative judgments; it must be audited without difficulty by an independent third party; and it must give results as close to real time as possible.
- It is a distinct advantage when selling to new customers to have them observe successful projects in actual working situations.
- Access is a sensitive issue, so we must provide for it through access and confidentiality agreements required from visitors.
- Preparation of documents that describe the objective of facility visits should be provided in advance.
- Facility personnel should have a clear agenda before we show up for a visit.
- Incentive bonuses should be offered to customers to facilitate plant visits. Make the visits a big deal. Use public relations staff effectively.
- Demonstrate that sharing of operating data has distinct benefits for the customers who do the sharing.
- Data sharing can utilize Web-based technology.

17

IMPROVING TECHNOLOGY

This chapter is intended especially for those of us who are interested in the entire process of developing and improving technology. But before getting down to business, we want to remind our readers of a few very important aspects of the commercialization process as we envision it. First, many of the truly ingenious people who come up with innovations that revolutionize some aspect of society, in either a major way or subtly, are involved in technology commercialization mainly because of the thrill of the innovation process. For them, making money is secondary. We admire their talent, dedication, and intensity. Second, we don't want to zero in on just one idea, we want to identify and develop a family of related ideas and innovations that potentially can revolutionize or create an entire industry. And we want to achieve that objective by making money at it, not because of avarice, but because that is an essential measure of success.

We said at the beginning of Chapter 4 that most of the remaining chapters of the book (Chapters 4 through 16) focus primarily on the tactics of commercializing individual ideas and concepts. But the final two chapters, this one and the next, are most meaningful when placed in the context of the overall strategic plan outlined in the first three chapters. Improving technologies and building on success are best viewed as part of an overall plan rather than simply as afterthoughts or serendipitous opportunities.

Commercialization of Innovative Technologies: Bringing Good Ideas to the Marketplace,
By C. Joseph Touhill, Gregory J. Touhill, and Thomas A. O'Riordan
Copyright © 2008 John Wiley & Sons, Inc.

Many of our colleagues believe that the commercialization world is conquered best by those radical concepts that sweep aside the status quo. This chapter is written more from the standpoint of the bull who walked down the hill to visit all the cows. Sometimes simpler approaches result in better and longer-lasting improvements. Great strides in improving the human condition can occur when enterprising people take existing technology and assemble several state-of-the-art ideas into a beautiful new and innovative system. This chapter celebrates taking advantage of this synergy.

17.1   FIGURE OUT WAYS TO MAKE THE INNOVATION BETTER

After we have gotten this far in the commercialization process, there isn't anybody in the world who knows and understands the idea and concept better than we do. Moreover, as we pointed out in Chapters 15 and 16, we didn't quit after we made the sale. We diligently tracked and monitored the technology to make certain that it worked right. Hence, it's only logical that we use that unique insight for purposes of making the product better. Look at all the upgrades and "builds" that are common in the software business. There's a very good chance that our upgrades can be more profitable than the first generation simply because all the hard work and development costs are behind us.

We must be careful about the conditions of sale for our existing customers when we embark upon improvements. Did we promise the customers that we would give them improvements if we made any? Did we say that we would give them these improvements without charge? Did we convey any ownership rights to them based on the original sale? What are the customers' responsibilities with regard to proprietary rights protection? If we obtained access to their facilities and data that assisted us in development of the improvement, what rights and/or recourse do they have related to them? Clearly, these are important questions that we have to review with our legal advisors. However, if we thought of these questions in advance, we probably provided for the answers in our sale, access, and data acquisition agreement terms and conditions executed earlier in the commercialization process.

We encourage the innovation team to create a budget for improvements early in the strategic planning process. In that way the team will be aware consciously of the need to explore the possibility of improving the technology before the endgame conveys it to its ultimate owner.

17.2   STRING TECHNOLOGIES TOGETHER TO FORM INTEGRATED SYSTEMS

There are lots of examples of great technologies whose life was extended by discovering another use (sometimes a completely unrelated use) for the product that otherwise seemed to reach maturity or even came to the end of its life. The most dramatic example is that old-time miracle drug, aspirin. First it was taken just for headaches, and now its benefits for mitigating heart disease are well recognized. In fact, it seems as though more aspirins are sold today to keep blood flowing smoothly than for extinguishing headaches. We believe that a good idea can become a great one when paired with other technologies, so that the integrated systems can do more than any of the components alone. In addition to extending the innovation life cycle, gathering good ideas and stringing them together can enhance overall profitability.

There are three types of improvements and extensions of technologies. First, we can take an innovation that we just developed and commercialized and tack on other technologies that we developed in parallel to form an integrated system. Or we can take two or more existing technologies and combine them so that they represent a new development and/or application that fulfills an untapped need. Finally, as in the aspirin example, we can take a single existing technology and simply apply it in a completely different way. In each case, the process, although it can be as intellectually challenging as the commercialization of a single brand-new concept, can be far more profitable. One of the reasons for higher profitability is because ideas strung together are probably at a higher level of development and demonstration. In other words, the difficult money has already been spent.

A benefit of developing an integrated system is that it makes the system more difficult to copy and hence tougher to compete against. This presumes, of course, that we have control over the intellectual property rights of all components of the system. By developing integrated systems, we help to build a reputation for commercialization at a more complex scale than with a single innovation. This added credibility is a great benefit in selling to larger companies with many locations.

In summary, we don't quit when we think we've got the perfect solution to a difficult problem. We look for linkages with other commercial stars in our stable and create integrated systems that can address more needs than we could with each one separately.

The next two sections show how imaginative thinking led to combining the capabilities of existing technology into innovative systems that saved taxpayers tons of money. More important, the creative approaches described saved the lives of many courageous American and Allied service men and women.

17.3 USING TECHNOLOGY TO INNOVATIVELY TRANSFORM THE BATTLEFIELD: RIPRNET[1]

September 2005 was a busy time for the members of the U.S. Central Command Air Forces (USCENTAF) as we prepared for the historic constitutional elections in Iraq. Iraqi and coalition planners were engaged with international observers and local election officials to prepare ballots, identify polling stations, and safeguard the election process and electorate. As the airspace control authority for the skies over Iraq, the Combined Forces Air Component Commander (CFACC) was leading efforts to secure the airspace over Iraq from attack.

Of primary concern was the possibility that a determined foe would hijack a civilian airliner and crash it into a high-value target in Baghdad, thereby undermining the confidence of the electorate during the crucial elections. At CFACC's direction, we were tasked to develop an integrated air defense system that would detect aircraft over Iraqi airspace, allow ground controllers to communicate with aircraft throughout the region, share the air picture with designated air defense organizations, and link all air defense command centers together with the CFACC. As the Director of Command, Control, Communications, and Computer (C4) Systems, I was tasked to "make it happen."

Over the course of several weeks leading up to September, I sought and received help from engineers in the United States in finding a "universal" data translator that enabled my technicians to integrate radar feeds from U.S. Air Force (USAF) long-range radars, civilian air traffic control radars, and U.S. Marine Corps (USMC) air defense radars. Led by my chief planner, Squadron Leader Patrick Del Guidice of the Royal Australian Air Force, installation of this equipment allowed us to feed all the radar inputs together into a common air picture that gave us greatly improved radar coverage across almost all Iraq, including important low-level surveillance in key areas.

Ready with the common air picture, we had to securely link all the key air defense centers together with reliable voice connectivity. In a tactical field environment where reliable electrical power is a luxury, we

[1]One of the authors, Colonel Gregory J. Touhill, was the key motivator in creating the system described in this section—RIPRNET. We decided that the story is best told in his voice (i.e., in the first person).

had to develop a zero-defect conferencing system where all players—the commander, air defense artillery, radar operators, and air defense airspace controllers—could be notified immediately, assess the threat, and react with appropriate and immediate orders. I assigned USAF Captain Terry Scott the daunting task of linking the command centers at the Combined Air Operations Center (CAOC) in Qatar, the Theater Air Control Center at Balad Air Base (north of Baghdad), the Multi-National Forces-Iraq (MNF-I) headquarters in Baghdad, and the civil defense authority in Baghdad—a distance over 1200 miles from top to bottom. I told him the job was easy—just give me three different methods of voice communication, make them secure, and get it all to me in two weeks. In a feat of combat daring-do, he coordinated with the U.S. Central Command at MacDill Air Force Base, Florida, the U.S. Army Signal Corps, the MNF-I, and a host of others to provide an integrated secure voice system that included voice-over-secure Internet routed protocol phones, standard secure telephone equipment over ordinary phone lines, and wideband "Red Switch" phone lines, all with automatic conferencing capability. Although this ordinarily would take several months, Terry made it happen in less than two weeks, an extraordinary achievement.

Armed with the ability to see aircraft on an integrated radar display and with the ability to communicate with all command elements a week before the election, CFACC was ready to exercise all parts of the system to combat the possible hijacker threat. Brigadier General Blair Hansen, CFACC's deputy, led the testing in a war game scenario. During the tests, we had a large cargo plane, usually a C-17 Globemaster II, fly an approach into Baghdad. The test was designed to determine how fast we could detect the aircraft and plot its course, attempt to contact the aircraft, and intercept it with fighter aircraft to determine its intent and ability to alert ground air defense and civil defense personnel. During the testing, the communications and radar systems worked as planned and we "communicators" celebrated, at least for a couple of hours (see Figure 17.1).

At the conclusion of the tests, Brigadier General Hansen gave us a new requirement: He needed to be able to listen to and talk with the pilots in the intercepting aircraft over Baghdad (over 1000 miles away), and he needed it in six days! From the testing of the system, Brigadier General Hansen found that current tactics at the time called for the Tactical Air Control Center to identify any available fighter aircraft, vector them to the potentially hostile aircraft for an intercept, and relay communication from the aircraft to the commander. Given the fact that an aircraft on final approach to Baghdad International Airport could suddenly veer to the right and into a high-value target in a matter of seconds, the time to relay a

FIGURE 17.1   Returning from a Baghdad test flight on a C-17.

message through the control center proved unacceptable; CFACC had to be able to communicate with the pilot. "This is the critical component of the entire air defense system and we need it now," said Brigadier General Hansen.

Ordinarily, creating this type of radio system takes over a year of planning and involves expensive acquisition of radios, long-haul communications lines, radio antennas and towers, and telephone interface equipment. We had six days and none of the above. It was time for a miracle. I quickly gathered my team at the base's British Officer's Club, the Muff, where I borrowed some paper towels to use as working papers and we sought to design a solution. Over Aussie beers and Coke Lite we formed a classic innovation team. Our inventor was Jeff Sapp, a civilian contractor who served as our chief radio engineer. Jeff had done some research into radio-over-Internet protocol routed network technology and had suggested it may be something we might want to investigate further. "Now is the time," I told my team. Our investor was Colonel Marty Edmonds, the Director of Communications for USCENTAF at Shaw Air Force Base, South Carolina. My predecessor in the desert, Marty knew the environment we operated in better than anyone and provided me with the resources—people and money—to meet the mission need. Our technologists were Captain Dave Canady and Mike Byard of my engineering team. Dave was deployed from the 3rd Combat Communications Group at Tinker Air Force Base, and Mike was deployed from Langley Air Force Base, Virginia. They were my smartest and most experienced field engineers and would lead the effort to integrate and install the solution in the field. As the team leader, I was the entrepreneur who had to bring all the pieces together.

Armed with an initial design on the paper towels, I called the team together in our trailer and outlined our objectives and my expected timelines during a secure conference call with our colleagues in the United States. Normally, the eight-hour time zone difference was a hindrance for us, but now it was an advantage. By distributing the workload between the forward deployed team members and their supporting colleagues in the United States, we could work on the problem virtually around the clock.

Our design was simple: Install radios around Baghdad tuned to the frequency of an intercepting allied fighter, interface it with a device that would digitize the signal, and pipe it over the computer network back to the Combined Air Operations Center, where CFACC could monitor the communications with the aircraft. Jeff selected the Telex IP-223 as the translation device based on his research, its low cost, and its ease of setup. Mike and Dave worked with Jeff to identify all the other components needed for the system and created an interface device between our air traffic radios audio jacks and the IP-223 input port so that they could work together.

Meanwhile, Colonel Marty Edmonds and his team at Shaw worked feverishly to get us the resources we needed. Marty coordinated with the U.S. Central Command at MacDill Air Force Base, Florida and with the help of Colonel Chris Wilhelm secured us the satellite channel needed to pipe the information from Baghdad back to the CAOC. This process normally takes months. In emergencies, you are lucky to get it done in a week. Marty and Chris helped us get it done in a day. Marty also worked to get us additional radios for our two radio sites. We "borrowed" some from other locations to fill the immediate need, but needed replacements before the rightful owners noticed their absence. Marty found replacements and got them airlifted to us right away; he remains on top of our hero list.

Installation of the radios and equipment was critical. We had to select locations that would provide excellent radio reception and transmission but also permit us to link the radios to our long-haul circuits. Once again Squadron Leader Del Guidice stepped to the plate and hit a home run. He coordinated with the units at Baghdad International Airport and Balad Air Base, found suitable locations and support gear, validated the installation

FIGURE 17.2   Sylvester, Canady, Byard, and McAlister in Baghdad.

plan with our chief technologists Canady and Byard, and organized the installation teams. Trained and led by Canady and Byard, the teams were ready and equipped to go to Baghdad and Balad three days after the initial tasking (see Figure 17.2).

Moving around the combat zone is not easy, particularly when you need air transport. That's where I stepped in. Being a seasoned traveler in the combat zone, I knew who to go to for help. I coordinated with the Air Mobility Division of the CAOC and secured a C-130 transport that would take my installation teams and their cargo to Baghdad and Balad. Brave airmen like Senior Airmen Daniel Urbanski (see Figure 17.3) climbed towers in Baghdad on day four, exposing themselves to potential sniper fire, to install the special radio antennas to link us with the interceptors. Canady and Byard traveled between the sites via U.S. Army Blackhawk helicopters, ensuring that everything was installed properly and that the long-haul lines were configured to pass the signal back properly. Meanwhile, Jeff Sapp and Squadron Leader Del Guidice worked with the CAOC networks team to install the computer, speakers, and microphone at the commander's battle station that would be used to link the commander to the aircraft.

FIGURE 17.3   Dan Urbanski.

By the end of day five, all the components were in place and the Radio-Over Internet Protocol Routed Network (RIPRNET, pronounced "Ripper-Net") was created and ready for testing. I coordinated with my counterpart, the Director of Operations, Colonel Wade "Biggles" Thompson, to conduct a test of the system with a live-fly exercise. The next day, the day before the elections, we tested the system successfully with F-16, F-18, and British Tornado aircraft over the skies of Baghdad as part of a test of the integrated air defense system. The RIPRNET innovation team did the impossible and delivered a working long-haul radio system to support the air defense of Baghdad with hours to spare.

Did the creation of RIPRNET make a difference? While the elections went off without a hitch, in the ensuing six months, there were eight instances where the RIPRNET system was used successfully to vector away potentially hostile aircraft that had ventured too close to high-value targets in the Baghdad area. RIPRNET also changed the way we conduct air defense. Rather than relay messages between the intercepting pilot through the Tactical Air Control Center, now the commander can speed his decision making by monitoring the communications directly and deciding how and when to act based on direct cues from the pilots.

RIPRNET changed the way we support convoys on the road in Iraq as well. Prior to its arrival in the combat theater, convoys would leave their support base and head out on the road armed with maps and low-power very high frequency (VHF) line-of-sight radios. At best, these radios could communicate only 10 miles from the vehicle. The Corps Support Command (COSCOM) would provide radio relay sites located periodically along the routes, and the USAF was tasked to augment the radio coverage with large Joint Surveillance, Targeting, and Acquisition Radar System (JSTARS) aircraft providing radio relay (see Figure 17.4). Use of JSTARS was not considered an effective or efficient means of performing this mission, as it was designed to use its powerful radar to track enemy ground targets rather than relay radio calls. Additionally, if it was relaying radio calls, it could not do its primary mission of hunting for enemies such as improvised explosive device (IED) bombers.

Enter my innovation team and the insertion of RIPRNET technology to create an integrated radio network along the main supply routes to improve radio coverage for convoys traveling up and down the roads of Iraq (see Figure 17.5). By implementing a RIPRNET-based radio network, coalition forces had an all-weather persistent secure radio net for personnel traveling in convoys. In addition to eliminating the need to deploy an additional three JSTARS aircraft, crews, and support personnel, we also freed over 200 soldiers who previously had to perform radio relay duties along the main supply routes, keeping them out of harm's way and allowing them either to be sent home or to be assigned to less risky duties.

The work of our innovation team was of great value to our commander, who nominated the team for special recognition. As a result, our team was

FIGURE 17.4   JSTARS aircraft.

FIGURE 17.5   Convoy leaving the logistics base.

awarded the 2006 U.S. Air Force Science and Engineering Achievement Award (see Figure 17.6). Most important, however, my entire installation team made it home safely with no injuries.

By way of an epilog to the story of RIPRNET, during January 2007, Colonel Greg Touhill received an e-mail message from Lt. Colonel Martin K. Schlacter calling Touhill's attention to an article about RIPRNET in Air Force Link, the official Web site of the U.S. Air Force.[2] We quote the article as follows:

> It [RIPRNET] enables, for the first time, the Army to pull hundreds of Soldiers back inside the wire to the main operating bases, rather than keeping them stationed at small outposts along roadsides," said Lt. Col. Marty Schlacter, the Combined Air Operations Center's Architectures and Integration Division chief. "It provides senior decision makers with the ability to determine the proper air and ground mix supporting convoy operations, thus freeing up aircraft for other high-priority missions."

> As the division chief, Colonel Schlacter oversaw the RIPRNET developers, installers, maintainers and support teams. He said the system also accelerates the response times for emergency and recovery forces by directly receiving distress calls and not relying on a third party.

[2]Francesca Popp, "Latest radio technology declared ready," Air Force Link, Jan. 19, 2007.

FIGURE 17.6 Colonel Greg Touhill accepting 2006 U.S. Air Force Science and Engineering Achievement Award on behalf of his RIPRNET team.

In his personal comments to Touhill, Schlacter said, "Also, I have an actual MEDEVAC report that proves that RIPRNET saved a soldier's life."

17.4   CLOSE AIR SUPPORT A PHONE CALL AWAY

Have you ever visited Afghanistan? Most folks have not had the opportunity. Afghanistan is a large country, almost half the size of the continental United States, with huge rugged mountains in the north and a dry, dusty, and inhospitable region in the south. When the author arrived at Bagram Air Base and remarked at the height of the mountains, a soldier from the United States Army's 10th Mountain Division and an Operation Enduring Freedom combat veteran, observed: "Of course they're big! We're at the tail end of the Himalayas!" For allied troops fighting the notorious Taliban in the region, the terrain posed tremendous challenges, but none more critical than in coordinating close air support to Allied troops engaged with the enemy.

Allied troops engaged in close contact with the enemy soon found themselves in a dangerous dilemma: They could not make contact with close support aircraft, as the mountains were blocking the line-of-sight radio communications between the ground personnel and the supporting aircraft. A-10 Thunderbolt II aircraft, renowned for their tank-killing nose cannon, patrolled over Afghanistan in support of Allied ground operations, but were limited by their UHF and VHF line-of-sight radios designed to communicate with ground personnel. If the radio signal from ground personnel could not directly "see" the aircraft's radio, the signal could not get through and ground personnel could not get close air support. With Allied personnel fighting enemy forces in the valleys and vales of Afghanistan, lives were at stake; we had to find a consistent and reliable means of providing timely and effective communications between ground and close air support forces.

Enter the innovative communications staff at the U.S. Central Command Air Forces (USCENTAF) and the brilliant engineers at the Air Armament Center (AAC). Forming an ad hoc innovation team, the group quickly determined the conditions they faced. The end state was a reliable, effective, and timely means of linking the Allied ground forces with the airborne A-10 close-support aircraft, no matter where either was. It had to operate in all weather conditions and couldn't result in the ground personnel having to "lug" any more gear. Additionally, because of the cost and long lead time to integrate new systems into the already complex aircraft, it had to be simple and not require an extensive aircraft modification.

Ugh! It can't be done, the naysayers said. Different options were pitched and discussed, mussed and fussed over, when someone (who, exactly, is unclear) said: "What we need is for the guys on the ground to call the airplanes—kind of like On-Star." Nonsense? No! In fact, this casual remark spurred some extremely creative and operationally effective thinking for the CENTAF and AAC innovation team. Focused on a clear objective, a phone call between the ground troops and the aircraft, they made history.

Like Gene Krantz's NASA team highlighted in *Apollo 13*, the team scoped the problem by looking at what they had available: an airplane with conventional UHF/VHF radios and ground teams equipped with UHF/VHF and satellite (SATCOM) radios. Unfortunately, the UHF/VHF radios were worthless to the ground troops if the aircraft were not in range of the signal. Therefore, the team had to devise a communications scheme that would alert the aircraft to reposition itself within range of the ground personnel.

The innovation team knew that the ground troops could contact the Air Support Operations Center (ASOC) at Bagram Air Base via their SATCOM radios and request air support. The challenge was communicating from the ASOC to the aircraft to reposition them, as the A-10s did not have the long-range SATCOM radios needed for the mountainous

Afghan environment; the team had to give the A-10s SATCOM capability. Modifying the airplane to incorporate SATCOM radios was planned but required costly and extensive modifications to the aircraft, so the team looked at alternatives.

Recall the phone call idea? What if we could install a SATCOM telephone, such as an Iridium phone, on the plane? Because the pilot couldn't keep it in the cockpit and monitor the phone, as he or she was busy controlling the aircraft, monitoring the radios, and performing other duties, this quickly was deemed impractical. But in analyzing the desired communications flow, the team needed a way to pipe a SATCOM-based telephone signal into the pilot's radio system to complete the communications chain.

The solution they developed is brilliantly elegant, yet simple. They created what is known as the Fighter Aircraft Communications Extension (FACE) pod (see Figure 17.7). Using a hollowed-out wing pod normally used for electronics jamming, the innovation team filled the pod with two Iridium telephones, power supplies, and a PRC-248 UHF/VHF radio. They sealed the pod and tipped it with both Iridium and UHF/VHF antennas. Powered by an electrical cord already used by the aircraft to support normal jamming pods, the FACE pod was ready to fly!

Now when Allied ground personnel in Afghanistan encounter enemy forces and need close air support, they use their SATCOM radio to call the ASOC for help. The ASOC controller validates the location of the ground personnel, picks up the phone, and calls the A-10s orbiting in predetermined locations over the country. The telephone signal goes through the satellite network and into the Iridium antenna, then into the telephone, which feeds the signal into the PRC-248 radio, which sends the signal back out the tip of the pod through the UHF/VHF antenna, which transmits the signal to the aircraft's normal UHF/VHF antenna and into the pilot's radio. For the pilot, the call for help appears just like a normal radio call directing him to new grid coordinates and instructions to contact the ground personnel for close air support—help from above! Once again, by using existing technology in a creative and imaginative way, American and Allied soldiers' lives were protected, and considerable money was saved to boot.

Sometimes the relationship between the various military services is strained unnecessarily. This is understandable, particularly in wartime, when lives are at stake, decision making is quick, and bodies and minds are strained. But good ideas can surmount these difficulties and engender cooperation when it is needed most. We have learned that good ideas in the military, just like in civilian life, generate satisfied customers who keep coming back for help and more innovations.

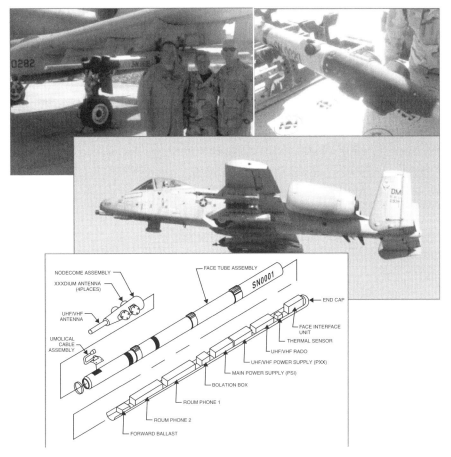

FIGURE 17.7   FACE pod technology. *Upper left*: A-10 pilot and communications support personnel at Bagram AB pose with the FACE pod mounted on the A-10. *Upper right*: Up-close view of the FACE pod antenna and power plug. *Middle*: A-10 in flight with FACE pod mounted under the left wing. *Bottom*: Schematic of the FACE pod.

17.5   REMEMBER THAT THE MOST EFFICIENT SALE IS TO A REPEAT CUSTOMER

The observation that it is easiest to sell to an existing customer is a truism that has become almost trite. Nevertheless, it is a fact, and believe it or not, some people tend to forget it. Our earliest customers were willing to take a chance, and because of our success in solving their problem, they are probably disposed to be receptive to our newer developments or to improvements to our proven technologies. This is an additional reason why continuing contact with the customer is very important, beyond the tracking and monitoring efforts discussed earlier.

Under the right conditions, customers can be extremely helpful in suggesting improvements. They tell us the areas that require improvement, suggest outcomes that they would like to achieve, and in some cases they can even generate a fix that we may want to incorporate in our product. Be careful that their participation is documented carefully and that there are clearly defined rights as to who owns what. Be professional and businesslike in arriving at equitable compensation for their help. Simply, it is harder to cultivate new potential customers, both in terms of time and money, than it is to treat old friends with kindness, generosity, and respect. We suggest that you work hard at it.

17.6   OFTEN IT IS MUCH EASIER TO INCREASE PROFIT MARGINS ON EXISTING TECHNOLOGY THAN TO START FROM SCRATCH

Innovation teams frequently get caught up by the dazzle and flash generated by their "toys." Interestingly, this happens far more often when the team is very successful and things are going well than when the going is hard. We all tend to overlook the potential for improving a good thing. Sometimes it's because of self-satisfaction, and sometimes it's simply laziness. The fact of the matter is that we should try to make good ideas better until the effort to do so doesn't match the benefit of the return. When this happens, it's time to move the ownership of the rights to the intellectual property to others, in accordance with the endgame strategy decided upon earlier.

The member of the innovation team who is best at improving a good product is the technologist.[3] Most technologists tend to be tinkerers, and they fill the role well. Inventors/innovators have the talent to do it but generally lack the temperament. They love the success of a concept and having proved that it works, turn their attention to the next marvel.

17.7   KEY POINTS

- This chapter is intended for those who are interested in linking technologies and making innovation improvements profitably.
- Evaluating and monitoring innovative technology generates unique insights on how to make a product better.

---

[3]Surely the two military examples (RIPRNET and FACE Pod) described above amplify on that point.

- Three types of product improvements are:
  - √ Combining a commercialized innovation with other technologies developed in parallel to form an integrated system.
  - √ Taking two or more existing technologies and combining them such that they represent a new development and/or application that fulfills an untapped need.
  - √ Taking an existing technology and simply applying it in a completely different way.
- Two examples of the imaginative use of existing technology to create innovative solutions to difficult problems have been given. Special attention was focused on system, monetary, and financial constraints within the context of the very short time period available for accomplishment.
- Earliest customers are likely to be most receptive to newer developments and improvements in proven technologies.
- Try to make good ideas better until the effort to do so doesn't match the benefit of the return.

18

BUILDING ON SUCCESS AND LEARNING FROM FAILURE

Well, we did it! We searched for good ideas; found some; picked out the really good ones; confirmed that the inventor's concept worked; perfected the idea; designed a prototype; showed that it functioned as expected; manufactured it; sold it; serviced it; and improved it. We commercialized our product and in doing so brought a good idea to the marketplace. Clearly, this was our intention when embarking on this adventure.

Now it's time to kick back and enjoy it! But let's not be too hasty. Is there anything else that needs to be done? The answer is yes! Before we move on to enlarge our stable of innovative technologies, the best thing we can do is take time to contemplate what went right and what went wrong and determine exactly why. Once we do that we'll know how to commercialize innovative technology better the next time and how to avoid our mistakes (or at least how to make them smaller and less frequent).

18.1 "CHASE THEM TO THE RIVER"

The first lesson that we'd like to share relative to building on success was provided by General George B. McClellan during the Civil War in

Commercialization of Innovative Technologies: Bringing Good Ideas to the Marketplace,
By C. Joseph Touhill, Gregory J. Touhill, and Thomas A. O'Riordan
Copyright © 2008 John Wiley & Sons, Inc.

September 1862. The essence of our lesson comes from an excerpt of McClellan's biography in *Wikipedia*.[1]

> Lee then continued his offensive by launching his Maryland Campaign, hoping to arouse pro-Southern sympathy in the slave state of Maryland. Lincoln then restored Pope's army to McClellan on September 2, 1862. Union forces accidentally found a copy of Lee's orders dividing his forces, but McClellan did not move swiftly enough to defeat the Confederates before they were reunited. At the Battle of Antietam near Sharpsburg, Maryland, on September 17, 1862, McClellan attacked Lee. Lee's army, while outnumbered, was not decisively defeated, because the Union forces did not manage to coordinate their attacks and because McClellan held back a large reserve.

> After the battle, Lee retreated back into Virginia. When McClellan failed to pursue Lee aggressively after Antietam, he was removed from command on November 5 and replaced by Maj. Gen. Ambrose Burnside on November 9. He was never given another command.

Despite having the Confederate battle plans given to him accidentally as a gift and having a clear manpower advantage, the cautious McClellan failed to capitalize on a situation that could have given Union forces a great victory and could potentially have shortened the Civil War by several years. Indecisiveness permitted Stonewall Jackson time to take Harper's Ferry and get most of his men back to Antietam as reinforcements. Even so, many historians call this deadly battle a draw. If only McClellan had chased Lee to the Potomac and trapped him there.[2]

Here are the lessons of this example that we want to convey that relate to the commercialization process:

- *Take advantage of good intelligence.* When we make a good discovery, we must analyze the information carefully so that its full

[1] http://www.en.wikipedia.org/wiki/George_McClellan. It was pointed out to us that *Wikipedia* isn't the most definitive source of information, so we read salient sections of Bruce Catton's *Terrible Swift Sword*, Vol. 2 of *The Centennial History of the Civil War*, Doubleday & Company, Garden City, New York, 1963. Based on our reading of Catton, we conclude that *Wikipedia* got the information substantially correct as conveyed in the quote we used above.

[2] As an interesting side note, most Army men at the time liked McClellan and regarded him as a fine engineer (technologist?) and a good organizer but a lousy field commander (entrepreneur?). He was also noted for having a highly inflated opinion of himself that eventually alienated everybody who came in contact with him (not a team player?). For greater insight into the strained relationship between McClellan and President Lincoln, we recommend appropriate sections of Doris Kearns Goodwin's book, **Team of Rivals: The Political Genius of Abraham Lincoln** (Simon & Schuster, New York, 2005).

benefit can be extracted. This pertains to the laboratory, pilot plant, prototype, customers, and competitors. Always remember the value of an exhaustive literature review, knowledge of the state of the art, and the value of homework.

- *Make the best of good opportunities.* When given the chance, make the best of every opportunity because often there are no second chances. Learn how to size up innovations quickly, and when good ones turn up, move fast.

- *Be decisive.* Indecision and caution must not be confused. Caution is the wisdom that comes with measuring risk in a rational and dispassionate way. Once acceptable risk is defined, act quickly and decisively. Indecision presumes that good things happen by default. That's not true! It's difficult to be indecisive when there is a thoughtful plan of action in place eagerly waiting to be implemented.

- *Demand coordination and organization.* We have emphasized throughout the book that teamwork is a core principle of commercialization. The innovation team works best when all of its members formulate and agree to strategic and tactical plans and then work toward their implementation in a disciplined manner. Loose cannons and clueless team members virtually guarantee failure.

- *Complete the job.* Despite his other missteps, McClellan still had the chance to seal victory at Antietam if only he had followed up and chased Lee to the Potomac, where the Southern forces would have been trapped with the river at their backs. We must finish our job by assuring that the innovation is fully developed technically and that the market is fully exploited. Moreover, we must create a business outcome that maximizes sales and profitability for whoever owns the concept after we are ready to move on (i.e., after we execute the foreseen endgame).

Thus, we must not let inattention, lack of interest, or timidity prevent us from victory and success. Victory means that the life of the innovation will be maximized. It also means that we will be in a strong position technically, financially, and managerially to uncover and develop other innovations.

18.2 INVESTING IN IMPROVEMENTS

In Chapter 17 we discussed how an innovation can be improved to optimize successful commercialization. In this section we build on that thought from the perspective that improvements really are investments. Recall from previous chapters that a strategy of preplanned product improvement can provide faster access to the market while allowing us to develop a customer base eager for the next version of our products.

Prudent investing in improvements helps in several different ways.

- *It permits us to optimize our return on investment for this innovation.* We suggested earlier that the most difficult money is spent in the early stages of commercialization. That's not a surprise because that's when there's the most uncertainty. Some approaches work and some don't, but all cost money. Once an innovation is demonstrated, subsequent improvements are easier and less costly.

- *It gives us experience that will be invaluable in developing our next great innovation.* Figuring out how to make an innovation better helps the innovation team by showing them ways to extend the inventor's concepts. Technologists learn tremendously from the process, and even inventors gain experience that may inspire them with their next creations.

- *Investing in improvements is very cost-effective and generates higher profit margins.* In addition to the point made in the first item, obtaining higher profit margins is often overlooked. Such improvements could involve making a product with lower-cost materials, fewer moving parts, better manufacturing techniques, and so on.

- *Improvements help to build a strong financial base for the next round of ideas.* If we are to realize our dream of a steady stream of innovations that will potentially revolutionize the marketplace in our expanding field of specialty, we need money to do it. As we have noted previously, higher margins are gained with less investment where improvements are evident.

These reasons are important because they all set the stage for the future and permit us to focus on the part of commercialization that interests us the most: *identifying new ideas in their infancy*.

18.3 IDENTIFYING NEW OPPORTUNITIES

By their nature, innovation team members, tend to have ants in their pants. They bore easily, and they are eager to get on with new ideas and concepts as soon as possible. The danger in this attitude is that they sometimes lose interest in very sound ideas too soon. Eagerness often breeds impatience, so the team must guard against this fault. The balance to this fault is that the innovation team is good at seeing promising ideas early. This talent develops over time based on the team's experience of what works and what doesn't. It also helps that the team works hard at keeping up with the state of the art in their sphere of specialization. Additionally, the team is imaginative and able to blend experiences and risk-taking proclivities so that we can identify good ideas and concepts in a way that allows us to see opportunity that others might not visualize.

The key for the team is to be disciplined in looking for new opportunities consciously and with an overall plan in mind. Sometimes that's hard to do. An old friend of ours, who is very good at finding ideas, said: "Many times I feel that there are so many good ideas out there that it's like drinking out of a fire hose!" Hence, the trick is to be able to prioritize. The team must pick out the opportunities that we can reasonably manage, and if we identify good ones that we believe have merit but we can't accommodate them in our own strategy, we should pass them on to others and be compensated appropriately for doing so.

After we have a few commercialization successes under our belt, it is imperative that we reexamine our fundamental strategy. Do we expand horizontally or vertically? Do we do more in our original area of specialty, or do we move into adjacent areas linked by common technologies, customers, or applications? Or do we embark upon a wholly new direction because of budding opportunities in technologies that are emerging where we cannot only ride the wave but can also create the wave? Decision making will be interesting and easier than when we started because the innovation team has matured and learned to work together efficiently and effectively. Some innovation teams disband after the original objective is achieved. Frankly, we think that's a shame. Having achieved success, our best days are ahead of us.

18.4 EVERYBODY MAKES MISTAKES, BUT THE BIGGEST ONE IS NOT LEARNING FROM THEM

Once an idea or concept has been discarded or commercialized and moved into its endgame, the team should take the time to analyze the details of the course that led to the innovation's fate. The evaluation must be highly analytical and unemotional. Achievements and mistakes must be documented and analyzed purposefully. Clearly, the objective is to identify what went right and what didn't. Success should be shared by all team members. Blame in the failure analysis must not be assigned to individuals. The purpose is to learn, not to punish.

Such learning will help to keep the innovation team together. Moreover, it will aid us in identifying and implementing promising ideas and concepts much better and more efficiently in future endeavors. As we said in the preceding section, it would be a shame to waste this magnificent learning process by quitting too soon. But the truth is that some people are uncomfortable with the pace of commercialization, and they simply don't enjoy it. Others get tired, and some just grow old. Thus, fresh talent must continuously be integrated into the innovation team. This can be done during the commercialization process so that the more recent additions can learn with live fire and real, consequential decision making. We must have a conscious plan in place to identify such persons and go out and get them to participate.

18.5   KEY POINTS

- We gave an example that pointed out the following lessons related to commercialization:
  - √ Take advantage of good intelligence.
  - √ Make the best of good opportunities.
  - √ Be decisive.
  - √ Demand coordination and organization.
  - √ Complete the job.
- Prudent investing in improvements helps in several different ways:
  - √ It permits us to optimize our return on investment for an innovation.
  - √ It gives us experience that will be invaluable in developing the next great innovation.
  - √ Investing in improvements is very cost-effective and generates higher profit margins.
  - √ Improvements help to build a strong financial base for the next round of ideas.
- Analyzing successes and failures helps us to focus on the part of commercialization that interests us the most: *identifying new ideas in their infancy*.
- After commercialization success, a key for the innovation team is to be disciplined in looking for new opportunities consciously with an overall plan in mind, and it is imperative that we reexamine our fundamental strategy.

- Once an idea or concept has been discarded or commercialized and moved into its endgame, the team should take the time to analyze the details of the course that determined the innovation's fate.
- Every effort should be made to keep the innovation team together and to integrate new talent into it.

BIBLIOGRAPHY

Allen, K. R., *Bringing New Technology to Market*, Prentice Hall, Upper Saddle River, NJ, 2002.

Chesbrough, H. W., *Open Innovation*, Harvard Business School Press, Watertown, MA, 2003.

Christensen, C. M., *The Innovator's Dilemma*, HarperCollins (Collins Business Essentials), New York, 2003.

Christensen, C. M., and Raynor, M. E., *The Innovator's Solution*, Harvard Business School Press, Watertown, MA, 2003.

Davidow, W. H., *Marketing High Technology*, Free Press, New York, 1986.

Dorf, R. C., and Byers, T. H., *Technology Ventures: From Idea to Enterprise, with Student DVD*, 2nd ed., McGraw-Hill, New York, 2006.

Gold, S. K., *Entrepreneur's Notebook: Practical Advice for Starting a New Business Venture*, Learning Ventures Press, Ocean Park, CA, 2006.

Goldberg, D. E., *The Entrepreneurial Engineer*, Wiley, Hoboken, NJ, 2006.

Govindarajan, V., and Trimble, C., *Ten Rules for Strategic Innovators*, Harvard Business School Press, Watertown, MA, 2005.

Jolly, V. K., *Commercializing New Technologies: Getting from Mind to Market*, Harvard Business School Press, Watertown, MA, 1997.

McGrath, R. G., and MacMillan, I., *The Entrepreneurial Mindset*, Harvard Business School Press, Watertown, MA, 2000.

Moore, G. A., *Crossing the Chasm*, HarperCollins (Collins Business Essentials), New York, 2002.

Speser, P. L., *The Art and Science of Technology Transfer*, Wiley, Hoboken, NJ, 2006.

Timmons, J. A., Zacharakis, A., and Spinelli, S., *Business Plans That Work*, McGraw-Hill, New York, 2004.

Wiefels, P., *The Chasm Companion*, HarperCollins (HarperBusiness), New York, 2002.

INDEX

Page references followed by t indicate material in tables.

Commercialization of Innovative Technologies: Bringing Good Ideas to the Marketplace,
By C. Joseph Touhill, Gregory J. Touhill, and Thomas A. O'Riordan
Copyright © 2008 John Wiley & Sons, Inc.